A guide to children's auth

4th Edition

Edited by
Viv Warren and **Mary Yardley**

LISU **mls**  **Loughborough University**

WARREN, Viv and YARDLEY, Mary, Editors
Who Next...? A guide to children's authors
Loughborough: LISU 2011

First published 1999, 4th edition 2011
ISBN 9781905499403

© LISU 2011

This edition supported by **mls** www.microlib.co.uk

Cover design by:
·I Bembrick, Design and Print, Loughborough University

side pages designed and typeset by:
Mary Ashworth and Sharon Fletcher, LISU

Printed by HSW Print, Cambrian Industrial Park, Clydach,
Tonypandy, Rhondda CF40 2XX

Published and distributed by:
LISU, Loughborough University, Loughborough, LE11 3TU
Tel +44 (0)1509 635680 · Fax +44 (0)1509 635699
Email lisu@lboro.ac.uk · http://www.lboro.ac.uk/departments/dis/lisu

Foreword

Why reading for pleasure matters
By Alan Gibbons

A reading child is a successful child. So says the Organisation for Economic Cooperation and Development. This body has concluded that reading for pleasure is even more important than a child's home background in determining academic and social success.

That shouldn't come as a surprise. Children who read regularly and for fun open up new worlds. They embark on journeys. They step into other people's shoes and walk around in them, as one truly great writer put it. They empathise with people from different backgrounds, different countries. They find it easier to understand, even change the world around them. Maybe most importantly, they embark on the most epic voyage of all, the one that takes them deep into their own identity and imagination.

But where do you start? There are so many books, stories of adventure, comedy and romance, spies and monsters and real life. There are picture books to read on Mum or Dad's knee, quick reads you can devour in an afternoon and extended, challenging series in which you follow a vast array of characters across the continents and down the centuries. The good news is that there are dedicated groups of book-mad people who spend hours choosing the right title for the right child. They're called librarians and they put together guides like this one.

There are signposts in these pages. Readers, teachers and parents can use them to find their way to great treasures.

Alan Gibbons is an award winning author and organiser of the Campaign for the Book

www.alangibbons.net

The Editors

Viv Warren and Mary Yardley are qualified librarians with many years' experience of working with children and young people in schools, in Schools Library Services and in public libraries. Mary and Viv became colleagues whilst working for East Sussex County Council, when Viv was Head of Library Services to Children and Young People and Mary, Head of Information Management.

Between them they have experience of:

- setting up and running school and college libraries
- formulating a variety of policies for library services in East Sussex
- advising schools on books and book provision
- advising parents and teachers on books and reading
- selecting stock for schools, Schools Library Services and public libraries
- running courses for teachers and parents on choosing and using books
- organising events to encourage parents and children to enjoy books together
- giving book talks to all ages
- setting up and running reading groups for both children and adults
- compiling up-to-date reading lists for all ages

Viv is now retired but keeps in touch - she is on the governing board of several schools and is chair of governors at an "outstanding" nursery school in Brighton. She delivers occasional book-related courses and has acted as co-ordinator for Family Learning events. Mary is currently working for Dorset Schools Library Service.

Contents

Acknowledgements ii

Introduction iv

How to Use this Guide vi

Author Lists for Ages: 5-7 1

                               8-11 44

                               12-14 105

                               14+ 168

Genres and Themes: Adoption, Adventure 197
    Ancient history 199
    Animals 200
    Apartheid, Ballet, Bullying 201
    Computers, Crime, Crusades, Death 202
    Detective mysteries 203
    Diaries, Disability, Dystopia 204
    Easy reader, Eating disorders, Environment 205
    Espionage, Fairy/folk, Family 206
    Fantasy 209
    Friends 211
    Genocide, Ghost/supernatural 213
    Historical 214
    Holocaust, Homosexuality, Horror 215
    Humour 216
    Illness, Immigration, Letters, Magic 219
    Martial arts 220
    Mystery, Mythology 221
    Other cultures, Other lands 222
    Philosophy, Pony/horse, Relationships, Romance 223
    School 224
    Science fiction 225
    Sea/boats, Slavery, Social issues 226
    Space, Sport, Stage, Superhero 228
    Teen pregnancy, Thrillers 229
    Time travel, Toys, Traditional, Transport 230
    Vampires, War 231

Graphic Novels 232

Short Stories 235

Current Children's Book Prizes 236

Exploring Further and Keeping up to Date 247

Index 253

Acknowledgements

As always we owe a debt of gratitude to many people without whose help this guide could not have been compiled.

Contributors who deserve a special measure of thanks are Dorset Schools Library Service; Karen Horsfield of Somerset Schools Library Service; Anna Morgan of "Bags of Books" bookshop, Lewes, East Sussex; Grace Ryan; and Dorne Fraser of Norfolk Library and Information Service.

The ideas and imagination of the many people who have contributed, help to give the book a wider scope and relevance, and we would like to acknowledge how difficult it is to find time to help with projects like ours with all the pressures there are in the workplace. Some of the people who contributed to the first round of information provision for this edition were unable to contribute further owing to staff shortages, and some have since lost their jobs.

Eileen Armstrong	Cramlington High School, Northumberland
Sally Ballard	Ranelagh School, Bracknell
Barbara Band	The Emmbrook School, Wokingham
Liz Broekmann & her team	Slough Library Service
Judy Cardnell	Colfe's School, Greenwich
Gill Clipsham	Buckinghamshire Libraries & Heritage
Paul Cunningham & SLS team	Suffolk Libraries and Heritage
Jill Currie	Plymouth Library Services
Caroline Fielding	Blackheath Bluecoats C of E Secondary School
Ellie Frost	Blessed Thomas Holford Catholic College, Altrincham
Mel Gibson	Senior Lecturer in Childhood Studies, & Trainer & Historian – Comics & Visual Literacies, Northumbria University
Lynne Hamer	Bath & North East Somerset Libraries
Susan Heyes & her teams	West Sussex Library Service
Gavin McQueen	London Borough of Richmond upon Thames
Judy Ottaway	
Tracey Paddon	Newport Central Library
Greta Paterson	East Sussex Library Service
Angela Robinson	Blackburn with Darwen Library Service
Linda Tomalin	Leicestershire Libraries

Helen Towers Hertfordshire Library Service
Laurel van Dommelen London Borough of Enfield Library Service
Jo Wesson Stoney Dean School, Amersham
Sue Yockney Dorset Schools Library Service

As always we are grateful to our publishers, LISU, at Loughborough University, and in particular to Mary Ashworth and Sharon Fletcher, who have guided us with unfailing patience.

Viv Warren   Mary Yardley

The publishers and editors are grateful to the following for permission to use reproductions from their original cover images:

Inside by J A Jarman
reproduced by permission of Andersen Press

Odd and the Frost Giants by Neil Gaiman
The Resistance by Gemma Malley
both reproduced by permission of Bloomsbury Publishing

Mezolith by Ben Haggarty, published by David Fickling Books.
Used by permission of The Random House Group Ltd.

Meerkat Mail and Spells by Emily Gravett
reproduced by permission of Macmillan Children's Books, London, UK

Diary of a Wimpy Vampire by Tim Collins
reproduced by permission of Michael O'Mara Books

The Shapeshifter - Dowsing the Dead by Ali Sparkes
reproduced by permission of OUP Oxford

Diary of a Wimpy Kid: Dog Days by Jeff Kinney (2011)
Devil's Kiss by Sarwat Chadda (2009)
The Enemy by Charlie Higson (2010)
Envy by Anna Godbersen (2009)
Spy Dog Secret Santa by Andrew Cope (2010)
all reproduced by permission of Penguin Books Ltd, London

The Abused Werewolf Rescue Group by Catherine Jinks
reproduced by permission of Quercus Publishing

Rebel Angels by Libba Bray
The 13 Treasures by Michelle Harrison
both reproduced by permission of Simon & Schuster

The Heartless Robots by Simon Bartram
reproduced by permission of Templar Publishing

Introduction

Who Next...? A guide to children's authors is designed as a tool to help parents, teachers and librarians in schools and public libraries to guide children who have already enjoyed stories by one writer to find other authors they will enjoy reading.

The book lists 759 writers of children's fiction, and with each name suggests other authors who write in a similar way. The idea is that you look up one of your favourite children's authors, then try reading a book by one of the other authors listed underneath. By moving from one entry to another, readers can expand the number of writers they enjoy. The same system has been used successfully in a similar guide to adult fiction, also published by LISU, *Who Else Writes Like...? A reader's guide to fiction authors*, which is now in its sixth edition.

The links that have been made between authors are of genre and theme, and also of styles of writing, or similar aspects of characterisation and settings. Of course no author writes exactly like another and readers will not agree with all the choices. Questioning *Who Next...?* may be one of the pleasures of using it, and a source for discussion and debate.

Most of the authors listed have written several books. We have tried to include books that are easily available, so you should be able to find the recommended titles in either a library or available from a bookshop/online supplier. Whilst recognising their importance in encouraging the love of reading, it was decided to exclude picture books for younger readers as the aim is to focus on the story rather than illustration. However, some classic picture books have been included as it is considered that they are multi-layered and work on any level for any age range of reader.

Also, we have tried to point out some titles aimed at young people with lower than average reading ages. These are in the main text and are indicated by BS after the title. This means that they have been produced by the publisher Barrington Stoke, who publishes books, written by popular authors, for children who have dyslexia, or who are struggling or reluctant readers – further information can be found on their website, www.barringtonstoke.co.uk. There are many other publishers who produce some titles with the same aim, but BS are specialists.

A new category added to this edition is entitled Easy reader and indicates that the author listed is a contributor to one of the many series which are aimed at helping children to master the art of reading.

We have also widened the age group to include 14-18 years. This section is not as comprehensive as the other age groups but is an attempt to highlight other titles that are often overlooked. Some of the stories involve difficult and often controversial material such as eating disorders, suicide and fatal illness and, therefore, should be recommended with sensitivity. Adults' authors that may be suitable for this age group can be found in the adult companion title Who Else Writes Like....?

Who Next...? is arranged by four 'audience age groups': children aged 5-7, 8-11, 12-14 and 14+. Where an author writes for more than one age group, this is shown. We have not attempted to define age ranges exactly, as this is limiting and our aim is to encourage children to read as widely as possible. We ask users of Who Next...? to bear in mind the preferences, abilities and needs of individual children.

We have also included in the text a selection of titles for each author, so that readers trying an author new to them have some idea of where to start.

At the end of Who Next...? are indexes of authors by theme and genre as well as a list of prize winners. There is also a section entitled Exploring Further, which suggests a small number of books, magazines and websites to enable readers to research further and to keep up to date.

We very much hope that this book will help many readers to enjoy more children's books.

Viv Warren   Mary Yardley

v

How to Use this Guide

Author Lists

We have arranged the lists of authors by age range then alphabetically by author surname.

So, to use *Who Next...?*, first select the appropriate age range, 5–7, 8–11, 12–14 or 14+. Then, in the alphabetical list, locate the author you want to match. There you will find the suggested alternative authors.

For example, a reader who is nine years old and who likes books by Kevin Crossley-Holland, might also enjoy stories by Geraldine McCaughrean, William Nicholson, Michelle Paver, Richard Platt, Philip Reeve, Rick Riordan, Rosemary Sutcliff or T H White.

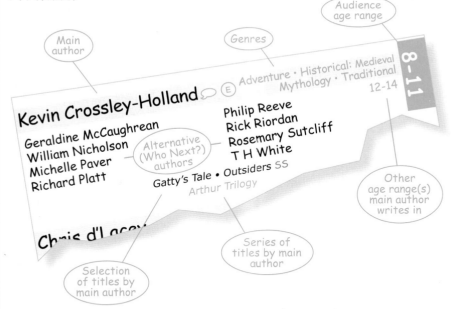

Where an author writes in a theme or genre, this is indicated. Do remember that some authors who frequently write in a particular category or for a specific age group sometimes produce a book in a quite different genre or for another age group. You can check this by reading the jacket details and summaries on the books themselves.

Barrington Stoke

Bradman   Adve.

ndreae   Te
  Beardsley   Rob
    ock • The Dirty Dozen (BS) • Hu
      Creaky Castle Series • Foc

BS indicates that this title is published by Barrington Stoke who specialise in resources for dyslexic and struggling readers www.barringtonstoke.co.uk.

Graphic Novels

GN indicates that this title is a Graphic Novel. Some titles can be found both as a straight text and as a Graphic Novel format. A list of all those titles featured in the text can be found on pages 232-234.

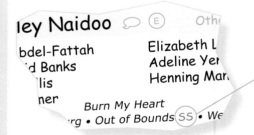

t Groening   Environment • F
  Jennings
  ry Pratchett   J
  Smith   /
                               S
      Futurama Series (GN) • The

Short Stories

ley Naidoo ⟨⟩ (E)   Oth

bdel-Fattah   Elizabeth L
 d Banks   Adeline Yer
  lis   Henning Mar.
   ner
      Burn My Heart
       rg • Out of Bounds (SS) • We

In this edition we have included some collections of short stories. These are indicated by the letters SS under the author entry. A list of all those indicated can be found on page 235.

Talking Books

Where some books by an author are available on CD and/or audio download as talking books, the symbol ⟨⟩ has been included by the author's name. (This does not necessarily imply that the listed titles for that author are available in this format.)

illiams ⟨⟩   Advent

eBooks

B Robert (E) Fc

The symbol (≡) by the author's name indicates that some of his/her books are available as ebooks, in one or more formats. It does not imply that the listed titles are available as ebooks. Given the rapidly developing ebook market, the absence of the symbol should not be seen as a definitive indication that ebooks are not available by that author.

Genres and Themes

If you only want a list of authors who write in a particular category or genre, such as Adventure or Animals, then turn straight to the Genre lists which start on page 197.

Current Children's Book Prizes

For this edition we have added a new list of current children's book prizes and these can be found on pages 236-237. The most long-lasting awards, listed in previous editions of the book, have been updated and are covered in detail on pages 238-246, together with their prize winners.

We believe you will find th s guide easy to use, but please remember, it is not nfallible. We have tried to ensure that you can navigate through a wealth of childrens literature for all ages, particularly as there are fewer specia ists to help now.
BUT, if you do need more information, ask -
library and bookshop staff are very willing to help.

Anne Adeney   Animals • Easy reader • Fairy/folk • Humour

Andy Blackford
Anne Cassidy
Penny Dolan
Sue Graves
Stella Gurney

Maggie Moore
Margaret Nash
Jillian Powell
Hilary Robinson
Barrie Wade

Agnes and the Giant • Ben and the Bear • The Big Duck
Five Teddy Bears • George and the Dragon • Lighthouse Mouse

Allan Ahlberg Ⓔ Animals • Easy reader • Family • Humour

Jonathan Allen
Giles Andreae
John Burningham
Chris d'Lacey
P D Eastman

Kes Gray
Daren King
David Orme
Julie Sykes

8-11

Burglar Bill • Chicken, Chips and Peas • Cops and Robbers
The Pencil • The Runaway Dinner • Shopping Expedition
Fast Fox, Slow Dog Series • Funnybones Series
The Gaskitts Series • Happy Families Series

Jenny Alexander   Adventure • Easy reader • Humour • Transport

Benedict Blathwayt
Jeff Brown

John Cunliffe
Jon Scieszka

Car-Mad Jack Series

Jonathan Allen   Humour • Magic

Allan Ahlberg
Terence Blacker
Humphrey Carpenter
Lauren Child

Jonathan Emmett
Ann Jungman
Jill Murphy
Shoo Rayner

I'm Not Cute! • I'm Not Sleepy! • When the Snow Comes

David Almond

Family · Fantasy

8-11
12-14

Neil Gaiman
Oliver Jeffers

Shaun Tan

The Boy Who Climbed into the Moon

Scoular Anderson

Animals · Easy reader · Humour · Magic

Simon Bartram
Tony Bradman
Julia Jarman
Frank Rodgers
Dee Shulman

Wendy Smith
Paul Stewart
Karen Wallace
Jeanne Willis
Philip Wooderson

Space Pirates Series • Stan the Dog Series • Wizzbang Wizard Series

Sorrel Anderson Ⓔ

Animals · Humour

Emily Bearn
Nick Butterworth
Hayley Daze

Joe Friedman
Daren King

The Clumsies Series

Giles Andreae Ⓔ

Animals · Fantasy · Friends · Humour

8-11

Allan Ahlberg
Jon Blake
Judy Brown
Lynley Dodd
Julia Jarman

Timothy Knapman
Alan MacDonald
Tony Mitton
Nick Sharratt
Mark Skelton

Billy Bonkers • Billy Bonkers 2: More Madness
The Chimpanzees of Happytown • Giraffes Can't Dance
Princess Pearl • Rumble in the Jungle
Captain Flinn and the Pirate Dinosaur Series

Laurence Anholt

Easy reader · Fairy/folk
Historical · Humour

8-11

Dosh Archer
Tony Bradman
Keith Brumpton
Ann Bryant
Lauren Child

Roald Dahl
Tony Mitton
Russell Punter
Bob Wilson
Chris Wormell

Bleeping Beauty • Seven for a Secret
Stone Girl, Bone Girl • Sunshine Boy
The One and Only Series • Seriously Silly Rhymes
Seriously Silly Stories

Dosh Archer

Laurence Anholt
Tony Bradman
Sam Lloyd

Jeremy Strong
Julie Sykes

Urgency Emergency! Series

Philip Ardagh 🗨

Jon Blake
Michael Broad
Jeff Brown

Alan MacDonald
Andy Stanton

Grubtown Tales Series

Ronda and David Armitage 🗨

Simon Bartram
Benedict Blathwayt
John Cunliffe
Mairi Hedderwick

Shirley Hughes
Sam Lloyd
Jane Simmons

The Lighthouse Keeper Series

Atinuke

Malorie Blackman
Ann Cameron

Mary Hoffman

Anna Hibiscus · Good Luck, Anna Hibiscus!
Have Fun, Anna Hibiscus! · Hooray for Anna Hibiscus
The No 1 Car Spotter

Antonia Barber 🗨

Michael Morpurgo
Linda Newbery

Mal Peet and Elspeth Graham
Jane Simmons

The Mousehole Cat

Simon Bartram 🗨

Scoular Anderson
Ronda and David Armitage
Martyn Beardsley
Bob Graham
Emily Gravett

Mini Grey
Oliver Jeffers
Timothy Knapman
Anna Maxted
David Orme

Dougal's Deep Sea Diary · Man on the Moon
Bob and Barry's Lunar Adventures Series

Klaus Baumgart

Friends · School

Joyce Lankester Brisley
Dorothy Edwards
Sally Gardner

Astrid Lindgren
Bel Mooney
Alf Prøysen

Laura's Star Series

Martyn Beardsley

Adventure · Family · Humour

8-11

Simon Bartram
Tony Bradman
Humphrey Carpenter
Anne Fine

Timothy Knapman
Tony Mitton
Chris Riddell
Karen Wallace

Sir Gadabout Series

Emily Bearn (E)

Adventure · Animals · Humour

Sorrel Anderson
Sue Bentley
Nick Butterworth
Hayley Daze
Ann Jungman

Michael Morpurgo
Chris Riddell
Geronimo Stilton
Jill Tomlinson
Alison Uttley

Tumtum and Nutmeg Series

David Bedford

Humour · Sport

8-11

Judy Brown
Keith Brumpton
Rob Childs
Alan Durant

Francesca Simon
Sophie Smiley
Martin Waddell

The Team Series

Ben 10

Adventure · Fantasy

H I Larry
Anna Maxted

David Orme

Ben 10 Comic Books Series GN

GN = Graphic novel

Raymond Briggs

John Grant
Emily Gravett
Satoshi Kitamura
Neal Layton
Alan MacDonald

Colin McNaughton
Laura North
Dav Pilkey
Andy Stanton

The Bear • Father Christmas
Fungus the Bogeyman • Jim and the Beanstalk • The Puddleman • Ug

Joyce Lankester Brisley

Family • Humour

Klaus Baumgart
Dorothy Edwards
Astrid Lindgren
Bel Mooney

Martine Murray
Jenny Oldfield
Alf Prøysen
Jenny Valentine

Milly Molly Mandy Stories

Michael Broad Adventure • Animals • Fantasy • Humour

Philip Ardagh
Jeff Brown
Andrew Cope
Alan MacDonald
Hilary McKay

Anna Maxted
Barbara Mitchelhill
Louis Sachar
Andy Stanton

Forget-Me-Not Series • Jake Cake Series • Monsterbook Series

Jeff Brown

Adventure • Fantasy

Jenny Alexander
Philip Ardagh
Michael Broad
Sally Gardner
John Grant

Megan McDonald
Dav Pilkey
Alf Prøysen
Andy Stanton

Flat Stanley Series

Judy Brown

Adventure • Fantasy • Sport

Giles Andreae
David Bedford
Janet Burchett and
 Sara Vogler

Vivian French
Astrid Lindgren
Colin McNaughton
Ian Whybrow

Pirate Princess Series • Super Soccer Boy Series

Marc Brown ⬭

Animals · Easy reader · Family
Friends · Humour

P D Eastman
John Grant
Shirley Hughes
James Marshall

Frank Rodgers
Dr Seuss
Francesca Simon
Ian Whybrow

Arthur Series

Anthony Browne

Animals · Family

John Burningham
Neil Gaiman
Mini Grey

O iver Jeffers
Satoshi Kitamura

*Bear's Magic Pencil • Changes • Little Beauty
Me and You • The Shape Game • Willy and Hugh*

Keith Brumpton ⬭

Fantasy · Humour · Sport

Laurence Anholt
David Bedford
Janet Burchett and
    Sara Vogler
Rob Childs

Paul Cooper
Rex Stone
Jeremy Strong
Martin Waddell
Philip Wooderson

Dino FC Series

Ann Bryant ⬭ Ballet · Easy reader · Friends · Humour · Magic

8-11

Laurence Anholt
Benedict Blathwayt
Darcey Bussell
Harriet Castor
Sue Graves

Beatrice Masini
James Mayhew
David Orme
Mo Willems
Anna Wilson

*Bad Cat, Ned! • But, Mum! • Hurry Up!
Jack's Party • Tag! • Who's at the Zoo?
Ballerina Dream Series*

Janet Burchett and Sara Vogler Ⓔ

Humour · Magic
Sport

Judy Brown
Keith Brumpton
Rob Childs
Paul Cooper

David Melling
Martin Waddell
Bob Wilson

*Fantastic Football Series
Gargoylz Series*

John Burningham

Animals · Family · Fantasy

Allan Ahlberg	Oliver Jeffers
Anthony Browne	Jill Tomlinson
Bob Graham	Martin Waddell

Avocado Baby • *Grandpa* • *The Magic Bed*
Mr Gumpy's Outing • *The Shopping Basket*

Darcey Bussell

Ballet · Magic

8-11

Ann Bryant	Natasha May
Harriet Castor	Daisy Meadows
Beatrice Masini	Anna Wilson

Magic Ballerina Series

Nick Butterworth

Adventure · Animals · Family · Humour

Sorrel Anderson	Lynley Dodd
Emily Bearn	Jan Fearnley
Helen Cooper	Mick Inkpen
John Cunliffe	Linda Newbery
Hayley Daze	Chris Riddell

Albert le Blanc • *Just Like Jasper*
My Mum is Fantastic • *Q Pootle 5* • *Thud!* • *The Whisperer*
Percy's Park Series • *Adventures of Jake Series*

Ann Cameron

Family · Friends · Humour · Other cultures

Atinuke	Shirley Hughes
Malorie Blackman	Julia Jarman
Dorothy Edwards	Francesca Simon

Banana Spaghetti
Julian Series

Humphrey Carpenter

Humour · Magic · School

Jonathan Allen	Tiffany Mandrake
Martyn Beardsley	Sue Mongredien
Terence Blacker	Jill Murphy
Maeve Friel	Julie Sykes
Ann Jungman	Kaye Umansky

Mr Majeika Series

Anne Cassidy   Animals · Easy reader · Fairy/folk · Humour

12-14
14+

Anne Adeney
Andy Blackford
Penny Dolan
Sue Graves
Stella Gurney

Maggie Moore
Jillian Powell
Hilary Robinson
Joan Stimson
Barrie Wade

Croc's Tooth • *Pippa and Poppa*
Wizard Wizzle Series

Harriet Castor Ballet · Friends

Ann Bryant
Darcey Bussell
Vivian French
Elizabeth Lindsay

Bel Mooney
Shoo Rayner
Anna Wilson

Ballet Magic
The Incredible Present
The Sleepover Club Series

Linda Chapman (E) Fantasy · Magic · Pony/horse

8-11

Sue Bentley
Maeve Friel
Pippa Funnell
Dick King-Smith
Elizabeth Lindsay

Kelly McKain
Daisy Meadows
Jenny Oldfield
Gwyneth Rees
Anna Wilson

Not Quite a Mermaid Series • *Skating School Series*
Sky Horses Series • *Stardust Series* • *Unicorn School Series*

Lauren Child (E) Fairy/folk · Family · Humour

8-11

Jonathan Allen
Laurence Anholt
Joe Friedman
Neil Gaiman
Kes Gray

Mini Grey
Astrid Lindgren
Alan Rusbridger
Dyan Sheldon
Kaye Umansky

Beware of the Story Book Wolves
Hubert Horatio Bartle Bobtor-Trent • *That Pesky Rat*
The Princess and the Pea
Who's Afraid of the Big Bad Book? • *Who Wants to be a Poodle? I Don't*
Charlie and Lola Series • *Clarice Bean Series*

Rob Childs

David Bedford
Keith Brumpton
Janet Burchett and
  Sara Vogler
Alan Durant

Alan MacDonald
Sophie Smiley
Martin Waddell
Bob Wilson

Keeper's Ball • Strike!
Wicked Catch! • Wicked Day!

Emma Chichester Clark

Animals · Friends · Humour

Alan Durant
Rose Impey
Paeony Lewis
Sam Lloyd
David McKee

James Marshall
Hiawyn Oram
Jane Simmons
Jill Tomlinson

Eliza and the Moonchild • Minty and Tink
Blue Kangaroo Series • Melrose and Croc Series

Alex Cliff

Adventure · Fantasy
8-11

Elizabeth Singer Hunt
H I Larry

Rex Stone
Jonny Zucker

Superpowers Series

Helen Cooper

Animals · Friends · Humour

Nick Butterworth
Bob Graham

Chris Wormell

Dog Biscuit • Pumpkin Soup

Paul Cooper

Animals · Humour

Tony Bradman
Keith Brumpton
Janet Burchett and
  Sara Vogler
Ted Dewan

Jonathan Emmett
Tony Mitton
Paul Stewart
Ian Whybrow

Pigs in Planes Series

E Some titles are available as ebooks

Andrew Cope Adventure · Animals · Humour

8-11

Michael Broad
Elizabeth Singer Hunt
Hilary McKay
Barbara Mitchelhill

Hiawyn Oram
Geronimo Stilton
Colin West
Jonny Zucker

Spy Dog Series · Spy Pups Series

June Crebbin Fantasy · Humour · Pony/horse

Chris d'Lacey
Roald Dahl
Alan Durant
Jan Fearnley
Anne Fine

Vivian French
Pippa Funnell
Diana Kimpton
Elizabeth Lindsay
Kelly McKain

The Dragon Test · Hal the Highwayman
Hal the Pirate · The King's Shopping
Merryfield Hall Riding School Series

John Cunliffe Friends · Humour

Jenny Alexander
Ronda and David Armitage
Andy Blackford
Benedict Blathwayt

Nick Butterworth
Sally Grindley
Jillian Powell

Postman Pat Series

Chris d'Lacey Animals · Family · Fantasy · Humour

8-11

Allan Ahlberg
Tony Bradman
June Crebbin

Vivian French
Pippa Goodhart
Michael Morpurgo

The Dragons of Wayward Crescent Series

Roald Dahl Fantasy · Humour

8-11

Laurence Anholt
June Crebbin
Paul Fleischman
Daren King
Tony Mitton

Laura North
Francesca Simon
Andy Stanton
Jeremy Strong
Bob Wilson

Dirty Beasts · Esio Trot · Fantastic Mr Fox
The Giraffe and the Pelly and Me · The Magic Finger
Revolting Rhymes

Lucy Daniels

Animals · Friends
8-11

Sue Bentley
Hayley Daze
Diana Kimpton
Dick King-Smith

Elizabeth Lindsay
Summer Waters
Holly Webb

*Animal Ark Pets Series • Dolphin Diaries Series
Little Animal Ark Series*

Hayley Daze

Animals · Magic

Sorrel Anderson
Emily Bearn
Sue Bentley
Nick Butterworth

Lucy Daniels
Summer Waters
Holly Webb

Puddle the Naughtiest Puppy Series

Ted Dewan

Animals · Humour

Paul Cooper
Ian Falconer
Colin McNaughton

Simon Puttock
Alison Uttley

Crispin Stories

Lynley Dodd

Animals · Humour

Giles Andreae
Nick Butterworth
Julia Donaldson
Emily Gravett

Mick Inkpen
Sam Lloyd
Daniel Postgate
Jill Tomlinson

Hairy McClarey Series

Penny Dolan ⊙ (E)

Animals · Easy reader
Ghost/supernatural · Humour

Anne Adeney
Andy Blackford
Anne Cassidy
Malachy Doyle
Sue Graves

Karina Law
Margaret Nash
Jillian Powell
Hilary Robinson
Joan Stimson

*In the Deep Dark Forest
The Little Red Hen • Lola Fanola
Mister Babbit's Rabbit • Mrs Bootle's Boots
Carlo's Circus Series • The Forest Family Series*

Julia Donaldson (E)

Lynley Dodd
Jan Fearnley
Bob Graham
Harry Horse
David McKee

David Melling
Chris Riddell
Tony Ross
Chris Wormell
Jane Yolen

Cave Baby • The Gruffalo
The Gruffalo's Child • Stick Man • The Troll • Zog
Princess Mirror-Belle Series

Malachy Doyle ⌢

Penny Dolan
Rose Impey
Geraldine McCaughrean
Margaret Mayo
Maggie Moore

Saviour Pirotta
Russell Punter
Barrie Wade
Karen Wallace
Ian Whybrow

Albert and Sarah Jane
Finn MacCool and the Giant's Causeway
The Football Ghosts • The Hound of Ulster • Jack and the Jungle
When a Zeeder Met a Xyder

Alan Durant ⌢

David Bedford
Rob Childs
Emma Chichester Clark
June Crebbin

Oliver Jeffers
Shoo Rayner
Paul Stewart
Mo Willems

Brown Bear Gets in Shape
A Dinosaur Called Tiny • Football Fever • Goal!
Nursery Crimes Series • Spider McDrew Series

P D Eastman (E)

Allan Ahlberg
Stan and Jan Berenstain
Marc Brown

Dr Seuss
Colin West
Mo Willems

Are You My Mother?
Go, Dog, Go! • Sam and the Firefly

⌢ Some titles are available as Talking books

Dorothy Edwards

5-7

Family · Friends · Humour

Klaus Baumgart
Joyce Lankester Brisley
Ann Cameron
Mairi Hedderwick
Mary Hoffman

Astrid Lindgren
Bel Mooney
Chris Powling
Dyan Sheldon
Jenny Valentine

My Naughty Little Sister Series

Jonathan Emmett

Adventure · Friends · Humour · Magic

Jonathan Allen
Paul Cooper
Jan Fearnley

Damian Harvey
Ann Jungman

*Foxes in the Snow • If We Had a Sailboat • The Pig's Knickers
Pigs Might Fly: Further Adventures of the Three Little Pigs
The Santa Trap • What Friends Do Best*
Conjuror's Cookbook Series

Ian Falconer

Animals · Humour

Ted Dewan
Colin McNaughton
Daniel Postgate

Simon Puttock
Michael Rosen

Olivia Series

Jan Fearnley

Animals · Family · Friends · Humour

Nick Butterworth
June Crebbin
Julia Donaldson

Jonathan Emmett
Frank Rodgers
Jeanne Willis

*Arthur and the Meanies
The Baby Dragon Tamer • Martha in the Middle • Milo Armadillo
Mr Wolf's Pancakes • Mr Wolf and the Three Bears*

Anne Fine

Family · Fantasy · Friends · School · Traditional

Martyn Beardsley
June Crebbin
Harry Horse
Hilary McKay
Bel Mooney

Michael Morpurgo
Linda Newbery
Jenny Nimmo
Jacqueline Wilson

8-11
12-14

*Friday Surprise • It Moved! • Jamie and Angus Forever
Notso Hotso • Under a Silver Moon • The Worst Child I Ever Had*
Killer Cat Series

Paul Fleischman

Roald Dahl   Louis Sachar

The Dunderheads

Vivian French

Judy Brown   Daisy Meadows
Harriet Castor   Simon Puttock
June Crebbin   Gwyneth Rees
Chris d'Lacey   Anna Wilson
Sally Grindley

Brian the Giant
Mouse in the House • Pig in Love
Draglins Series • The Tiara Club Series

Joe Friedman

Sorrel Anderson   Mick Inkpen
Lauren Child

Boobela and Worm Series

Maeve Friel

8-11

Terence Blacker   Sue Mongredien
Humphrey Carpenter   Jill Murphy
Linda Chapman   Laura Owen
Kelly McKain   Wendy Smith
Daisy Meadows   Valerie Thomas

Felix and the Kitten
Felix on the Move • Felix Takes the Blame
Tiger Lily Series • Witch in Training Series

Pippa Funnell

8-11

Linda Chapman   Elizabeth Lindsay
June Crebbin   Kelly McKain
Diana Kimpton   Jenny Oldfield

Tilly's Pony Tails Series

Go to back for lists of: Authors by Genre • Graphic novels
Short stories • Prize winners • Exploring further

Neil Gaiman Ⓔ

Animals · Family · Fantasy

David Almond
Anthony Browne
Lauren Child
Mini Grey

Oliver Jeffers
Colin McNaughton
Shaun Tan
Colin Thompson

8-11
12-14
14+

Crazy Hair
The Day I Swapped My Dad for Two Goldfish
Instructions • *The Wolves in the Walls*

Sally Gardner Ⓔ

Fantasy

Klaus Baumgart
Jeff Brown

Hilda Offen

8-11
12-14

Magical Children Series

Pippa Goodhart

Animals · Easy reader · Fantasy · School

Chris d'Lacey
Mick Gowar
Mary Hoffman
Geraldine McCaughrean

Alan MacDonald
Michael Morpurgo
Jill Tomlinson

Ashok's Dog • *Big Cat*
Dogball • *Dragon Magic* • *Glog* • *Nature Detectives*
Maxine and Minnie Series

Mick Gowar

Adventure · Easy reader · Friends · Humour

Tony Bradman
Pippa Goodhart
Geraldine McCaughrean

Tony Ross
Joan Stimson

Sir Otto
Finn's Fortune Series • *Sheriff Stan Series*

Bob Graham

Animals · Family · Friends · Humour · Magic

Simon Bartram
John Burningham
Helen Cooper
Julia Donaldson
Kes Gray

Mini Grey
Shirley Hughes
Maggie Moore
Tony Ross
Hannah Shaw

April Underhill Tooth Fairy • *How to Heal a Broken Wing*
Jethro Byrd, Fairy Child • *Miracle on Separation Street*
Tales from the Waterhole • *The Trouble with Dogs*

John Grant

Tony Bradman
Raymond Briggs
Jeff Brown
Marc Brown

Neal Layton
Alan MacDonald
Dav Pilkey
Nick Sharratt

Littlenose Series

Sue Graves

Anne Adeney
Ann Bryant
Anne Cassidy
Penny Dolan
Damian Harvey

Maggie Moore
Margaret Nash
David Orme
Joan Stimson

A Cake for Tea
Blackbeard's Treasure • Don in a Mess
I Wish • Too Sleepy • Tubby Tabby

Emily Gravett

Simon Bartram
Raymond Briggs
Lynley Dodd
Kes Gray
Mini Grey

Oliver Jeffers
Timothy Knapman
Hannah Shaw
Colin Thompson
Chris Wormell

Little Mouse's Big Book of Fears
Meerkat Mail • The Rabbit Problem
Spells • Wolf Won't Bite • Wolves

Kes Gray

8-11

Allan Ahlberg
Benedict Blathwayt
Lauren Child
Bob Graham

Emily Gravett
Nick Sharratt
Jenny Valentine

Billy's Bucket • Cluck O'Clock
Mum and Dad Glue • My Mum Goes to Work • Vesuvius Poovius
Daisy Series

💬 Some titles are available as Talking books

Mini Grey

Simon Bartram
Anthony Browne
Lauren Child
Neil Gaiman
Bob Graham

Emily Gravett
Hiawyn Oram
Hannah Shaw
Colin Thompson
Chris Wormell

The Adventures of the Dish and the Spoon
Biscuit Bear • Egg Drop • Three by the Sea
Traction Man is Here • Traction Man Meets Turbodog

Sally Grindley Adventure · Animals · Friends

Stan and Jan Berenstain
John Cunliffe
Vivian French

Barbara Mitchelhill
Margaret Ryan
Karen Wallace

8-11

Cat-a-Wall • Crazy Chameleons
Little Elephant Thunderfoot • Mouldylocks and the Three Clares
Bear Detective Series • Poppy and Max Series

Stella Gurney Adventure · Easy reader · Humour / Other cultures · School

Anne Adeney
Anne Cassidy
Maggie Moore

Margaret Nash
Hilary Robinson
Barrie Wade

Kassia's Surprise • Mr Bickle and the Ghost
My Dad the Hero • Sally Sails the Seas • Will's Boomerang

Damian Harvey Historical · Humour · Magic · Mythology

Jonathan Emmett
Sue Graves
Maggie Moore
Jillian Powell
Hilary Robinson

Barrie Wade
Karen Wallace
Ian Whybrow
Jeanne Willis

Big Bad Bart • Captain Cool
Eric Bloodaxe the Viking King • King Midas's Golden Touch
Snail's Legs • The Wizard's Wish
The Mudcrusts Series • Robo-Runners Series
Tales of Robin Hood Series

E Some titles are available as ebooks

19

Mairi Hedderwick Family

Ronda and David Armitage
Dorothy Edwards
Shirley Hughes
Astrid Lindgren

James Mayhew
Jill Murphy
Michael Rosen

Katie Morag Series

Mary Hoffman (E)

Adventure · Family · Friends
Humour · Other cultures
12-14

Atinuke
Malorie Blackman
Dorothy Edwards

Fippa Goodhart
Hiawyn Oram
David Orme

The Colour of Home
Grace Series

Harry Horse (E)

Adventure · Animals · Environment

Julia Donaldson
Anne Fine
Michael Morpurgo

Linda Newbery
Alison Uttley

The Last Castaways
The Last Cowboys • *The Last Gold Diggers* • *The Last Polar Bears*
Little Rabbit Series

Shirley Hughes (E)

Family · Humour · War 1939-45

Ronda and David Armitage
Marc Brown
Ann Cameron
Bob Graham

Mairi Hedderwick
Mick Inkpen
Michael Rosen
Martin Waddell

Dogger • *Ella's Big Chance*
Helpers • *Jonadab and Rita* • *The Lion and the Unicorn*
Lucy and Tom Go to School
Alfie Stories • *Olly and Me Series*

Elizabeth Singer Hunt

Adventure · Other lands
8-11

Alex Cliff
Andrew Cope
H I Larry

Hilary McKay
Rex Stone
Jonny Zucker

Jack Stalwart Series

Rose Impey

Animals · Family · Humour · Traditional

8-11

Emma Chichester Clark
Malachy Doyle
Karina Law
James Marshall
Tony Mitton

Sue Mongredien
Hiawyn Oram
Alan Rusbridger
Margaret Ryan

Monster and Frog Series · Nipper McFee Series
Scout and Ace Series · Titchy Witch Series

Mick Inkpen

Animals · Humour · Toys

Nick Butterworth
Lynley Dodd
Joe Friedman
Shirley Hughes
Paeony Lewis

David McKee
Beatrix Potter
Tony Ross
Mo Willems
Jane Yolen

Baggy Brown
Blue Nose Island Series · Kipper Series

Julia Jarman

Adventure · Animals · Historical: Tudor
Magic · Other cultures

8-11
14+

Scoular Anderson
Giles Andreae
Malorie Blackman
Ann Cameron
Beatrix Potter

Chris Powling
Alan Rusbridger
Dee Shulman
Jacqueline Wilson

Class Two at the Zoo · Class Three All at Sea
Grandma's Seaside Bloomers · Henry Eighth Has to Choose
Hey! What's That Nasty Whiff? · Jessame to the Rescue and Other Stories

Oliver Jeffers

Death · Fantasy · Friends · Humour

8-11

David Almond
Simon Bartram
Anthony Browne
John Burningham
Alan Durant

Neil Gaiman
Emily Gravett
Neal Layton
Shaun Tan
Chris Wormell

The Great Paper Caper
The Heart and the Bottle · How to Catch a Star
The Incredible Book Eating Boy · Lost and Found · The Way Back Home

Ann Jungman 💬

Jonathan Allen
Emily Bearn
Terence Blacker
Humphrey Carpenter
Jonathan Emmett

Jill Murphy
Shoo Rayner
Margaret Ryan
Geronimo Stilton

*Broomstick Series • Romans Series
Septimouse Series • Vlad the Drac Series*

Diana Kimpton

Sue Bentley
June Crebbin
Lucy Daniels
Pippa Funnell

Elizabeth Lindsay
Kelly McKain
Holly Webb

*Amy Wild, Animal Talker Series
Pony-Mad Princess Series*

Daren King

Allan Ahlberg
Sorrel Anderson
Roald Dahl
Dick King-Smith
Michael Morpurgo

Jenny Nimmo
Chris Powling
Dee Shulman
Jeremy Strong

*Mouse Noses on Toast
Peter the Penguin Pioneer
Frightfully Friendly Ghosties Series*

Dick King-Smith 💬

Linda Chapman
Lucy Daniels
Daren King
Bel Mooney
Michael Morpurgo

Martine Murray
Linda Newbery
Daniel Postgate
Jill Tomlinson

*The Adventurous Snail
All Because of Jackson • Dinosaur Trouble
Emily's Legs • Hairy Hezekiah • Horse Pie
The Sophie Stories*

Satoshi Kitamura

Raymond Briggs
Anthony Browne

Neal Layton
Nick Sharratt

Millie's Marvellous Hat
Stone Age Boy

Timothy Knapman

Giles Andreae
Simon Bartram
Martyn Beardsley
Emily Gravett

H I Larry
Colin McNaughton
Nick Sharratt
Ian Whybrow

Mungo Series

H I Larry

Ben 10
Alex Cliff
Elizabeth Singer Hunt

Timothy Knapman
Rex Stone
Jonny Zucker

Zac Power Series

Karina Law

Penny Dolan
Rose Impey

Jillian Powell

Marlowe's Mum and the Tree House
The Truth About Hansel and Gretel
The Truth About Those Billy Goats

Michael Lawrence

Tony Bradman
Shoo Rayner

Francesca Simon
Jeremy Strong

A Pair of Jacks Series

Neal Layton

Raymond Briggs
John Grant
Oliver Jeffers

Satoshi Kitamura
Jill Murphy

Mammoth Academy Series

Paeony Lewis
Family · Friends

Emma Chichester Clark
Mick Inkpen

Ian Whybrow

Florence and Arnold Stories

Astrid Lindgren
Adventure · Friends
Humour · Other cultures

Klaus Baumgart
Joyce Lankester Brisley
Judy Brown
Lauren Child

Dorothy Edwards
Mairi Hedderwick
Megan McDonald

Emil Series · Pippi Longstocking Series

Elizabeth Lindsay
Adventure · Animals · Magic · Pony/horse
8-11

Harriet Castor
Linda Chapman
June Crebbin
Lucy Daniels
Pippa Funnell

Diana Kimpton
Daisy Meadows
Jenny Oldfield
Gwyneth Rees
Summer Waters

Magic Pony Series · Silverlake Fairy School Series

Sam Lloyd
Animals · Humour

Dosh Archer
Ronda and David Armitage
Emma Chichester Clark

Lynley Dodd
Jane Simmons
Karen Wallace

Inspector Croc Investigates
Mr Pusskins Series

Geraldine McCaughrean Ⓔ
Traditional
8-11
12-14

Malachy Doyle
Pippa Goodhart
Mick Gowar

Margaret Mayo
Saviour Pirotta
Russell Punter

Fig's Giant · Jalopy · St George and the Dragon

Go to back for
lists of:
Authors by Genre
Graphic novels
Short stories
Prize winners
Further reading

24

Alan MacDonald

Giles Andreae
Philip Ardagh
Raymond Briggs
Michael Broad
Rob Childs

Pippa Goodhart
John Grant
Bel Mooney
Dav Pilkey
David Henry Wilson

8-11

Dirty Bertie Series
History of Warts Series
Iggy the Urk Series • Troll Trouble Series

Megan McDonald

8-11

Jeff Brown
Astrid Lindgren
Hilary McKay
Bel Mooney
Martine Murray

Alf Prøysen
Francesca Simon
Andy Stanton
Jenny Valentine

Judy Moody Series • Stink Series

Kelly McKain

Linda Chapman
June Crebbin
Maeve Friel
Pippa Funnell
Diana Kimpton

Daisy Meadows
Jenny Oldfield
Gwyneth Rees
Anna Wilson

8-11

Fairy House Series
Pony Camp Diaries Series

Hilary McKay

Michael Broad
Andrew Cope
Anne Fine

Elizabeth Singer Hunt
Megan McDonald
Julie Sykes

8-11
12-14

Charlie Small Series

David McKee

Emma Chichester Clark
Julia Donaldson
Mick Inkpen

Tony Ross
Hannah Shaw
Jane Yolen

Not Now, Bernard
Two Monsters • Who Is Mrs Green?
Elmer Series

Colin McNaughton

Jon Blake
Raymond Briggs
Judy Brown
Ted Dewan
Ian Falconer

Neil Gaiman
Timothy Knapman
Dav Pilkey
Margaret Ryan
Dr Seuss

Captain Abdul's Little Treasure
Captain Abdul's Pirate School • Here Come the Aliens!
Jolly Roger and the Pirates of Abdul the Skinhead • Nighty Night!
Not Last Night but the Night Before
Preston Pig Stories

Tiffany Mandrake
Fantasy · Friends · Humour · Magic · School

Humphrey Carpenter
Jill Murphy
Martine Murray

Laura Owen
Jenny Valentine

Little Horrors Series

James Marshall
Animals · Easy reader · Humour

Andy Blackford
Marc Brown
Emma Chichester Clark

Rose Impey
Shoo Rayner

Fox on Stage • Fox Outfoxed

Beatrice Masini
Ballet · Friends

8-11

Ann Bryant
Darcey Bussell
Natasha May

James Mayhew
Anna Wilson

Ballet Academy Series

Anna Maxted
Friends · Humour · Space

8-11

Simon Bartram
Ben 10

Michael Broad
David Orme

Tom and Matt Series

💬 Some titles are available as Talking books

Natasha May
5-7

Ballet · Friends

Darcey Bussell
Beatrice Masini

Anna Wilson

Poppy Love Series

James Mayhew

Ballet · Historical

Ann Bryant
Mairi Hedderwick

Beatrice Masini
Anna Wilson

Ella Bella Ballerina Series
Katie Series

Margaret Mayo

Fairy/folk

Malachy Doyle
Geraldine McCaughrean
Tony Mitton
Maggie Moore

Laura North
Saviour Pirotta
Russell Punter
Barrie Wade

First Fairy Tales Series

Daisy Meadows ⬭ Ⓔ

Magic

8-11

Terence Blacker
Darcey Bussell
Linda Chapman
Vivian French
Maeve Friel

Elizabeth Lindsay
Kelly McKain
Gwyneth Rees
Margaret Ryan
Anna Wilson

The Dance Fairies Series • The Ocean Fairies Series
The Sporty Fairies Series • Rainbow Magic Series

David Melling

Animals · Family · Ghost/supernatural
Humour · Magic

8-11

Janet Burchett and
Sara Vogler

Julia Donaldson

The Ghost Library • Hugless Douglas • Three Wishes
Goblins Series

Barbara Mitchelhill

Detective mysteries · Family · Humour

8-11

Michael Broad
Andrew Cope
Sally Grindley

Chris Riddell
Francesca Simon
Geronimo Stilton

Damian Drooth Supersleuth Series

27

Tony Mitton 🗩

Giles Andreae
Laurence Anholt
Martyn Beardsley
Paul Cooper
Roald Dahl

Rose Impey
Margaret Mayo
Laura North
Alan Rusbridger
Kaye Umansky

Bumpus Jumpus Dinosaurumpus
Jolly Olly Octopus • Rainforest Romp • Super Safari
Happy Ever After Series • Raps Series • Rap Rhymes Series

Sue Mongredien 🗩

Sue Bentley
Humphrey Carpenter
Maeve Friel

Rose Impey
Laura Owen
Kaye Umansky

Frightful Families Series
Kitten Club Series • Oliver Moon Series
Secret Mermaid Series

Bel Mooney 🗩

Klaus Baumgart
Joyce Lankester Brisley
Harriet Castor
Dorothy Edwards
Anne Fine

Dick King-Smith
Alan MacDonald
Megan McDonald
Jenny Oldfield
Jacqueline Wilson

Mr Tubs is Lost! • Who Loves Mr Tubs?
Kitty and Friends Series

Maggie Moore

Anne Adeney
Andy Blackford
Anne Cassidy
Malachy Doyle
Bob Graham

Sue Graves
Stella Gurney
Damian Harvey
Margaret Mayo
Barrie Wade

The Fun Run • The Magic Word
Persephone and the Pomegranate Seeds
Snow White • Thor's Hammer • The Three Little Pigs

Michael Morpurgo Ⓔ

Animals · Fairy/folk · Family

Antonia Barber
Emily Bearn
Chris d'Lacey
Anne Fine
Pippa Goodhart

Harry Horse
Daren King
Dick King-Smith
Linda Newbery
Jenny Nimmo

8-11
12-14

Animal Tales
Cool as a Cucumber • *It's a Dog's Life* • *Little Albatross*
Mr Skip • *This Morning I Met a Whale*
Mudpuddle Farm Series

Jill Murphy Ⓔ

Humour · Magic

Jonathan Allen
Terence Blacker
Humphrey Carpenter
Maeve Friel
Mairi Hedderwick

Ann Jungman
Neal Layton
Tiffany Mandrake
Laura Owen
Valerie Thomas

8-11

Peace at Last
Large Family Series • *The Worst Witch Series*

Martine Murray Ⓔ

Adventure · Family · Humour

Joyce Lankester Brisley
Dick King-Smith
Megan McDonald

Tiffany Mandrake
Chris Riddell
Jenny Valentine

Henrietta Series

Margaret Nash

Animals · Easy reader · Family
Humour · Other cultures

Anne Adeney
Andy Blackford
Tony Bradman
Penny Dolan
Sue Graves

Stella Gurney
David Orme
Jillian Powell
Hilary Robinson
Joan Stimson

Ben's Escape from the Blitz
The Bossy Cockerel
Chief Five Hands • *Dog Knows Best*
A Jacket for Buzz • *Mum's Red Hat*

Ⓔ Some titles are available as ebooks

Linda Newbery

 Animals

8-11
12-14
14+

Antonia Barber
Nick Butterworth
Anne Fine
Harry Horse
Dick King-Smith

Michael Morpurgo
Mal Peet and
    Elspeth Graham
Jane Simmons

Cat Tales Series

Jenny Nimmo

Animals · Family · Fantasy · Magic

8-11

Anne Fine
Daren King
Michael Morpurgo

Mal Peet and
    Elspeth Graham
Colin West

The Beasties
Delilah and the Dishwasher Dogs · Invisible Vinnie
Matty Mouse · The Stone Mouse · The Witch's Tears

Laura North

Fairy/folk · Humour · Mythology

Raymond Briggs
Roald Dahl
Margaret Mayo

Tony Mitton
Saviour Pirotta
Margaret Ryan

Cinderella's Big Foot · Jack and the Bean Pie
Sleeping Beauty: 100 Years On · Theseus and the Minotaur

Hilda Offen

Adventure · Family
Ghost/supernatural · Humour · Magic

Malorie Blackman
Sally Gardner
Hiawyn Oram

Daniel Postgate
Alf Prøysen
Kaye Umansky

The Galloping Ghost · Knee-High to a Knight
Watch Out for Witches · The Wizard's Warning
Rita Series

Jenny Oldfield

Friends · Humour · Magic · School

8-11

Sue Bentley
Joyce Lankester Brisley
Linda Chapman
Pippa Funnell
Elizabeth Lindsay

Kelly McKain
Bel Mooney
Francesca Simon
Summer Waters
Holly Webb

Definitely Daisy Series · My Magical Pony Series
Pearl's Dressing-Up Dreams Series

Hiawyn Oram
Adventure · Animals · Humour · Magic

Malorie Blackman
Emma Chichester Clark
Andrew Cope
Mini Grey
Mary Hoffman

Rose Impey
Hilda Offen
Laura Owen
Gwyneth Rees
Alan Rusbridger

Mona the Vampire Series
Rumblewick Letters Series

David Orme
Adventure · Easy reader · Humour · Science fiction

Allan Ahlberg
Simon Bartram
Ben 10
Ann Bryant
Sue Graves

Mary Hoffman
Anna Maxted
Margaret Nash
Jillian Powell
Colin West

Boffin Boy Series GN
Freddy's Family Series

Laura Owen
Adventure · Humour · Magic

Maeve Friel
Tiffany Mandrake
Sue Mongredien
Jill Murphy

Hiawyn Oram
Wendy Smith
Valerie Thomas
Kaye Umansky

8-11

Winnie the Witch Series

Mal Peet and Elspeth Graham
Animals · Other lands
Traditional

Antonia Barber
Linda Newbery

Jenny Nimmo
Jane Simmons

8-11

Cloud Tea Monkeys

Dav Pilkey
Humour

Jon Blake
Raymond Briggs
Jeff Brown
John Grant
Alan MacDonald

Colin McNaughton
Andy Stanton
Geronimo Stilton
Rex Stone

8-11

Captain Underpants Series
The Dumb Bunnies Series · *Ricky Ricotta Series*

Saviour Pirotta
Mythology

Malachy Doyle
Geraldine McCaughrean
Margaret Mayo

Laura North
Russell Punter
Barrie Wade

First Greek Myths Series • Once Upon a World Series

Daniel Postgate
Adventure • Animals • Family
Ghost/supernatural • Humour

Lynley Dodd
Ian Falconer
Dick King-Smith

Hilda Offen
Frank Rodgers
Jane Simmons

AbracaDebra • Big Mum Plum
Cosmo and the Pirates • Smelly Bill: Love Stinks
Smelly Bill Stinks Again • Smelly Bill's Whiffy Weekend

Beatrix Potter
Animals • Family

Sue Bentley
Mick Inkpen
Julia Jarman
Chris Riddell

Jill Tomlinson
Alison Uttley
Holly Webb

The Tale of Benjamin Bunny
The Tale of Peter Rabbit

Jillian Powell
Animals • Easy reader • Family • Humour • School

Anne Adeney
Anne Cassidy
John Cunliffe
Penny Dolan
Damian Harvey

Karina Law
Margaret Nash
David Orme
Hilary Robinson

Craig's Crocodile • Ellie's Star
Izzie's Idea • My Nan • Ron's Race • Tall Tilly
Get Up and Go Series • Rosie's Rides Series • Tilly and Todd Series

Chris Powling
Adventure • Family • Ghost/supernatural • Humour

8-11

Dorothy Edwards
Julia Jarman
Daren King
Margaret Ryan

Dyan Sheldon
Bob Wilson
Philip Wooderson

Kit's Castle
On the Ghost Trail • Treasure at the Boot-fair
My Sister's Name is Rover Series

Alf Prøysen

Klaus Baumgart
Joyce Lankester Brisley
Jeff Brown

Megan McDonald
Hilda Offen
Jill Tomlinson

Mrs Pepperpot Series

Russell Punter

Easy reader · Fairy/folk · Humour · Traditional

Laurence Anholt
Malachy Doyle
Geraldine McCaughrean

Margaret Mayo
Saviour Pirotta

The Chilly Little Penguin
Danny the Dragon • Dick Whittington • Percy and the Pirates
The Scaredy Cat • There Was a Crooked Man

Simon Puttock

Animals · Humour

Ted Dewan
Ian Falconer

Vivian French

Love from Louisa

Shoo Rayner

Adventure · Animals · Humour

8-11

Jonathan Allen
Harriet Castor
Alan Durant
Ann Jungman
Michael Lawrence

James Marshall
Alan Rusbridger
Mark Skelton
Paul Stewart
Martin Waddell

Viking Vik and the Wolves
Axel Storm Series • Little Horrors Series
Monster Boy Series • Ricky Rocket Series

Gwyneth Rees ○ E

Magic

8-11

Linda Chapman
Vivian French
Elizabeth Lindsay
Kelly McKain

Daisy Meadows
Hiawyn Oram
Summer Waters

Cosmo Series • Fairy Dust Series

Go to back for lists of: Authors by Genre • Graphic novels
Short stories • Prize winners • Exploring further

Chris Riddell

Animals · Fantasy · Humour

Martyn Beardsley
Emily Bearn
Nick Butterworth
Julia Donaldson
Barbara Mitchelhill

Martine Murray
Beatrix Potter
Hannah Shaw
Jenny Valentine
Ian Whybrow

The Emperor of Absurdia
Wendel's Workshop
Ottoline Series

Hilary Robinson

Animals · Humour

Anne Adeney
Stan and Jan Berenstain
Andy Blackford
Anne Cassidy
Penny Dolan

Stella Gurney
Damian Harvey
Margaret Nash
Jillian Powell
Nick Sharratt

Batty Betty's Spells • Croc by the Rock
How to Teach a Dragon Manners • Pet to School Day
The Royal Jumble Sale • Ted's Party Bus

Frank Rodgers

Animals · Humour · Magic

Scoular Anderson
Marc Brown
Jan Fearnley
Daniel Postgate
Alan Rusbridger

Wendy Smith
Kaye Umansky
Colin West
Jeanne Willis

Little T Series • Mr Croc Series
Pirate Penguins Series • The Witch's Dog Series

Michael Rosen

Death · Magic · Toys

Ian Falconer
Mairi Hedderwick

Shirley Hughes

Michael Rosen's Sad Book
Red Ted and the Lost Things

Tony Ross

Animals · Family · Friends

Julia Donaldson
Mick Gowar
Bob Graham

Mick Inkpen
David McKee
Jane Yolen

Little Princess Series

Alan Rusbridger Ⓔ

Animals · Humour

Lauren Child	Hiawyn Oram
Rose Impey	Shoo Rayner
Julia Jarman	Frank Rodgers
Tony Mitton	Jill Tomlinson

The Coldest Day at the Zoo
The Smelliest Day at the Zoo • The Wildest Day at the Zoo

Margaret Ryan

Adventure · Family · Humour · Magic

8-11

Sally Grindley	Laura North
Rose Impey	Chris Powling
Ann Jungman	Dyan Sheldon
Colin McNaughton	Dee Shulman
Daisy Meadows	Karen Wallace

Kevin and the Pirate Test
Scratch and Sniff • Smuggler and the Smelly Fish
Canterbury Tales Series • Roodica the Rude Series • Weird Street Series

Louis Sachar Ⓔ

Humour

8-11
12-14

Michael Broad	Jeremy Strong
Paul Fleischman	David Henry Wilson
Andy Stanton	

Marvin Redpost Series

Jon Scieszka

Transport

Jenny Alexander	Benedict Blathwayt

Melvin Might? • Smash! Crash!

Dr Seuss Ⓔ

Easy reader · Environment · Humour

Stan and Jan Berenstain	Colin McNaughton
Marc Brown	Nick Sharratt
P D Eastman	Mo Willems

The Cat in the Hat • Fox in Socks
Green Eggs and Ham • How the Grinch Stole Christmas • The Lorax

Ⓔ Some titles are available as ebooks

35

Nick Sharratt

Giles Andreae
John Grant
Kes Gray
Satoshi Kitamura
Timothy Knapman

Hilary Robinson
Dr Seuss
Mo Willems
Jeanne Willis

Caveman Dave
The Green Queen • *Monday Run-day*
Pointy-hatted Princesses • *Shark in the Park* • *Smart Aunties*

Hannah Shaw

Bob Graham
Emily Gravett
Mini Grey

David McKee
Chris Riddell
Chris Wormell

Erroll • *Evil Weasel*

Dyan Sheldon

Lauren Child
Dorothy Edwards
Chris Powling

Margaret Ryan
Jacqueline Wilson
Jenny Valentine

Drusilla and her Brothers
What Mona Wants, Mona Gets

Dee Shulman

Scoular Anderson
Julia Jarman
Daren King

Margaret Ryan
Wendy Smith

Hetty the Yeti
Haunted Mouse Series

Jane Simmons

Ronda and David Armitage
Antonia Barber
Emma Chichester Clark
Sam Lloyd

Linda Newbery
Mal Peet and Elspeth Graham
Daniel Postgate

Beryl Goes Wild • *Ship's Cat Doris*
Ebb and Flo Series

Francesca Simon

Family · Humour · School

8-11

David Bedford
Marc Brown
Ann Cameron
Roald Dahl
Michael Lawrence

Megan McDonald
Barbara Mitchelhill
Jenny Oldfield
Ian Whybrow
David Henry Wilson

Horrid Henry Series

Mark Skelton

Animals · Humour · Time travel

8-11

Giles Andreae
Shoo Rayner

Andy Stanton

Monkey Pirates Series

Sophie Smiley

Adventure · Disability · Family · Humour · Sport

David Bedford
Rob Childs

Martin Waddell

*Football Fever • Man of the Match
Puppy on the Pitch • Snow Goalie*

Wendy Smith

Family · Friends · Humour · Magic

Scoular Anderson
Terence Blacker
Maeve Friel
Laura Owen

Frank Rodgers
Dee Shulman
Kaye Umansky
Jacqueline Wilson

Mrs Magic Series • Space Twins Series

Andy Stanton

Humour

8-11

Philip Ardagh
Raymond Briggs
Michael Broad
Jeff Brown
Roald Dahl

Megan McDonald
Dav Pilkey
Louis Sachar
Mark Skelton

Mr Gum Series

Paul Stewart

Family · Humour · Science fiction

8-11
12-14

Scoular Anderson
Paul Cooper
Alan Durant

Shoo Rayner
Jeremy Strong

*Dogbird
Dogbird and Other Mixed-up Tales • The Were-Pig*

Geronimo Stilton

Adventure · Animals
8-11

Emily Bearn
Terence Blacker
Andrew Cope

Ann Jungman
Barbara Mitchelhill
Dav Pilkey

Geronimo Stilton Series

Joan Stimson

Animals · Easy reader · Humour

Anne Cassidy
Penny Dolan
Mick Gowar

Sue Graves
Margaret Nash

Amazing Shane • Dan's Gran's Goat
The Dinosaur Next Door • Hunky Monkey

Rex Stone

Adventure · Fantasy
8-11

Keith Brumpton
Alex Cliff
Elizabeth Singer Hunt

H I Larry
Dav Pilkey

Dinosaur Cove Series

Jeremy Strong Adventure · Family · Fantasy · Humour

8-11
12-14

Dosh Archer
Jon Blake
Keith Brumpton
Roald Dahl
Daren King

Michael Lawrence
Louis Sachar
Paul Stewart
Julie Sykes
Jeanne Willis

Dinosaur Pox
Giant Jim and the Hurricane • My Brother's Famous Bottom
Pirate School Series

Julie Sykes Ⓔ

Animals · Humour

Allan Ahlberg
Dosh Archer
Terence Blacker
Humphrey Carpenter

Hilary McKay
Jeremy Strong
Colin West
Jeanne Willis

The Pet Sitter Series

Shaun Tan

8-11
12-14

Fantasy · Magic · Other cultures

David Almond
Neil Gaiman

Oliver Jeffers
Colin Thompson

Eric · The Lost Thing · The Red Tree

Valerie Thomas

Humour · Magic

Terence Blacker
Maeve Friel

Jill Murphy
Laura Owen

Winnie the Witch Series

Colin Thompson Ⓔ

Environment · Fantasy · Historical

Neil Gaiman
Emily Gravett

Mini Grey
Shaun Tan

Castles · Falling Angels
How to Live Forever · The Paperbag Princess · Paradise Garden

Jill Tomlinson

Animals · Humour · Magic

Emily Bearn
John Burningham
Emma Chichester Clark
Lynley Dodd
Pippa Goodhart

Dick King-Smith
Beatrix Potter
Alf Prøysen
Alan Rusbridger
Alison Uttley

The Owl Who Was Afraid of the Dark
The Penguin Who Wanted to Find Out

Kaye Umansky Ⓔ

Detective mysteries · Family
Fantasy · Humour · Magic
8-11

Humphrey Carpenter
Lauren Child
Tony Mitton
Sue Mongredien
Hilda Offen

Laura Owen
Frank Rodgers
Wendy Smith
Karen Wallace
Jeanne Willis

Alien Alby · Goblinz and the Witch · I Don't Like Gloria!
Pongwiffy Series · Sir Quinton Quest Series

Some titles are available as Talking books

39

Alison Uttley

Animals

Emily Bearn
Ted Dewan
Harry Horse

Beatrix Potter
Jill Tomlinson

Little Grey Rabbit Series

Jenny Valentine (E)

Family · Humour

12-14
14+

Joyce Lankester Brisley
Dorothy Edwards
Kes Gray
Megan McDonald

Tiffany Mandrake
Martine Murray
Chris Riddell
Dyan Sheldon

Iggy and Me Series

Martin Waddell

Adventure · Fairy/folk · Mythology · Sport

David Bedford
Keith Brumpton
Janet Burchett and
   Sara Vogler
John Burningham

Rob Childs
Shirley Hughes
Shoo Rayner
Sophie Smiley
Bob Wilson

Captain Small Pig • *Cup Final Kid* • *Little Dracula and Millicent*
Tales of Sinbad the Sailor Series

Barrie Wade

Fairy/folk · Humour · Mythology · Traditional

Anne Adeney
Andy Blackford
Anne Cassidy
Malachy Doyle
Stella Gurney

Damian Harvey
Margaret Mayo
Maggie Moore
Saviour Pirotta

Emperor's New Clothes • *Gelert The Brave* • *Icarus, the Boy Who Flew*
Rumpelstiltskin • *The Three Billy Goats Gruff*

Karen Wallace (E)

Fairy/folk · Family
Humour · Mythology

12-14
8-11

Scoular Anderson
Martyn Beardsley
Stan and Jan Berenstain
Malachy Doyle
Sally Grindley

Damian Harvey
Sam Lloyd
Margaret Ryan
Kaye Umansky
Philip Wooderson

Alfie Takes Action • *Alice Knows Best* • *The Elves and the Shoemaker*
The Emperor's New Clothes
Detective Dog Series • *Monster Mountain Series*
Princess PJ Series • *Tales of King Arthur Series*

Summer Waters *Adventure · Animals · Magic*

Sue Bentley
Lucy Daniels
Hayley Daze

Elizabeth Lindsay
Jenny Oldfield
Gwyneth Rees

Silver Dolphins Series

Holly Webb *Adventure · Animals · Magic*

8-11

Sue Bentley
Lucy Daniels
Hayley Daze

Diana Kimpton
Jenny Oldfield
Beatrix Potter

Ellie the Forgotten Puppy
Jess the Lonely Puppy • Misty the Abandoned Kitten
Animal Magic Series • Molly's Magic Series
My Naughty Little Puppy Series

Colin West *Animals · Family · Humour*

Stan and Jan Berenstain
Andrew Cope
P D Eastman
Jenny Nimmo

David Orme
Frank Rodgers
Julie Sykes
Philip Wooderson

Big Wig • Go Tell It to the Toucan • Moose and Mouse
My Funny Family Series

Ian Whybrow *Adventure · Animals · Humour · Letters*

Judy Brown
Marc Brown
Paul Cooper
Malachy Doyle
Damian Harvey

Timothy Knapman
Paeony Lewis
Chris Riddell
Francesca Simon
David Henry Wilson

Animal Soup • The Flying Diggers
Tim, Ted and the Pirates • Whizz the Fleabag
Harry Series • Little Wolf Series

Go to back for lists of: Authors by Genre • Graphic novels
Short stories • Prize winners • Exploring further

Mo Willems Animals

Stan and Jan Berenstain
Andy Blackford
Ann Bryant
Alan Durant

P D Eastman
Mick Inkpen
Dr Seuss
Nick Sharratt

Don't Let the Pigeon Drive the Bus
Don't Let the Pigeon Stay Up Late • The Pigeon Finds a Hot Dog
The Pigeon Wants a Puppy
Elephant and Piggie Series

Jeanne Willis Animals · Humour

Scoular Anderson
Jan Fearnley
Damian Harvey
Frank Rodgers

Nick Sharratt
Jeremy Strong
Julie Sykes
Kaye Umansky

Big Bad Bun • Grill Pan Eddy
Mayfly Day • Misery Moo • Old Dog • Tadpole's Promise
Crazy Jobs Series

Anna Wilson Animals · Ballet · Friends · School

Ann Bryant
Darcey Bussell
Harriet Castor
Linda Chapman
Vivian French

Kelly McKain
Beatrice Masini
Natasha May
James Mayhew
Daisy Meadows

8-11

Terry the Flying Turtle
Nina Fairy Ballerina Series

Bob Wilson Friends · Humour · Sport

Laurence Anholt
Janet Burchett
and Sara Vogler
Rob Childs

Roald Dahl
Chris Powling
Martin Waddell

Fearless Dave • Helpful Helen the Robot
Stanley Bagshaw Series

GN = Graphic novel

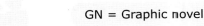

David Henry Wilson

Adventure · Family · Humour

Alan MacDonald
Louis Sachar

Francesca Simon
Ian Whybrow

Jeremy James Series

Jacqueline Wilson ⌕ Ⓔ

Adventure · Family
Fantasy · Humour

Malorie Blackman
Anne Fine
Julia Jarman

Bel Mooney
Dyan Sheldon
Wendy Smith

8-11
12-14

The Dinosaur's Packed Lunch • Monster Eyeballs • The Monster Storyteller
My Brother Bernadette • Sleepovers • The Werepuppy

Philip Wooderson

Adventure · Historical · Humour

Scoular Anderson
Keith Brumpton
Chris Powling

Karen Wallace
Colin West

Arf and the Happy Campers
Arf and the Metal Detector GN • Arf and the Tarantula
The Nile Files Series

Chris Wormell

Fairy/folk · Fantasy

Laurence Anholt
Helen Cooper
Julia Donaldson
Emily Gravett

Mini Grey
Oliver Jeffers
Hannah Shaw

Ferocious Wild Beasts • In the Woods • One Smart Fish
The Saddest King • Scruffy Bear and the Six White Mice • The Wild Girl

Jane Yolen ⌕ Ⓔ

Animals · Friends · Humour

Benedict Blathwayt
Julia Donaldson
Mick Inkpen

David McKee
Tony Ross

How Do Dinosaurs Clean Their Rooms?
How Do Dinosaurs Say Goodnight? • How Do Dinosaurs Say I Love You?

Jonny Zucker ⌕

Adventure · Family · Science fiction

Alex Cliff
Andrew Cope

Elizabeth Singer Hunt
H I Larry

8-11

Max Flash Series

Deborah Abela
Adventure • Detective mysteries

Enid Blyton
Carol Hedges

Anthony Read

Max Remy: Spyforce Series

Richard Adams
Animals • Environment • Fantasy

David Clement-Davies
Colin Dann

Timothee de Fombelle
Brian Jacques

Watership Down

Allan Ahlberg
Family • Fantasy • Humour

5-7

Giles Andreae
Ian Beck

Alf Prøysen
Shoo Rayner

The Bear Nobody Wanted
The Boy, the Wolf, the Sheep and the Lettuce • Woof!
The Gaskitts Series

Joan Aiken
Adventure • Family • Fantasy
Ghost/supernatural

12-14

Paul Bajoria
Linda Buckley-Archer
Frances Hardinge
Robin Jarvis

Garry Kilworth
Penelope Lively
William Nicholson
Philip Pullman

The Wolves of Willoughby Chase Series

Louisa May Alcott
Family

Jeanne Birdsall
Frances Hodgson Burnett
Hilary McKay

L M Montgomery
Johanna Spyri
Laura Ingalls Wilder

Good Wives • Jo's Boys • Little Women

Some titles are available as Talking books

David Almond

Death · Family · Fantasy

Thomas Bloor
Lucy Christopher
Oliver Jeffers
Clive King
Elizabeth Laird

Linda Newbery
Andrew Norriss
Michelle Paver
Shaun Tan

5-7
12-14

My Dad's a Birdman • *My Name is Mina*
Skellig • *Slog's Dad* • *The Savage* GN

R J Anderson

Fairy/folk · Fantasy
Ghost/supernatural · Magic

Holly Black
Herbie Brennan
Michelle Harrison
Robin Jarvis

Katherine Langrish
Mary Norton
David Lee Stone

12-14

Arrow • *Knife* • *Rebel*

Giles Andreae

Humour

Allan Ahlberg
Martyn Beardsley
Tony Bradman
Neil Gaiman

Shoo Rayner
Mark Skelton
Karen Wallace

5-7

Billy Bonkers • *Billy Bonkers 2*
Luke Lancelot and the Golden Shield
Luke Lancelot and the Treasure of the Kings

Laurence Anholt

Humour

Jason Hightman
Sam Llewellyn
Dav Pilkey

Shoo Rayner
Francesca Simon

5-7

Seriously Silly Rhymes Series
Seriously Silly Stories Series

Roy Apps

Adventure · Fantasy · Humour · School · Vampires

Matt Crossick
Tommy Donbavand
Morris Gleitzman

Paul Jennings
Daren King
Jeremy Strong

Fang Gang Series

(E) Some titles are available as ebooks

8-11

8-11

Philip Ardagh 💬
Adventure • Humour
5-7

Steve Barlow and
   Steve Skidmore
Lauren Child
Steve Cole
Ceci Jenkinson

Sam Llewellyn
Philip Ridley
Lemony Snicket
Cat Weatherill

The Green Men of Gressingham BS
The Red Dragons of Gressingham BS
Eddie Dickens Trilogy • *Grubtown Tales Series*
Henry's House Series • *Unlikely Exploits Series*

Louise Arnold 💬
Friends • Ghost/supernatural

Eva Ibbotson
Penelope Lively

Nick Shadow

The Invisible Friend Series

Ros Asquith 💬
Friends • Humour
12-14

Guy Bass
Meg Cabot
Cathy Cassidy
Grace Cavendish
Karen McCombie

Hilary McKay
Helena Pielichaty
Gwyneth Rees
Dyan Sheldon
Jacqueline Wilson

Letters From an Alien Schoolboy
Fibby Libby Series • *Girl Writer Series*
Trixie Tempest, Teenage Tearaway Series

Steve Augarde Ⓔ
Fantasy • War
12-14

Holly Black
Sally Gardner
Diana Wynne Jones
Elizabeth Kay

Katherine Langrish
Jenny Nimmo
Terry Pratchett

Touchstone Trilogy

Paul Bajoria
Adventure • Historical • Thrillers
12-14

Joan Aiken
Linda Buckley-Archer
Andrew Lane
Caroline Lawrence

Chris Priestley
Anthony Read
Justin Richards

The Printer's Devil Trilogy

E D Baker

Fairy/folk · Humour · Magic

Cressida Cowell
Anna Dale
Jason Hightman

Liz Kessler
Philip Pullman

The Tale of the Frog Princess Series

Blue Balliett

Adventure · Detective mysteries · School

Rick Riordan
Matthew Skelton

Lemony Snicket

*The Calder Game • Chasing Vermeer
The Danger Box • The Wright 3*

Lynne Reid Banks

Family · Fantasy
12-14

Betty G Birney
Clive King
Penelope Lively

E Nesbit
Mary Norton

*Harry the Poisonous Centipede
Harry the Poisonous Centipede Goes to Sea
Harry the Poisonous Centipede's Big Adventure • I, Houdini
Indian in the Cupboard Series*

Dominic Barker

*Adventure · Detective mysteries
Fantasy · Humour*
12-14

Ian Beck
Betty G Birney
Charlie Higson
Diana Kimpton

Wendy Orr
Terry Pratchett
Justin Richards
Steve Voake

*Adam and the Arkonauts
Blart Series • Mickey Sharp Series*

Steve Barlow and Steve Skidmore

*Humour
Mythology*

Philip Ardagh
Adam Blade
Steve Cole
Terry Deary
Andy Griffiths

Mark Haddon
Steve Jackson and
    Ian Livingstone
Katherine Langrish
John Vornholt

*I Hero Series • Mad Myths Series
Tales of the Dark Forest Series*

J M Barrie

Fantasy

Frank L Baum
Lewis Carroll
C S Lewis
Geraldine McCaughrean

Mary Norton
Philippa Pearce
P L Travers

Peter Pan

Guy Bass

Fantasy · Humour · Space

Ros Asquith
Steve Cole

Anna Maxted
Dav Pilkey

Alien Escape! • Alien Invasion!
Secret Santa: Agent of X.M.A.S.
Dinkin Dings Series • Gormy Ruckles Series

Michelle Bates

Animals

Lauren Brooke
Jenny Dale
Lucy Daniels

Stacy Gregg
Jenny Oldfield
Anna Sewell

Sandy Lane Stables Series

Frank L Baum

Fantasy

J M Barrie
Lewis Carroll
C S Lewis

Geraldine McCaughrean
Philip Pullman
P L Travers

The Wizard of Oz

Nina Bawden

Family · War 1939-45

Theresa Breslin
Berlie Doherty
Jackie French
Adèle Geras

Judith Kerr
Sophie McKenzie
Michelle Magorian
Linda Newbery

Carrie's War

Andy Baxter

Thrillers

Adam Blade
Linda Chapman
Alex Cliff
Elizabeth Singer Hunt

H I Larry
Rex Stone
Jonny Zucker

Beastly! Series

Martyn Beardsley

Humour
5-7

Giles Andreae
Tony Bradman

Shoo Rayner
Karen Wallace

Sir Gadabout Series

Ian Beck ⬭ Ⓔ

Fairy/folk · Family
12-14

Allan Ahlberg
Dominic Barker
Heather Dyer

Ted Hughes
Elizabeth Kay
Angie Sage

Tom Trueheart Series

David Bedford

Friends · Sport
5-7

Bob Cattell
Rob Childs

Tom Palmer
Bali Rai

The Team Series

Jeanne Birdsall ⬭ Ⓔ

Family

Louisa May Alcott
Lucy M Boston
Frances Hodgson Burnett
Hilary McKay

L M Montgomery
Johanna Spyri
P L Travers
Laura Ingalls Wilder

The Penderwicks Series

Betty G Birney ⬭ Ⓔ

Adventure · Animals · Family
Humour · School

Lynne Reid Banks
Dominic Barker
Malorie Blackman
Michael Bond

Annette Butterworth
Jenny Dale
Roddy Doyle
Livi Michael

The Princess and the Peabodys
According to Humphrey Series

Holly Black ⬭

Fantasy
14+

R J Anderson
Steve Augarde
Herbie Brennan
Georgia Byng
Sally Gardner

Debi Gliori
Michelle Harrison
Chris Mould
Justin Richards
Emily Rodda

The Spiderwick Chronicles

8-11

Terence Blacker Ⓔ

Malorie Blackman
Tony Bradman
Rob Childs

Michael Coleman
David Walliams

The Angel Factory • Missing, Believed Crazy
The Transfer • You Have Ghost Mail
Ms Wiz Series

Malorie Blackman Ⓔ

Betty G Birney
Terence Blacker
Theresa Breslin
Gillian Cross
John Fardell

Alan Gibbons
Sally Grindley
Julia Jarman
Helena Pielichaty
Kate Thompson

A.N.T.I.D.O.T.E. • Cloud Busting • Dangerous Reality
Hostage • Jack Sweettooth

Adam Blade

Steve Barlow and
    Steve Skidmore
Andy Baxter
Linda Chapman
Alex Cliff
Timothee de Fombelle

David Grimstone
Steve Jackson and
    Ian Livingstone
Dan Lee
Rick Riordan
David Lee Stone

Beast Quest Series • The Chronicles of Avantia Series

Thomas Bloor

David Almond
Gillian Cross
Sally Gardner

Derek Landy
Lemony Snicket
Robert Swindells

Beast Beneath the Skin • Blood Willow • Bomber Boys BS
The Dragon and the Warlord ES • Worm in the Blood

Judy Blume

Meg Cabot
Anne Fine
Sara Pennypacker

Dyan Sheldon
Jacqueline Wilson

Fudge Series
The Pain and the Great One Series

Enid Blyton Ⓔ Adventure · Detective mysteries · School

Deborah Abela
Paul Haven
David Miller
Mary Norton

Arthur Ransome
Ali Sparkes
Lauren St John
Trenton Lee Stewart

Famous Five Series · Malory Towers Series
Secret Seven Series · St Clare's Series

Michael Bond Ⓔ Animals · Family

Betty G Birney
Chris d'Lacey
Dick King-Smith

A A Milne
Wendy Orr

Olga Da Polga Series · Paddington Bear Series

Pseudonymous Bosch Adventure · Magic · Mystery

Henry Chancellor
Kate di Camillo
Neil Gaiman
Rick Riordan

J K Rowling
Angie Sage
Trenton Lee Stewart

12-14

Secret Series

Lucy M Boston Adventure · Family · Fantasy

Jeanne Birdsall
Frances Hodgson Burnett
Elizabeth Goudge

E Nesbit
Philippa Pearce
P L Travers

The Children of Green Knowe

Frank Cottrell Boyce Ⓔ Adventure · Crime Family · Humour

Morris Gleitzman
Paul Jennings
Andrew Norriss

Philip Ridley
Louis Sachar
David Walliams

12-14

Cosmic · Desirable · Framed · Millions

John Boyne Ⓔ Death · Family · Illness

Yanker Glatshteyn

Suzanne LaFleur

12-14

Noah Barleywater Runs Away

8-11

Chris Bradford (E)

Adventure · Other lands · Sport

12-14

Jason Hightman
Derek Landy
Dan Lee
Joshua Mowll

Bali Rai
Rick Riordan
Jeff Stone
Mark Walden

Young Samurai Series

Tony Bradman

Adventure · Environment · Humour · Sport

5-7

Giles Andreae
Martyn Beardsley

Terence Blacker
Rob Childs

Aftershock • The Dirty Dozen BS *• Hurricane • The Two Jacks* BS
Creaky Castle Series • Football Fever Series
The Greatest Adventures in the World Series
Tales of Terror Series

Christiana Brand

Family · Humour

Debi Gliori
Sam Llewellyn
Lois Lowry

E Nesbit
P L Travers

Nurse Matilda Series

Herbie Brennan (E)

Adventure · Humour · Letters

12-14

R J Anderson
Holly Black
Roald Dahl
Anna Dale
Joseph Delaney

Michelle Harrison
Anthony Horowitz
Daisy Meadows
Andrew Newbound
David Lee Stone

Faerie Wars Series

Theresa Breslin (E)

Fantasy · Historical · Humour · Magic

12-14

Nina Bawden
Malorie Blackman
Berlie Doherty

Caroline Lawrence
J K Rowling

Starship Rescue BS
Dream Master Series • The Magic Factory Series

BS = Published by Barrington Stoke
specialists in resources for dyslexic and struggling readers

Raymond Briggs

Fantasy · Humour

Neil Gaiman
René Goscinny

Michael Lawrence
Dav Pilkey

5-7

Father Christmas GN • Fungus the Bogeyman GN
Jim and the Beanstalk

Lauren Brooke

Pony/horse

Michelle Bates
Pippa Funnell
Stacy Gregg

Elizabeth Lindsay
Kelly McKain
Anna Sewell

12-14

Chestnut Hill Series • Heartland Series

Ann Bryant

Friends · Humour · School

Darcey Bussell
Cindy Jefferies
Ceci Jenkinson
Beatrice Masini
Daisy Meadows

Jenny Oldfield
Caroline Plaisted
Noel Streatfeild
Anna Wilson

5-7

Ballerina Dream Series • School Friends Series • Step Chain Series

Linda Buckley-Archer

Adventure · Historical
Science fiction

Joan Aiken
Paul Bajoria
Chris Priestley

Anthony Read
Trenton Lee Stewart

12-14

Time Quake Trilogy

Frances Hodgson Burnett

Family
Historical: Victorian

Louisa May Alcott
Jeanne Birdsall
Lucy M Boston
Elizabeth Goudge

L M Montgomery
E Nesbit
Gwyneth Rees

Little Lord Fauntleroy • A Little Princess • The Secret Garden

Darcey Bussell

Ballet · Magic

Ann Bryant
Beatrice Masini
Daisy Meadows

Noel Streatfeild
Anna Wilson

5-7

Magic Ballerina Series

8-11

Annette Butterworth Adventure · Animals · Humour

Betty G Birney
Andrew Cope
Roddy Doyle

Liv Michael
Jil Murphy
Dodie Smith

Adventures of Jake Series

Betsy Byars Animals · Family · Humour · School

Lucy Christopher
Michael Morpurgo

Philippa Pearce

The Midnight Fox

Georgia Byng (E) Adventure · Fantasy · Humour
Social issues

Holly Black
Lauren Child
Sally Grindley

Anthony McGowan
Lemony Snicket

Molly Moon Series

Meg Cabot (E) Family · Friends

12-14

Ros Asquith
Judy Blume
Cathy Cassidy
Lauren Child
Geri Halliwell

Megan McDonald
Sara Pennypacker
Dyan Sheldon
Jacqueline Wilson

Allie Finkle's Rules For Girls Series

Lewis Carroll (E) Fantasy

J M Barrie
Frank L Baum
C S Lewis

Geraldine McCaughrean
P L Travers

Alice's Adventures in Wonderland
Through the Looking-Glass and What Alice Found There

Cathy Cassidy (E) Family · Social issues · Thrillers

12-14

Ros Asquith
Meg Cabot
Pippa Funnell
Rose Impey
Diana Kimpton

Hilary McKay
Sara Pennypacker
Jean Ure
Jacqueline Wilson

Cherry Crush • Ginger Snaps • Sundae Girl
Daizy Star Series

Bob Cattell

Other cultures · Sport

David Bedford   Michael Coleman
Rob Childs

Butter-Finger • Shine on Butter-Finger
Glory Gardens Series

Grace Cavendish   Detective mysteries · Historical: Tudor

12-14

Ros Asquith   Mary Hooper
Sally Gardner   Richard Platt
Julia Golding   Lauren St John

The Lady Grace Mysteries

Philip Caveney   Adventure · Fantasy · Science fiction

12-14

Paul Haven   Graham Marks
Hergé   Jill Marshall
Anthony Horowitz   David Miller
Allan Frewin Jones

Alec Devlin Series • Sebastian Darke Series

Henry Chancellor

Adventure · Fantasy

12-14

Pseudonymous Bosch   Sarah Prineas
Andrew Lane   Rick Riordan
Joan Lennon   Trenton Lee Stewart
David Miller

The Remarkable Adventures of Tom Scatterhorn Series

Linda Chapman   Animals · Family · Fantasy · Magic

5-7

Andy Baxter   Pippa Funnell
Adam Blade   Elizabeth Lindsay
Louise Cooper   Daisy Meadows
Annie Dalton   Titania Woods
Heather Dyer

My Secret Unicorn Series
Not Quite a Mermaid Series • Stardust Series

Simon Cheshire

Adventure · Detective mysteries
Humour · School

Andrew Lane   Kaye Umansky
Chris Priestley   Mark Walden

Bottomby • Pants on Fire!
Saxby Smart: Private Detective Series

Lauren Child

Philip Ardagh
Georgia Byng
Meg Cabot

Jack Gantos
Megan McDonald
Jenny Oldfield

Clarice Bean Series

Rob Childs Ⓔ

David Bedford
Terence Blacker
Tony Bradman
Bob Cattell

Michael Coleman
Alan Gibbons
Tom Palmer

Keeper's Ball • Moving the Goalposts GN
County Cup Series

Lucy Christopher ◯

David Almond
Betsy Byars

Sharon Creech
Ally Kennen

Flyaway

David Clement-Davies Ⓔ

Richard Adams
Colin Dann
Brian Jacques

Garry Kilworth
Michelle Paver

The Alchemists of Barbal • Fire Bringer • The Sight • The Telling Pool

Alex Cliff ◯ Ⓔ

Andy Baxter
Adam Blade

David Grimstone
Jeff Stone

Superpowers Series

Steve Cole ◯

Philip Ardagh
Steve Barlow and
   Steve Skidmore
Guy Bass
Anna Maxted

Andrew Norriss
Sebastian Rook
Henry Winkler
Jenny Zucker

Z-Rex
Astrosaurs Series • Astrosaurs Academy Series
Cows in Action Series • Slime Squad Series

Michael Coleman

Adventure · Computers · Sport

Terence Blacker
Bob Cattell
Rob Childs

Chris d'Lacey
Alan Gibbons

Danger Signs BS
Foul Football Series

8-11

Eoin Colfer

Adventure · Detective mysteries
Fantasy · Humour

12-14

Roddy Doyle
Debi Gliori
Matt Haig
Michelle Harrison
Garry Kilworth

Andrew Lane
Andrew Newbound
Ian Ogilvy
Philip Ridley
Steve Voake

Arctic Incident GN • *Half Moon Investigations*
The Legend of Captain Crow's Teeth • *The Legend of Spud Murphy*
The Supernaturalist
Artemis Fowl Series

Louise Cooper

Animals · Fantasy · Magic

Linda Chapman
Lucy Daniels

Diana Kimpton
Jenny Oldfield

Sea Horses • *Short and Scary* SS • *Short and Spooky* SS
Creatures Series • *Mermaid Curse Series*

Susan Cooper

Adventure · Fantasy · Historical
Sea/boats

Paul Dowswell
Charlie Fletcher
Cornelia Funke
Alan Garner
John Gordon

Geraldine McCaughrean   12-14
William Nicholson
Jenny Nimmo
Angie Sage
J R R Tolkien

The Boggart • *Victory*
The Dark is Rising Series

Andrew Cope

Animals · Humour

Annette Butterworth
Joshua Doder

Roddy Doyle
Livi Michael

5-7

Spy Dog Series • *Spy Pups Series*

SS = Short stories

Zizou Corder Ⓔ

Adventure · Ancient history
Animals · Crime · Fantasy
12-14

Kate di Camillo
Alan Garner
Michael Hoeye
Erin Hunter

Livi Michael
Daniel Pennac
Ali Sparkes
Lauren St John

Halo · *Lee Raven: Boy Thief*
Lionboy Series

Cressida Cowell

Fantasy · Historical · Humour

E D Baker
Chris d'Lacey
Lucinda Hare
Diana Hendry
Jason Hightman

Eva Ibbotson
Shoo Rayner
Dugald Steer
Geronimo Stilton

How to Train Your Dragon Series

Sharon Creech Ⓔ

Diaries · Family · Fantasy · Humour

Lucy Christopher
Kate di Camillo
Berlie Doherty

Sally Grindley
Suzanne LaFleur

The Castle Corona · *Hate That Cat*
Heartbeat · *Love That Dog* · *The Unfinished Angel*

Richmal Crompton Ⓔ

Family · Humour · School

René Goscinny
Paul Jennings
Alan MacDonald

Anthony McGowan
Francesca Simon

Just William Series

Gillian Cross  Ⓔ

Adventure · Historical: Roman
Humour · School · Thriller
12-14

Malorie Blackman
Thomas Bloor
Siobhan Dowd
Sally Gardner

Mark Haddon
Gene Kemp
Bali Rai
Di Toft

The Great Elephant Chase · *Wolf*
The Demon Headmaster Series

GN = Graphic novel

Matt Crossick

Ghost/supernatural · Humour · School

Roy Apps
Tommy Donbavand

Barry Hutchison
Louis Sachar

Too Ghoul for School Series

Kevin Crossley-Holland

Adventure · Historical: Medieval
Mythology · Traditional

Geraldine McCaughrean
William Nicholson
Michelle Paver
Richard Platt

Philip Reeve
Rick Riordan
Rosemary Sutcliff
T H White

12-14

Gatty's Tale · Outsiders SS
Arthur Trilogy

Chris d'Lacey

Adventure · Family
Fantasy · Social issues

Michael Bond
Michael Coleman
Cressida Cowell
Cornelia Funke
Kenneth Grahame

Lucinda Hare
Elizabeth Kay
A A Milne
Ian Ogilvy
Steve Voake

5-7

Fly, Cherokee, Fly
Horace: a Teddybear Story · Shrinking Ralph Perfect
The Last Dragon Chronicles

Roald Dahl

Fantasy · Humour

Herbie Brennan
Daren King
Philip Ridley

Jamie Rix
Andy Stanton
David Walliams

5-7

The BFG · Charlie and the Chocolate Factory
Danny the Champion of the World
James and the Giant Peach · Matilda

Anna Dale Ⓔ

Adventure · Magic

E D Baker
Herbie Brennan
Joseph Delaney
Maeve Friel

Eva Ibbotson
Jill Marshall
Jill Murphy

Dawn Undercover · Spellbound
Whispering to Witches

Jenny Dale   Animals

Michelle Bates
Betty G Birney
Lucy Daniels
Pippa Funnell

Diana Kimpton
Ingrid Lee
Jenny Oldfield
Holly Webb

Best Friends Series • Kitten Tales • Puppy Tales

Annie Dalton   Family • Fantasy

Linda Chapman
Catherine Fisher
Meg Harper
Diana Hendry

Hazel Marshall
Jill Marshall
William Nicholson

Friday Forever • Ways to Trap a Yeti BS
Lilac Peabody Series • Mel Beeby, Agent Angel Series

Lucy Daniels   Animals • Diaries

5-7

Michelle Bates
Louise Cooper
Jenny Dale
Pippa Funnell
Diana Kimpton

Ingrid Lee
Elizabeth Lindsay
Anna Sewell
Holly Webb

Animal Ark Series
Dolphin Diaries Series • Little Animal Ark Series

Colin Dann ⊚ Ⓔ   Adventure • Animals

Richard Adams
David Clement-Davies
Kenneth Grahame
Brian Jacques

Garry Kilworth
Dick King-Smith
Jenny Oldfield
Dodie Smith

Farthing Wood Series

Katie Davies   Animals • Family • Friends • Humour

Ally Kennen

Anthony McGowan

The Great Hamster Massacre
The Great Rabbit Rescue

Go to back for lists of: Authors by Genre • Graphic novels
Short stories • Prize winners • Exploring further

Timothee de Fombelle Ⓔ

Adventure · Environment
Fantasy
12-14

Richard Adams
Adam Blade
Neil Gaiman

Ted Hughes
Kenneth Oppel
Steve Voake

Toby Alone · Toby and the Secrets of the Tree

Terry Deary Ⓔ

Historical · Humour
Mythology · War 1939-45

Steve Barlow and
   Steve Skidmore
René Goscinny

Caroline Lawrence
Richard Platt
Dugald Steer

The Fire Thief · Flight of the Fire Thief · Ghost for Sale BS
The Hat Trick BS *· Pitt Street Pirates* BS *· War Games* BS
Horrible Histories Series

Joseph Delaney Ⓔ

Ghost/supernatural · Magic

Herbie Brennan
Anna Dale
Tommy Donbavand
Jeanne DuPrau
Barry Hutchison

Sebastian Rook
Angie Sage
Justin Somper
J R R Tolkien
Pat Walsh

12-14

The Last Apprentice Series · Wardstone Chronicles Series

Narinder Dhami Ⓔ

Animals · Other cultures
School · Sport

Rose Impey
Hilary McKay
Tom Palmer

Helena Pielichaty
Bali Rai
Jacqueline Wilson

12-14

Changing Places · Grow Up, Dad! BS
Beautiful Game Series

Kate di Camillo Ⓔ

Adventure · Animals · Family
Magic · Other lands

Pseudonymous Bosch
Zizou Corder
Sharon Creech
Elizabeth Goudge

Michael Hoeye
Brian Jacques
Daren King
Wendy Orr

Because of Winn-Dixie · The Magician's Elephant
The Miraculous Journey of Edward Tulane
The Tale of Despereaux · The Tiger Rising

8-11

Joshua Doder

Adventure · Animals · Humour

Andrew Cope
Roddy Doyle
Michael Hoeye

Livi Michael
Wendy Orr
Kaye Umansky

Grk Series

Berlie Doherty (E)

Adventure · Family · Fantasy
Historical
12-14

Nina Bawden
Theresa Breslin
Sharon Creech
Anne Fine

Adèle Geras
Penelope Lively
Geraldine McCaughrean
Linda Newbery

Granny Was a Buffer Girl • *The Sailing Ship Tree*
Spellhorn • *The Starburster* • *Street Child*

Tommy Donbavand (E)

Horror · Humour · Vampires
12-14

Roy Apps
Matt Crossick
Joseph Delaney

Barry Hutchison
Derek Landy

Scream Street Series

Siobhan Dowd (E)

Adventure · Detective mysteries
Social issues
12-14
14+

Gillian Cross
Mark Haddon

Lauren St John

The London Eye Mystery

Paul Dowswell (E)

Historical: Victorian · Sea/boats · War
12-14

Susan Cooper
Elizabeth Laird

Michael Molloy

The Adventures of Sam Witchall Series

Roddy Doyle

Animals · Humour

Betty G Birney
Annette Butterworth
Eoin Colfer

Andrew Cope
Joshua Doder
Jeremy Strong

The Giggler Treatment
The Meanwhile Adventures • *Rover Saves Christmas*

Fiona Dunbar

Family · Magic

Anne Fine
Rose Impey
Karen McCombie

Gwyneth Rees
Margaret Ryan
Jacqueline Wilson

Jinx Series

Helen Dunmore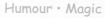

Adventure · Family · Friends
School · Sea/boats
12-14

Anne Fine
Frances Hardinge

Liz Kessler

Ingo Series

Jeanne DuPrau

Fantasy · Science fiction

Joseph Delaney
Cornelia Funke
Diana Wynne Jones

Livi Michael
Angie Sage

Ember Series

Heather Dyer

Humour · Magic

Ian Beck
Linda Chapman
Eva Ibbotson

Gwyneth Rees
Louis Sachar

*The Boy in the Biscuit Tin • The Fish in Room 11
The Girl with the Broken Wing*

John Fardell

Adventure · Humour · Mystery

Malorie Blackman
Julia Jarman

Joan Lennon

*The Flight of the Silver Turtle • Manfred the Baddie
The Secret of the Black Moon Moth*

Anne Fine

Diaries · Family · Humour · School
5-7
12-14

Judy Blume
Berlie Doherty
Fiona Dunbar
Helen Dunmore

Gene Kemp
Karen McCombie
Helena Pielichaty
Jacqueline Wilson

*Charm School • Eating Things on Sticks • Frozen Billy
Goggle Eyes • Jennifer's Diary • Under a Silver Moon*

8-11

Catherine Fisher 💬 Ⓔ

Fantasy · Friends · Mystery
Thrillers
12-14

Annie Dalton
Alan Garner
Robin Jarvis
Diana Wynne Jones

Garry Kilworth
William Nicholson
Michelle Paver
Katherine Roberts

Book of the Crow Series • Oracle Series • The Snow Walker Trilogy

Charlie Fletcher 💬

Fantasy · Friends
12-14

Susan Cooper
Alan Garner
Derek Landy
C S Lewis

E Nesbit
Philip Reeve
Robert Westall

Stone Heart Trilogy

Michael Ford

Adventure · Ancient history
12-14

David Grimstone
Caroline Lawrence

Kate Thompson

Spartan Warrior Series

Jackie French Ⓔ

Family · Magic · War 1939-45

Nina Bawden
Morris Gleitzman
Anne Holm

Judith Kerr
Ian Serraillier
Robert Westall

Hitler's Daughter

Maeve Friel 💬

Magic
5-7

Anna Dale
Eva Ibbotson
Daisy Meadows
Jill Murphy

Laura Owen
Gwyneth Rees
Emily Rodda

Tiger Lily Series • Witch in Training Series

Cornelia Funke 💬

Adventure · Fantasy
12-14

Susan Cooper
Chris d'Lacey
Jeanne DuPrau
Jason Hightman
Eva Ibbotson

Andrew Newbound
Jenny Nimmo
Sarah Prineas
Matthew Skelton
Pat Walsh

*Dragon Rider • Igraine the Brave
Princess Pigsty • Reckless • The Thief Lord
Ghosthunters Series • The Inkheart Trilogy*

Pippa Funnell Ⓔ

Adoption • Pony/horse

Lauren Brooke
Cathy Cassidy
Linda Chapman
Jenny Dale
Lucy Daniels

Stacy Gregg
Deborah Kent
Diana Kimpton
Kelly McKain
Holly Webb

5-7

Tilly's Pony Tails Series

Neil Gaiman Ⓔ

Family • Fantasy
Ghost/supernatural • Humour

Giles Andreae
Pseudonymous Bosch
Raymond Briggs
Timothee de Fombelle
John Gordon

Oliver Jeffers
Caro King
Marcus Sedgwick
Trenton Lee Stewart
Shaun Tan

5-7
12-14
14+

The Day I Swapped My Dad for Two Goldfish
The Graveyard Book • Odd and the Frost Giants • Wolves in the Walls

Jack Gantos

Family • Humour • School • Social issues

Lauren Child
Morris Gleitzman
Gene Kemp
Jeff Kinney

Andrew Norriss
Louis Sachar
David Walliams

14+

Joey Pigza Series

Sally Gardner Ⓔ

Fantasy • Historical • Magic
Other lands

Steve Augarde
Holly Black
Thomas Bloor
Grace Cavendish

Gillian Cross
Frances Hardinge
Mary Hooper

5-7
12-14

I, Coriander • The Red Necklace • Silver Blade

Alan Garner ⌬

Adventure • Fantasy • Magic

Susan Cooper
Zizou Corder
Catherine Fisher
Charlie Fletcher
John Gordon

Philip Pullman
J R R Tolkien
Pat Walsh
T H White

A Bag of Moonshine • Elidor
The Moon of Gomrath • The Weirdstone of Brisingamen
The Stone Book Quartet

Adèle Geras Ⓔ

Ballet · Diaries · Family · Historical

12-14

Nina Bawden
Berlie Doherty
Beatrice Masini

Linda Newbery
Noel Streatfeild

Good Luck, Louisa • Louisa on Screen
The Historical House Trilogy

Alan Gibbons Ⓔ

Adventure · Computers · Fantasy
Social issues · Sport

12-14
14+

Malorie Blackman
Rob Childs
Michael Coleman

Diana Hendry
Paul Shipton

The Legendeer Trilogy • Total Football Series

Yanker Glatshteyn

Friends · Holocaust · War 1939-45

12-14

John Boyne
Morris Gleitzman

Robert Westall

My Story: The Storm to Come

Morris Gleitzman Ⓔ

Animals · Family · Humour
War 1939-45

12-14

Roy Apps
Frank Cottrell Boyce
Jackie French
Jack Gantos
Yanker Glatshteyn

Mark Haddon
Anne Holm
Paul Jennings
Judith Kerr
Jeff Kinney

Now • Once • Then • Toad Heaver • Toad Rage • Toad Surprise

Debi Gliori Ⓔ

Family · Fantasy · Humour · Magic

Holly Black
Christiana Brand
Eoin Colfer
Kes Gray
Matt Haig

Nigel Hinton
Sam Llewellyn
Laura Owen
Terry Pratchett
Margaret Ryan

Deep Fear • Deep Trouble • Deep Water
Pure Dead Brilliant • Pure Dead Gorgeous • Pure Dead Magic
Witch Baby and Me Series

Ⓔ Some titles are available as ebooks

Julia Golding Ⓔ Adventure · Fantasy · Historical · Stage

Grace Cavendish
John Gordon
Katherine Langrish

Matthew Skelton
Noel Streatfeild

12-14

Ship Between the Worlds
Cat Royal Series • The Companions Quartet

Harriet Goodwin Adventure · Death · Fantasy
Ghost/supernatural · Mythology

Sam Osman
Marcus Sedgwick

Ali Sparkes

The Boy Who Fell Down Exit 43 • Gravenhunger

John Gordon Ⓔ Fantasy · Ghost/supernatural

Susan Cooper
Neil Gaiman
Alan Garner
Julia Golding

Angie Sage
Marcus Sedgwick
Pat Walsh

The Giant Under the Snow

René Goscinny Historical: Roman · Humour

Raymond Briggs
Richmal Crompton
Terry Deary
Hergé

Andrew Norriss
Dav Pilkey
Jeremy Strong

Asterix Series GN

Elizabeth Goudge  Fantasy

Lucy M Boston
Frances Hodgson Burnett

Kate di Camillo
E Nesbit

The Little White Horse

Candy Gourlay Ⓔ Family · Illness · Other lands · Sport

Pete Johnson

Michael Morpurgo

12-14

Tall Story

Kenneth Grahame Ⓔ Animals · Fantasy

Chris d'Lacey
Colin Dann
Brian Jacques

Dick King-Smith
A A Milne
Wendy Orr

The Reluctant Dragon • The Wind in the Willows

Kes Gray 💬 Ⓔ

Debi Gliori
Anna Maxted

Francesca Simon
Kaye Umansky

Daisy Series · Nelly the Monster Sitter Series

Stacy Gregg Ⓔ

Pony/horse
12-14

Michelle Bates
Lauren Brooke
Pippa Funnell
Deborah Kent

Diana Kimpton
Kelly McKain
Jenny Oldfield
Anna Sewell

Pony Club Secrets

Andy Griffiths 💬 Ⓔ

Humour · School

Steve Barlow and
   Steve Skidmore
Michael Lawrence

Dav Pilkey
Jamie Rix
Jeremy Strong

Help! I'm Trapped in my Best Friend's Nose
Help! My Parents Think I'm a Robot · Robot Riot! · Treasure Fever!
Bum Series

David Grimstone

Friends · Historical: Roman

Adam Blade
Alex Cliff

Michael Ford
Kate Thompson

Gladiator Boy Series

Sally Grindley 💬

Death · Family · Letters · Other cultures
5-7

Malorie Blackman
Georgia Byng
Sharon Creech
Julia Jarman

Elizabeth Laird
Helena Pielichaty
Jean Ure

Bravo Max · Dear Max · Feather Wars · Hurricane Wills · Relax Max

Mark Haddon 💬 Ⓔ Adventure · Humour · Science fiction · Space

12-14
14+

Steve Barlow and
   Steve Skidmore
Gillian Cross
Siobhan Dowd
Morris Gleitzman

Sam Llewellyn
Anthony McGowan
Andrew Norriss
Philip Ridley
Louis Sachar

Boom!
Agent Z Series

Matt Haig Ⓔ

Fantasy · Magic

Eoin Colfer
Debi Gliori

Katherine Langrish
John Vornholt

14+

The Runaway Troll • *Shadow Forest*

Geri Halliwell Ⓔ

Adventure · Friends · School

Meg Cabot
Carol Hedges

Jill Marshall

Ugenia Lavender Series

Dennis Hamley

Diaries · Family · War 1939-45

Sophie McKenzie
Linda Newbery

Ian Serraillier
Robert Westall

Coming in to Land
The Diary of a World War II Pilot • *The War and Freddy*

Frances Hardinge Ⓔ

Fantasy

Joan Aiken
Helen Dunmore
Sally Gardner

Diana Wynne Jones
Matthew Skelton
Trenton Lee Stewart

12-14

Fly By Night • *Gullstruck Island*
Twilight Robbery • *Verdigris Deep*

Lucinda Hare Ⓔ

Fantasy

Cressida Cowell

Chris d'Lacey

Dragon Whisperer Series

Meg Harper

Friends · Humour

Annie Dalton
Diana Hendry

Karen McCombie

My Mum and Other Horror Stories
Saint Jenni Series

Michelle Harrison Ⓔ

Fairy/folk · Fantasy

R J Anderson
Holly Black

Herbie Brennan
Eoin Colfer

12-14

The 13 Treasure Series

8-11

Paul Haven
Adventure · Crime · Mystery · Other lands

Enid Blyton
Philip Caveney
Allan Frewin Jones

Sam Osman
Rick Riordan

The Seven Keys of Balabad

Carol Hedges
Adventure

Deborah Abela
Geri Halliwell

Charlie Higson
Jill Marshall

12-14

Spy Girl Series

Diana Hendry (E)
Family · Fantasy · Social issues

Cressida Cowell
Annie Dalton
Alan Gibbons

Meg Harper
Jill Murphy
J K Rowling

Harvey Angell and the Ghost Child BS
Swan Boy • *You Can't Kiss it Better*

Hergé ⌐

Adventure · Historical

Philip Caveney
René Goscinny

Charlie Higson
Andrew Lane

Tintin Series GN

Jason Hightman ⌐

Adventure · Fantasy

Laurence Anholt
E D Baker
Chris Bradford

Cressida Cowell
Cornelia Funke
William Nicholson

The Saint of Dragons • *Samurai*

Charlie Higson ⌐ (E)
Adventure · Computers · Humour

Dominic Barker
Carol Hedges
Hergé
Anthony Horowitz

Derek Landy
Jill Marshall
Joshua Mowll
Mark Walden

12-14
14+

Monstroso
Young Bond Series

Nigel Hinton

Adventure · Fantasy

Debi Gliori
Mary Norton

Robert C O'Brien

12-14

Beaver Towers Series

Michael Hoeye

Adventure · Animals · Fantasy · Humour

8-11

Zizou Corder
Kate di Camillo
Joshua Doder
Brian Jacques
Robin Jarvis

Garry Kilworth
Dick King-Smith
Ian Ogilvy
S F Said
E B White

Hermux Tantamoq Adventure Series

Anne Holm

War 1939-45

Jackie French
Morris Gleitzman
Judith Kerr

Ian Serraillier
Sandi Toksvig
Robert Westall

I Am David

Mary Hooper

Animals · Ghost/supernatural
Historical · Humour

Grace Cavendish
Sally Gardner

Dyan Sheldon
Jean Ure

12-14

Witch House BS
Katie Series

Anthony Horowitz

Adventure · Humour

Herbie Brennan
Philip Caveney
Charlie Higson
Derek Landy
Joshua Mowll

Tom Palmer
Philip Ridley
Nick Shadow
Mark Walden

12-14

*Granny • Groosham Grange
Return to Groosham Grange • The Switch
Diamond Brothers Series • Power of 5 Series*

BS = Published by Barrington Stoke
specialists in resources for dyslexic and struggling readers

Ted Hughes

Ian Beck
Timothee de Fombelle
Clive King

Geraldine McCaughrean
Robert C O'Brien
Mal Peet and Elspeth Graham

The Dreamfighter and Other Creation Tales
How the Whale Became and Other Stories
The Iron Man • The Iron Woman

Elizabeth Singer Hunt Adventure

5-7

Andy Baxter
Steve Jackson and
   Ian Livingstone
H I Larry

Barbara Mitchelhill
Rex Stone
Jonny Zucker

Jack Stalwart Series

Erin Hunter ⓔ Adventure · Animals · Fantasy · Magic

Zizou Corder
Elizabeth Kay
Garry Kilworth

Michelle Paver
S F Said
Ali Sparkes

Seekers Series • Warrior Series
Warriors Manga: Seekers Series GN • Warriors: Manga Series GN

Barry Hutchison ⓔ Fantasy · Horror · Sport

Matt Crossick
Joseph Delaney
Tommy Donbavand

Derek Landy
Tom Palmer
Bali Rai

Away from Home • Twin Trouble
Ben 10 Stories Series • Invisible Fiends Series

Eva Ibbotson ⓔ
Adventure · Fantasy
Ghost/supernatural · Humour

12-14

Louise Arnold
Cressida Cowell
Anna Dale
Heather Dyer
Maeve Friel

Cornelia Funke
Liz Kessler
Caro King
Emily Rodda
Kate Saunders

The Beasts of Clawstone Castle • The Dragonfly Pool
Journey to the River Sea • The Ogre of Oglefort
The Secret of Platform 13 • Which Witch?

GN = Graphic novel

8-11

Rose Impey

Cathy Cassidy
Narinder Dhami
Fiona Dunbar
Lois Lowry
Karen McCombie

Barbara Mitchelhill
Gwyneth Rees
Margaret Ryan
Jean Ure

Hothouse Flower • Introducing Scarlett Lee
My Scary Fairy Godmother • The Shooting Star

Steve Jackson and Ian Livingstone

Adventure
Fantasy

Steve Barlow and
    Steve Skidmore
Adam Blade

Elizabeth Singer Hunt
H I Larry
Katherine Roberts

Fighting Fantasy Series

Brian Jacques

Adventure · Animals · Fantasy

12-14

Richard Adams
David Clement-Davies
Colin Dann
Kate di Camillo
Kenneth Grahame

Michael Hoeye
Robin Jarvis
Garry Kilworth
Robert C O'Brien
S F Said

Redwall Series

Julia Jarman

Family · Ghost/supernatural · Historical

5-7
14+

Malorie Blackman
John Fardell
Sally Grindley

Caroline Lawrence
Paul Shipton

Ghost Writer • The Jessame Stories
Jessame to the Rescue and Other Stories
The Time-travelling Cat Series

Robin Jarvis

Fantasy

12-14

Joan Aiken
R J Anderson
Catherine Fisher
Michael Hoeye

Brian Jacques
Allan Frewin Jones
Robert C O'Brien
S F Said

The Deptford Histories Series
The Mouselets of Deptford Series
Tales from the Wyrd Museum Series
The Whitby Witches Series

Cindy Jefferies
Friends · School

Ann Bryant
Kelly McKain
Helena Pielichaty

Caroline Plaisted
Noel Streatfeild

Fame School Series

Oliver Jeffers
Death · Fantasy · Humour

5-7

David Almond
Neil Gaiman

Shaun Tan

The Great Paper Caper
The Incredible Book Eating Boy • *The Heart and the Bottle*

Ceci Jenkinson (E)
Adventure · Humour · Magic · School

Philip Ardagh
Ann Bryant

Francesca Simon
Jeremy Strong

Oli and Skipjack's Tales of Trouble! Series

Paul Jennings
Fantasy · Humour

12-14

Roy Apps
Frank Cottrell Boyce
Richmal Crompton
Morris Gleitzman
Dav Pilkey

Philip Ridley
Andy Stanton
Jeremy Strong
David Walliams

Uncovered! SS • *Unreal!* SS • *Unseen!* SS

Pete Johnson (E)
Adventure · Crime · Ghost/supernatural
Humour · Vampires

12-14

Candy Gourlay
Allan Frewin Jones
Jeff Kinney

Marcus Sedgwick
R L Stine
Robert Swindells

Avenger • *Help! I'm a Classroom Gambler*
How to Train Your Parents • *Trust Me, I'm a Troublemaker*
The Vampire Blog
Spook School Series

Allan Frewin Jones (E)
Adventure · Animals · Fantasy

Philip Caveney
Paul Haven
Robin Jarvis

Pete Johnson
Robert Swindells

Sundered Lands Series • *Talisman Series*

Diana Wynne Jones (E)

Fantasy · Ghost/supernatural
Magic
12-14

Steve Augarde
Jeanne DuPrau
Catherine Fisher
Frances Hardinge
Elizabeth Kay

Ross Mackenzie
Michael Molloy
Sarah Prineas
J K Rowling
Di Toft

Enchanted Glass · House of Many Ways
The Chrestomanci Series

Elizabeth Kay

Fantasy · Magic

Steve Augarde
Ian Beck
Chris d'Lacey

Erin Hunter
Diana Wynne Jones
Jenny Nimmo

The Tree Devil
The Divide Trilogy

Gene Kemp

Humour · School

Gillian Cross
Anne Fine
Jack Gantos

Hilary McKay
Lauren St John

Nothing Scares Me · The Turbulent Term of Tyke Tyler

Ally Kennen

Death · Family
12-14
14+

Lucy Christopher
Katie Davies

Di Toft

Sparks

Deborah Kent

Animals · Historical

Pippa Funnell
Stacy Gregg
Elizabeth Lindsay

Jenny Oldfield
Anna Sewell

Saddle the Wind Series

Judith Kerr (E)

War 1939-45

Nina Bawden
Jackie French
Morris Gleitzman
Anne Holm
Michelle Magorian

Michael Morpurgo
Linda Newbery
Ian Serraillier
Sandi Toksvig
Robert Westall

Bombs on Aunt Dainty
A Small Person Far Away · When Hitler Stole Pink Rabbit

8-11

75

P B Kerr

Hazel Marshall	Sam Osman
Jenny Nimmo	Argie Sage
Kenneth Oppel	Cat Weatherill

One Small Step
Children of the Lamp Series

Liz Kessler

E D Baker	Eva Ibbotson
Helen Dunmore	

Emily Windsnap Series • Philippa Fisher Series

Garry Kilworth Ⓔ

Joan Aiken	Michael Hoeye
David Clement-Davies	Erin Hunter
Eoin Colfer	Brian Jacques
Colin Dann	Michelle Paver
Catherine Fisher	

Jigsaw • Silver Claw
The Welkin Weasels Series

Diana Kimpton

Dominic Barker	Lucy Daniels
Cathy Cassidy	Pippa Funnell
Louise Cooper	Stacy Gregg
Jenny Dale	Kelly McKain

Amy Wild Animal Talker Series • The Pony Mad Princess Series

Caro King

Neil Gaiman	Ross Mackenzie
Eva Ibbotson	Ali Sparkes
C S Lewis	

The Seven Sorcerers • Shadow Spell

Clive King

David Almond	Andrew Norriss
Lynne Reid Banks	Robert C O'Brien
Ted Hughes	Arthur Ransome

Stig of the Dump

Daren King

Animals · Ghost/supernatural · Humour

5-7

Roy Apps
Roald Dahl
Kate di Camillo
David Melling

Wendy Orr
Steve Voake
Karen Wallace

Mouse Noses on Toast • *Peter the Penguin Pioneer*
Frightfully Friendly Ghosties Series

Dick King-Smith

Animals · Family · Friends · Humour

5-7

Michael Bond
Colin Dann
Kenneth Grahame
Michael Hoeye
Ingrid Lee

A A Milne
Jenny Oldfield
Dodie Smith
Geronimo Stilton
E B White

Harry's Mad • *Just Binnie* • *The Mouse Family Robinson*
Ninnyhammer • *The Sheep-pig* • *The Twin Giants*

Jeff Kinney Ⓔ

Bullying · Diaries · Friends · Humour · School

12-14

Jack Gantos
Morris Gleitzman
Pete Johnson
Michael Lawrence

Charlie Small
Andy Stanton
David Walliams

Diary of a Wimpy Kid Series

Suzanne LaFleur ⚬ Ⓔ

Death · Family · Illness

12-14

John Boyne
Sharon Creech

Elizabeth Laird
Jacqueline Wilson

Love, Aubrey

Elizabeth Laird ⚬ Ⓔ

Adventure · Family · Historical
Other cultures · Social issues

12-14

David Almond
Paul Dowswell
Sally Grindley

Suzanne LaFleur
Michael Molloy
Michael Morpurgo

Crusade • *Lost Riders* • *Red Sky in the Morning*
Secret Friends • *Secrets of the Fearless*

⚬ Some titles are available as **Talking books**

77

Derek Landy Ⓔ
Fantasy · Ghost/supernatural · Horror
12-14

Thomas Bloor
Chris Bradford
Tommy Donbavand
Charlie Fletcher
Charlie Higson

Anthony Horowitz
Barry Hutchison
Chris Priestley
Marcus Sedgwick

Skulduggery Pleasant Series

Andrew Lane Ⓔ
Crime · Detective mysteries

Paul Bajoria
Henry Chancellor
Simon Cheshire
Eoin Colfer

Hergé
Caroline Lawrence
William Nicholson
Anthony Read

Young Sherlock Holmes Series

Katherine Langrish Ⓔ
Fairy/folk · Fantasy
Historical: Viking

R J Anderson
Steve Augarde
Steve Barlow and
   Steve Skidmore
Julia Golding

Matt Haig
Ian Ogilvy
Paul Stewart
John Vornholt

Dark Angels
Troll Trilogy

H I Larry Ⓔ
Adventure · Thrillers
5-7

Andy Baxter
Elizabeth Singer Hunt
Steve Jackson and
   Ian Livingstone

Dan Lee
Rex Stone
Jonny Zucker

Zac Power Series

Caroline Lawrence Ⓔ
Detective mysteries
Historical: Roman
12-14

Paul Bajoria
Theresa Breslin
Terry Deary
Michael Ford
Julia Jarman

Andrew Lane
Katherine Roberts
Paul Shipton
Lauren St John
Rosemary Sutcliff

The Roman Mysteries Series

Michael Lawrence Ⓔ

Fantasy · Humour

Raymond Briggs
Andy Griffiths
Jeff Kinney

Dav Pilkey
Jamie Rix
Charlie Small

5-7
12-14

Young Blackbeard • *Young Dracula* BS
Young Monsters BS • *Young Wizards*
Alldus Lexicon Series
Jiggy McCue Series • *A Pair of Jacks Series*

Dan Lee Ⓔ

Thrillers

Adam Blade
Chris Bradford
H I Larry

Jeff Stone
Jonny Zucker

Tangshan Tigers Series

Ingrid Lee

Animals

Jenny Dale
Lucy Daniels
Dick King-Smith

Holly Webb
Anna Wilson

Dog Lost • *Dustbin Cat*

Joan Lennon Ⓔ

Adventure · Detective mysteries
Fantasy · Historical

Henry Chancellor
John Fardell
Barbara Mitchelhill

Sam Osman
Lauren St John
J R R Tolkien

The Night of the Kelpies BS • *The Seventh Tide*
Slightly Jones Mystery Series • *Wickit Chronicles*

C S Lewis Ⓔ

Fantasy

J M Barrie
Frank L Baum
Lewis Carroll
Charlie Fletcher
Caro King

E Nesbit
Philip Pullman
J R R Tolkien
T H White

Chronicles of Narnia

Elizabeth Lindsay

Animals · Magic

Lauren Brooke
Linda Chapman
Lucy Daniels

Deborah Kent
Kelly McKain
Jenny Oldfield

5-7

Magic Pony Series • *Silverlake Fairy School Series*

Penelope Lively

Joan Aiken
Louise Arnold
Lynne Reid Banks
Berlie Doherty

Sophie McKenzie
Philippa Pearce
Kate Thompson

The Ghost of Thomas Kempe

Sam Llewellyn Ⓔ

Laurence Anholt
Philip Ardagh
Christiana Brand
Debi Gliori
Mark Haddon

Joshua Mowll
Ian Ogilvy
Marcus Sedgwick
Andy Stanton
T H White

Little Darlings
Abbot Dagger's Academy Series • Monster of Lyonesse Series

Lois Lowry

Christiana Brand
Rose Impey

L M Montgomery
Lemony Snicket

The Willoughbys

Geraldine McCaughrean Ⓔ

J M Barrie
Frank L Baum
Lewis Carroll
Susan Cooper

Kevin Crossley-Holland
Berlie Doherty
Ted Hughes
Michael Morpurgo

The Death Defying Pepper Roux • The Kite Rider
Not the End of the World • Peter Pan in Scarlet
Smile! • Tamburlaine's Elephants

Karen McCombie Ⓔ

Ros Asquith
Fiona Dunbar
Anne Fine
Meg Harper
Rose Impey

Megan McDonald
Hilary McKay
Sara Pennypacker
Gwyneth Rees
Margaret Ryan

Ally's World Series • Indie Kidd Series
Sadie Rocks Series • Stella etc Series

Alan MacDonald

Humour · Magic

Richmal Crompton
David Melling
Dav Pilkey
Louis Sachar

Francesca Simon
Andy Stanton
Kaye Umansky

5-7

Dirty Bertie Series
History of Warts Series • Troll Trouble Series

8-11

Megan McDonald

Family · Humour

Meg Cabot
Lauren Child
Karen McCombie
Sara Pennypacker

Shoo Rayner
Gwyneth Rees
Dyan Sheldon
Francesca Simon

5-7

Judy Moody Series • The Sisters Club Series • Stink Series

Anthony McGowan

Fantasy · Friends · Humour

Georgia Byng
Richmal Crompton
Katie Davies
Mark Haddon

Jamie Rix
Charlie Small
Jeremy Strong
Andy Stanton

12-14
14+

Einstein's Underpants and How They Saved the World
Bare Bum Gang Series

Kelly McKain

Diaries · Friends · Humour · School

Lauren Brooke
Pippa Funnell
Stacy Gregg
Cindy Jefferies
Diana Kimpton

Elizabeth Lindsay
Hilary McKay
Bali Rai
Margaret Ryan

5-7

Pony Camp Diaries • Totally Lucy Series

Hilary McKay

Family · Humour · Social issues

Louisa May Alcott
Ros Asquith
Jeanne Birdsall
Cathy Cassidy
Narinder Dhami

Gene Kemp
Karen McCombie
Kelly McKain
Barbara Mitchelhill

5-7
12-14

Swop! BS • Wishing for Tomorrow
The Casson Family Series • The Exiles Series

Ross Mackenzie
Fantasy · Magic

Diana Wynne Jones
Caro King

Jenny Nimmo
J K Rowling

Zac and the Dream Pirates

Sophie McKenzie
Time Travel · War 1939-45

Nina Bawden
Dennis Hamley

Penelope Lively

12-14
14+

Time Train to the Blitz

Michelle Magorian
Family · War 1939-45

Nina Bawden
Judith Kerr
Linda Newbery
Philippa Pearce

Ian Serraillier
Sandi Toksvig
Robert Westall

12-14

Back Home · Goodnight Mister Tom

Graham Marks
Adventure · Fantasy · Science fiction
Thrillers · Time travel

Philip Caveney

A i Sparkes

12-14
14+

Faultline · Kaï-ro · Playing with Phyre · Snatched! · Takedown
I Spy Series

Hazel Marshall
Fantasy · Historical

Annie Dalton
P B Kerr

Paul Stewart

Troublesome Angels Series

Jill Marshall
Adventure · Ancient history · Humour

Philip Caveney
Anna Dale
Annie Dalton
Geri Halliwell

Carol Hedges
Charlie Higson
D Toft

Doghead · Doghead Bites Back
Jane Blonde Series

Beatrice Masini
Ballet · Friends · School

Ann Bryant
Darcey Bussell

Adèle Geras
Anna Wilson

5-7

Ballet Academy Series

Anna Maxted

Adventure · Family · Humour

5-7

Guy Bass
Steve Cole

Kes Gray
Francesca Simon

Tom and Matt Series

Daisy Meadows

Friends · Magic

5-7

Herbie Brennan
Ann Bryant
Darcey Bussell
Linda Chapman
Maeve Friel

Gwyneth Rees
Emily Rodda
Margaret Ryan
Anna Wilson
Titania Woods

The Jewel Fairies Series · The Party Fairies Series
The Pet Keeper Fairies Series · The Weather Fairies Series

David Melling

Ghost/supernatural · Humour · Magic

5-7

Daren King
Alan MacDonald

Kaye Umansky

Goblins Series

Livi Michael

Animals · Family · Fantasy · Humour

Betty G Birney
Annette Butterworth
Andrew Cope
Zizou Corder
Joshua Doder

Jeanne DuPrau
Michael Molloy
Di Toft
Cat Weatherill

Faerie Hunt · Sky Wolves · The Whispering Roads
Frank and the .... Series

David Miller

Adventure

12-14

Enid Blyton
Philip Caveney
Henry Chancellor

Joshua Mowll
Arthur Ransome
Ali Sparkes

Leopard's Claw · Sea Wolf · Shark Island

A A Milne

Animals

Michael Bond
Chris d'Lacey
Kenneth Grahame

Dick King-Smith
E B White

The House at Pooh Corner · Winnie the Pooh

8-11

Barbara Mitchelhill

Elizabeth Singer Hunt
Rose Impey
Joan Lennon

Hilary McKay
Philip Ridley

Damian Drooth Super Sleuth Series

Michael Molloy

Paul Dowswell
Diana Wynne Jones
Elizabeth Laird

Livi Michael
Justin Somper

The House on Falling Star Hill
Night Witches Series • Peter Raven Series • Witch Trade Trilogy

L M Montgomery Ⓔ

Louisa May Alcott
Jeanne Birdsall
Frances Hodgson Burnett

Lois Lowry
Johanna Spyri
Laura Ingalls Wilder

Anne of Avonlea • Anne of Green Gables • Anne of the Island

Michael Morpurgo Ⓔ

Betsy Byars
Candy Gourlay
Judith Kerr
Elizabeth Laird
Geraldine McCaughrean

Jenny Nimmo
Philippa Pearce
Mal Peet and Elspeth Graham
Lauren St John
Sandi Toksvig

Born to Run • An Elephant in the Garden
The Kites are Flying • Running Wild • Shadow • War Horse

Chris Mould Ⓔ

Holly Black
Ian Ogilvy
Chris Priestley

Marcus Sedgwick
Lemony Snicket

Fangs 'n' Fire SS
Something Wickedly Weird Series

SS = Short stories

Joshua Mowll

Adventure · Family · Fantasy
Other cultures · Space
12-14

Chris Bradford
Charlie Higson
Anthony Horowitz
Sam Llewellyn

David Miller
Chris Priestley
Robert Swindells

The Great Space Race
The Guild Trilogy

Jill Murphy ⬭ Ⓔ

Fantasy · Humour · Magic · School
5-7

Annette Butterworth
Anna Dale
Maeve Friel
Diana Hendry
Laura Owen

J K Rowling
Louis Sachar
Kate Saunders
Kaye Umansky
Ursula Moray Williams

Dear Hound
The Worst Witch Series

E Nesbit ⬭ Ⓔ

Family · Fantasy

Lynne Reid Banks
Lucy M Boston
Christiana Brand
Frances Hodgson Burnett

Charlie Fletcher
Elizabeth Goudge
C S Lewis

Five Children and It
The Phoenix and the Carpet • The Railway Children

Linda Newbery Ⓔ

Animals · Family · Social issues
War 1939-45
5-7
12-14
14+

David Almond
Nina Bawden
Berlie Doherty
Adèle Geras
Dennis Hamley

Judith Kerr
Michelle Magorian
Philippa Pearce
Ian Serraillier

At the Firefly Gate • Blitz Boys
Lob • Nevermore • Polly's March
Cat Tales Series

Andrew Newbound

Adventure · Fantasy
Ghost/supernatural

Herbie Brennan
Eoin Colfer

Cornelia Funke

Demon Strike

8-11

William Nicholson (E) Adventure · Dystopia · Fantasy

12-14

Joan Aiken
Susan Cooper
Kevin Crossley-Holland
Annie Dalton
Catherine Fisher

Jason Hightman
Andrew Lane
Kenneth Oppel
Philip Reeve

Wind on Fire Trilogy

Jenny Nimmo

Family · Fantasy · Ghost/supernatural
Science fiction
5-7

Steve Augarde
Susan Cooper
Cornelia Funke
Elizabeth Kay
P B Kerr

Ross Mackenzie
Michael Morpurgo
Mal Peet and Elspeth Graham
J K Rowling
Cat Weatherill

The Witch's Tears
Charlie Bone Series • The Snow Spider Trilogy

Andrew Norriss (E) Family · Fantasy · Humour
Science fiction

David Almond
Frank Cottrell Boyce
Steve Cole
Jack Gantos

René Goscinny
Mark Haddon
Clive King

Aquila • Aquila 2: the Adventure Continues ... • Ctrl-Z
The Portal • The Touchstone • The Unluckiest Boy in the World

Mary Norton

Adventure · Family · Fantasy

R J Anderson
Lynne Reid Banks
J M Barrie
Enid Blyton
Nigel Hinton

Alf Prøysen
P L Travers
Cat Weatherill
E B White

The Borrowers Series

Robert C O'Brien

Environment · Fantasy

Nigel Hinton
Ted Hughes
Brian Jacques

Robin Jarvis
Clive King
Marcus Sedgwick

Mrs Frisby and the Rats of Nimh

Ian Ogilvy

Eoin Colfer
Chris d'Lacey
Michael Hoeye
Katherine Langrish
Sam Llewellyn

Chris Mould
Paul Stewart
David Lee Stone
E B White

Measle Stubbs Adventure Series

Jenny Oldfield Animals · Family · Humour · Pony/horse

5-7

Michelle Bates
Ann Bryant
Lauren Child
Louise Cooper
Jenny Dale

Colin Dann
Stacy Gregg
Deborah Kent
Dick King-Smith
Elizabeth Lindsay

Live the Dream! • *Pet School* BS
Definitely Daisy Series • *Horses of Half Moon Ranch Series*
My Magical Pony Series

Kenneth Oppel Ⓔ Adventure · Animals · Fantasy

Social issues

12-14

Timothee de Fombelle
P B Kerr
William Nicholson

Philip Reeve
Justin Somper

Matt Cruse Series • *Silverwing Series*

Wendy Orr Ⓔ Adventure · Animals · Family · Humour

Dominic Barker
Michael Bond
Kate di Camillo
Joshua Doder

Kenneth Grahame
Daren King
E B White

Nim at Sea • *Nim's Island*

Sam Osman Adventure · Fantasy · Mystery · Other lands

12-14

Harriet Goodwin
Paul Haven
P B Kerr
Joan Lennon

Ellen Renner
Rick Riordan
Ali Sparkes

Quicksilver • *Serpent's Gold*

BS = Published by Barrington Stoke
specialists in resources for dyslexic and struggling readers

8-11

Laura Owen

Maeve Friel
Debi Gliori
Jill Murphy

Kaye Umansky
Ursula Moray Williams

Winnie the Witch Series

Tom Palmer *Detective mysteries · Friends · Sport · Thrillers*

David Bedford
Rob Childs
Narinder Dhami
Anthony Horowitz

Barry Hutchison
Helena Pielichaty
Bali Rai

Football Academy Series
Foul Play (Football Detective) Series

Michelle Paver

Animals · Fantasy
12-14

David Almond
David Clement-Davies
Kevin Crossley-Holland
Catherine Fisher
Erin Hunter

Garry Kilworth
Daniel Pennac
J K Rowling
Paul Stewart
J R R Tolkien

Chronicles of Ancient Darkness Series

Philippa Pearce *Adventure · Animals · Family · Fantasy*

J M Barrie
Lucy M Boston
Betsy Byars
Penelope Lively
Michelle Magorian

Michael Morpurgo
Linda Newbery
Arthur Ransome
Kate Saunders
E B White

The Battle of Bubble and Squeak · A Dog So Small
Minnow on the Say · Tom's Midnight Garden · The Way to Sattin Shore

Mal Peet and Elspeth Graham

Animals · Other lands
Traditional
5-7

Ted Hughes
Michael Morpurgo

Jenny Nimmo

Cloud Tea Monkeys

Ⓔ Some titles are available as ebooks

Daniel Pennac

Animals

Zizou Corder
Michelle Paver

S F Said

Dog • Eye of the Wolf

Sara Pennypacker

Family • Friends

Judy Blume
Meg Cabot
Cathy Cassidy

Karen McCombie
Megan McDonald

Clementine Series

8-11

Helena Pielichaty

Diaries • Friends • Letters • School

Ros Asquith
Malorie Blackman
Narinder Dhami
Anne Fine

Sally Grindley
Cindy Jefferies
Tom Palmer
Bali Rai

12-14

Only Love, Simone
After School Club Series • Girls FC Series

Dav Pilkey

Humour

Laurence Anholt
Guy Bass
Raymond Briggs
René Goscinny
Andy Griffiths

Paul Jennings
Michael Lawrence
Alan MacDonald
Jamie Rix
Francesca Simon

5-7

Captain Underpants Series

Caroline Plaisted

Friends

Ann Bryant
Cindy Jefferies

Jean Ure
Holly Webb

Brownies Series

Richard Platt

Diaries • Historical

Grace Cavendish
Kevin Crossley-Holland
Terry Deary

Dugald Steer
Karen Wallace

Castle Diary • Egyptian Diary
Pirate Diary • Roman Diary

Chris Powling
Adventure · Ghost/supernatural · Humour

Jeremy Strong
Karen Wallace
5-7

Best in the World BS · *On the Ghost Trail* · *Thin Ice* BS

Terry Pratchett Ⓔ
Fantasy · Humour

Steve Augarde
Dominic Barker
Debi Gliori

Philip Ridley   12-14
Paul Stewart   14+
David Lee Stone

The Amazing Maurice and His Educated Rodents · *The Carpet People*
The Bromeliad Trilogy · *Johnny Maxwell Stories*

Chris Priestley ⌾ Ⓔ
Adventure · Detective mysteries
Ghost/supernatural · Historical · Thrillers

Paul Bajoria
Linda Buckley-Archer
Simon Cheshire
Derek Landy
Chris Mould

Joshua Mowll   12-14
Philip Pullman
Anthony Read
Marcus Sedgwick

The Dead of Winter · *New World*
Tom Marlowe Adventure Series

Sarah Prineas ⌾ Ⓔ
Fantasy · Magic

Henry Chancellor
Cornelia Funke

Diana Wynne Jones
Angie Sage

The Magic Thief Series

Alf Prøysen ⌾
Magic

Allan Ahlberg
Mary Norton

Ursula Moray Williams   5-7

Mrs Pepperpot Stories

Philip Pullman ⌾
Adventure · Fairy/folk
Fantasy · Historical: Victorian

Joan Aiken
E D Baker
Frank L Baum
Alan Garner
C S Lewis

Chris Priestley   12-14
Anthony Read
Philip Reeve
Justin Richards
J R R Tolkien

Aladdin and the Enchanted Lamp
Count Karlstein, or the Ride of the Demon Huntsman
The Firework-maker's Daughter · *I Was a Rat! or The Scarlet Slippers*
The Scarecrow and His Servant
His Dark Materials Trilogy

8-11

Bali Rai Ⓔ

Friends · Other cultures · School · Sport

David Bedford
Chris Bradford
Gillian Cross
Narinder Dhami
Barry Hutchison

Kelly McKain
Tom Palmer
Helena Pielichaty
Jacqueline Wilson

12-14
14+

Soccer Squad Series

Arthur Ransome

Adventure · Family

Enid Blyton
Clive King

David Miller
Philippa Pearce

Swallows and Amazons Series

Shoo Rayner

Adventure · Humour · Space

Allan Ahlberg
Giles Andreae
Laurence Anholt
Martyn Beardsley

Cressida Cowell
Megan McDonald
Louis Sachar
Mark Skelton

5-7

Axel Storm Series • Ricky Rocket Series
Scaredy Cats Series • Viking Vik Series

Anthony Read

Detective mysteries · Historical: Victorian

Deborah Abela
Paul Bajoria
Linda Buckley-Archer
Andrew Lane

Chris Priestley
Philip Pullman
Justin Richards

Baker Street Boys Series

Gwyneth Rees ⚬ Ⓔ

Fairy/folk · Magic

Ros Asquith
Frances Hodgson Burnett
Fiona Dunbar
Heather Dyer
Maeve Friel

Rose Impey
Karen McCombie
Megan McDonald
Daisy Meadows
Jean Ure

5-7

Cosmo and the Great Witch Escape
The Magic Princess Dress • The Making of May
Fairy Series • Mum Series

Philip Reeve

Adventure · Humour
12-14

Kevin Crossley-Holland
Charlie Fletcher
William Nicholson
Kenneth Oppel

Philip Pullman
Justin Somper
Paul Stewart
Kate Thompson

Here Lies Arthur • *No Such Thing as Dragons*
Larklight Series

Ellen Renner Ⓔ Adventure · Detective mysteries · Fantasy

Sam Osman

Lemony Snicket

Castle of Shadows • *City of Thieves*

Justin Richards Ⓔ

Adventure · Detective mysteries
Ghost/supernatural · School

Paul Bajoria
Dominic Barker
Holly Black
Philip Pullman

Anthony Read
Nick Shadow
Karen Wallace

The Chaos Code
Agent Alfie Series • *Dr Who Series*
School of Night Series • *Time Runners Series*

Philip Ridley Family · Fantasy · Humour · Magic

Philip Ardagh
Frank Cottrell Boyce
Eoin Colfer
Roald Dahl
Mark Haddon

Anthony Horowitz
Paul Jennings
Barbara Mitchelhill
Terry Pratchett

Kasper in the Glitter • *Krindle Krax* • *Scribbleboy*
Vinegar Street • *Zinder Zunder* • *Zip's Apollo*

Rick Riordan Ⓔ

Adventure · Humour · Mythology
12-14

Blue Balliett
Adam Blade
Pseudonymous Bosch
Chris Bradford
Henry Chancellor

Kevin Crossley-Holland
Paul Haven
Sam Osman
Katherine Roberts
Paul Shipton

The Maze of Bones
Heroes of Olympus Series
Kane Chronicles Series • *Percy Jackson Series*

Jamie Rix 💬 Ⓔ
Diaries · Humour

Roald Dahl
Andy Griffiths
Michael Lawrence

Anthony McGowan
Dav Pilkey
Jeremy Strong

The Incredible Luck of Alfie Pluck
Grizzly Tales Series • The Revenge Files of Alistair Fury Series

Katherine Roberts
Adventure · Fantasy · Historical
Mythology · Pony/horse
12-14

Catherine Fisher
Steve Jackson and
   Ian Livingstone
Caroline Lawrence
Rick Riordan

Anna Sewell
Paul Shipton
Dugald Steer
J R R Tolkien

I am the Great Horse
The Seven Fabulous Wonders Series

Emily Rodda 💬
Adventure · Detective mysteries
Fairy/folk · Fantasy

Holly Black
Maeve Friel
Eva Ibbotson

Daisy Meadows
Titania Woods

Bob and the House Elves
Fairy Charm Series

Sebastian Rook
Adventure · Horror · Thrillers

Steve Cole
Joseph Delaney

Justin Somper

Vampire Dusk (Plague) Series

J K Rowling 💬
Fantasy · Magic · School
12-14

Pseudonymous Bosch
Theresa Breslin
Diana Hendry
Diana Wynne Jones
Ross Mackenzie

Jill Murphy
Jenny Nimmo
Michelle Paver
Kaye Umansky

The Tales of Beedle the Bard SS
The Harry Potter Series

SS = Short stories

93

Margaret Ryan

Family · Humour
5-7

Fiona Dunbar
Debi Gliori
Rose Impey
Karen McCombie

Kelly McKain
Daisy Meadows
Kate Saunders
Jean Ure

Roodica the Rude Series • Weird Street Series

Louis Sachar (E)

Humour · School · Social issues
5-7
12-14

Frank Cottrell Boyce
Matt Crossick
Heather Dyer
Jack Gantos
Mark Haddon

Alan MacDonald
Jill Murphy
Shoo Rayner
David Walliams
Henry Winkler

Holes • Small Steps

Marvin Redpost Series • Wayside School Series

Angie Sage (E)

Animals · Magic

Ian Beck
Pseudonymous Bosch
Susan Cooper
Joseph Delaney
Jeanne DuPrau

John Gordon
P B Kerr
Sarah Prineas
Lemony Snicket
John Vornholt

Araminta Spook Series • Septimus Heap Series

S F Said ⬭ (E)

Adventure · Animals · Science fiction

Michael Hoeye
Erin Hunter
Brian Jacques

Robin Jarvis
Daniel Pennac

The Outlaw Varjak Paw • Varjak Paw

Kate Saunders

Fantasy · Magic · School

Eva Ibbotson
Jill Murphy
Philippa Pearce

Margaret Ryan
Kaye Umansky

Beswitched • Magicalamity

The Belfry Witches Series

⬭ Some titles are available as Talking books

Marcus Sedgwick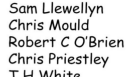

Family · Humour · Magic

12-14

Neil Gaiman	Sam Llewellyn
Harriet Goodwin	Chris Mould
John Gordon	Robert C O'Brien
Pete Johnson	Chris Priestley
Derek Landy	T H White

The Raven Mysteries

Ian Serraillier

War 1939-45

Jackie French	Michelle Magorian
Dennis Hamley	Linda Newbery
Anne Holm	Sandi Toksvig
Judith Kerr	Robert Westall

The Silver Sword

Anna Sewell

Animals · Pony/horse

Michelle Bates	Stacy Gregg
lauren Brooke	Deborah Kent
Lucy Daniels	Katherine Roberts

Black Beauty

Nick Shadow

Horror

Louise Arnold	Justin Richards
Anthony Horowitz	

Midnight Library Series

Dyan Sheldon

Adventure · Humour · Magic

5-7
12-14

Ros Asquith	Mary Hooper
Judy Blume	Megan McDonald
Meg Cabot	

The Difficult Job of Keeping Time
Drusilla and Her Brothers • What Mona Wants, Mona Gets

Paul Shipton

Historical · Humour · Mythology

Alan Gibbons	Rick Riordan
Julia Jarman	Katherine Roberts
Caroline Lawrence	

The Pig Scrolls • The Pig That Saved the World

8-11

Francesca Simon

Family · Humour
5-7

Laurence Anholt
Richmal Crompton
Kes Gray
Ceci Jenkinson
Alan MacDonald

Anna Maxted
Megan McDonald
Dav Pilkey
Jean Ure
Henry Winkler

The Horrid Henry Series

Mark Skelton

Animals · Humour · Time travel
5-7

Giles Andreae
Shoo Rayner

Andy Stanton

Monkey Pirates Series

Matthew Skelton

Fantasy
12-14

Blue Balliett
Cornelia Funke

Julia Golding
Frances Hardinge

Endymion Spring • The Story of Cirrus Flux

Charlie Small

Adventure · Diaries · Humour

Jeff Kinney
Michael Lawrence

Anthony McGowan
David Walliams

The Charlie Small Journals

Dodie Smith

Adventure · Animals

Annette Butterworth
Colin Dann

Dick King-Smith
E B White

One Hundred and One Dalmatians • The Starlight Barking

Lemony Snicket

Fantasy · Humour

Philip Ardagh
Blue Balliett
Thomas Bloor
Georgia Byng
Lois Lowry

Chris Mould
Ellen Renner
Angie Sage
Trenton Lee Stewart
R L Stine

A Series of Unfortunate Events

Justin Somper

Fantasy · Horror

12-14

Joseph Delaney
Michael Molloy
Kenneth Oppel

Philip Reeve
Sebastian Rook
R L Stine

Vampirates Series

Ali Sparkes

Adventure · Family · Fantasy

12-14

Enid Blyton
Zizou Corder
Harriet Goodwin
Erin Hunter
Caro King

Graham Marks
David Miller
Sam Osman
Di Toft

Dark Summer • Frozen in Time • Wishful Thinking
Monster Makers Series • The Shapeshifter Series

Johanna Spyri

Family

Louisa May Alcott
Jeanne Birdsall

L M Montgomery
Laura Ingalls Wilder

Heidi

Lauren St John

Adventure · Animals · Detective mysteries
Other lands · Thrillers

Enid Blyton
Grace Cavendish
Zizou Corder
Siobhan Dowd

Gene Kemp
Caroline Lawrence
Joan Lennon
Michael Morpurgo

Dolphin Song • The Elephant's Tale
The Last Leopard • The White Giraffe
Laura Marlin Mystery Series

Andy Stanton

Humour

5-7

Roald Dahl
Paul Jennings
Jeff Kinney
Sam Llewellyn

Alan MacDonald
Anthony McGowan
Mark Skelton
David Walliams

The Story of Matthew Buzzington BS
Mr Gum Series

Dugald Steer Ⓔ *Adventure · Historical · Magic*

Cressida Cowell
Terry Deary
Richard Platt

Katherine Roberts
T H White

Alienology · Dragonology · Monsterology
Mythology · Piratology · Wizardology
Dragonology Chronicles Series

Paul Stewart *Animals · Fantasy · Historical · Horror*

5-7
12-14

Katherine Langrish
Hazel Marshall
Ian Ogilvy
Michelle Paver

Terry Pratchett
Philip Reeve
David Lee Stone
Steve Voake

Barnaby Grimes Series
The Edge Chronicles Series · Far Flung Adventures Series

Trenton Lee Stewart *Adventure · Mystery*

12-14

Enid Blyton
Pseudonymous Bosch
Linda Buckley-Archer
Henry Chancellor

Neil Gaiman
Frances Hardinge
Lemony Snicket

The Mysterious Benedict Society Series

Geronimo Stilton *Animals · Humour*

5-7

Cressida Cowell
Dick King-Smith

Jeremy Strong

Geronimo Stilton GN
Geronimo Stilton Series

R L Stine Ⓔ *Horror*

12-14

Pete Johnson
Lemony Snicket

Justin Somper
Robert Swindells

Goosebumps Series

David Lee Stone *Fantasy · Historical: Roman*

12-14

R J Anderson
Adam Blade
Herbie Brennan

Ian Ogilvy
Terry Pratchett
Paul Stewart

The Illmoor Chronicles

Jeff Stone

Adventure · Martial arts

Chris Bradford
Alex Cliff

Dan Lee

Five Ancestors Series

Rex Stone

Adventure · Animals

5-7

Andy Baxter
Elizabeth Singer Hunt

H I Larry
Jonny Zucker

Dinosaur Cove Series

Noel Streatfeild

Ballet · Family · Stage

Ann Bryant
Darcey Bussell
Adèle Geras

Julia Golding
Cindy Jefferies

Ballet Shoes • Ballet Shoes for Anna

Jeremy Strong

Animals · Family · Humour

5-7
12-14

Roy Apps
Roddy Doyle
René Goscinny
Andy Griffiths
Ceci Jenkinson

Paul Jennings
Anthony McGowan
Chris Powling
Jamie Rix
Geronimo Stilton

Batpants! • The Beak Speaks
Doctor Bonkers! • Weird • We Want to be on Telly
Hundred-Mile-an-Hour-Dog Series
My Brother's Famous Bottom Series • Pirate School Series

Rosemary Sutcliff

Historical: Medieval/Roman · Mythology

Kevin Crossley-Holland
Caroline Lawrence

T H White

Beowulf: Dragonslayer
The Eagle of the Ninth Series • The King Arthur Trilogy

Robert Swindells

Adventure · Ghost/supernatural
Science fiction · War 1939-45

12-14

Thomas Bloor
Pete Johnson
Allan Frewin Jones
Joshua Mowll

R L Stine
Kate Thompson
Robert Westall

Blitzed • Nightmare Stairs • Room 13
The Shade of Hettie Daynes • Shrapnel • Timesnatch

Shaun Tan

Fantasy · Humour
5-7
12-14

David Almond   Oliver Jeffers
Neil Gaiman

Eric • The Lost Thing • The Red Tree

Kate Thompson (E)

Fantasy · Ghost/supernatural
Historical: Roman
12-14
14+

Malorie Blackman   Penelope Lively
Michael Ford   Philip Reeve
David Grimstone   Robert Swindells

Wanted!
The Missing Link Trilogy
The New Policeman Trilogy • The Switchers Trilogy

Di Toft

Fantasy · Horror · Humour

Gillian Cross   Jill Marshall
Diana Wynne Jones   Livi Michael
Ally Kennen   Ali Sparkes

Wolven Series

Sandi Toksvig (E)

Other cultures · War 1939-45

Anne Holm   Michael Morpurgo
Judith Kerr   Ian Serraillier
Michelle Magorian

Hitler's Canary

J R R Tolkien (E)

Adventure · Fantasy
12-14
14+

Susan Cooper   C S Lewis
Joseph Delaney   Michelle Paver
Alan Garner   Philip Pullman
Joan Lennon   Katherine Roberts

The Hobbit GN • *Lord of the Rings Series*

P L Travers (E)

Family · Fantasy · Humour · Magic

J M Barrie   Christiana Brand
Frank L Baum   Lewis Carroll
Jeanne Birdsall   Mary Norton
Lucy M Boston

Mary Poppins Series

9-11

Kaye Umansky Ⓔ

Simon Cheshire
Joshua Doder
Kes Gray
Alan MacDonald
David Melling

Jill Murphy
Laura Owen
J K Rowling
Kate Saunders
Jean Ure

Clover Twig and the Incredible Flying Cottage BS
Meet the Weirds • The Silver Spoon of Solomon Snow
Solomon Snow and the Stolen Jewel • Wilma's Wicked Spell
Goblinz Series • Pongwiffy Series

Jean Ure Ⓔ Diaries · Ghost/supernatural · Letters · School

12-14

Cathy Cassidy
Sally Grindley
Mary Hooper
Rose Impey
Caroline Plaisted

Gwyneth Rees
Margaret Ryan
Francesca Simon
Kaye Umansky
Jacqueline Wilson

Boys Beware • Hunky Dory • Ice Lolly
Secret Meeting • Star Crazy • Sugar and Spice
Girlfriends Series • Sandy Simmons Series

Steve Voake Ⓔ

Fantasy · Science fiction · Thrillers
12-14

Dominic Barker
Eoin Colfer
Chris d'Lacey

Timothee de Fombelle
Daren King
Paul Stewart

Blood Hunters • The Dreamwalker's Child
Fightback • The Starlight Conspiracy • The Web of Fire
Daisy Dawson Series • Hooey Higgins Series

John Vornholt

Fantasy

Steve Barlow and
   Steve Skidmore
Matt Haig

Katherine Langrish
Angie Sage

The Troll King Trilogy

Mark Walden Ⓔ

Adventure · Thrillers
12-14

Chris Bradford
Simon Cheshire

Charlie Higson
Anthony Horowitz

H.I.V.E. Series

Karen Wallace Ⓔ

Adventure · Historical

5-7
12-14

Giles Andreae	Richard Platt
Martyn Beardsley	Chris Powling
Daren King	Justin Richards

Crunchbone Castle Chronicles • Lady Violet Winters Series

David Walliams Ⓔ

Friends · Humour · Social issues

12-14

Terence Blacker	Jeff Kinney
Frank Cottrell Boyce	Louis Sachar
Roald Dahl	Charlie Small
Jack Gantos	Andy Stanton
Paul Jennings	

Billionaire Boy • Boy in the Dress • Mr Stink

Pat Walsh

Fantasy · Historical · Magic

Joseph Delaney	Alan Garner
Cornelia Funke	John Gordon

The Crowfield Curse • The Crowfield Demon

Cat Weatherill

Adventure · Fantasy · Magic

Philip Ardagh	Jenny Nimmo
P B Kerr	Mary Norton
Livi Michael	

Barkbelly • Snowbone • Wild Magic

Holly Webb Ⓔ

Friends

5-7

Jenny Dale	Ingrid Lee
Lucy Daniels	Caroline Plaisted
Pippa Funnell	Anna Wilson

Rose • Rose and The Lost Princess • Rose and the Magician's Mask
Molly's Magic Series • My Naughter Little Puppy Series

Robert Westall

Adventure · Ghost/supernatural
War 1939-45
12-14

Charlie Fletcher	Judith Kerr
Jackie French	Michelle Magorian
Yanker Glatshteyn	Ian Serraillier
Dennis Hamley	Robert Swindells
Anne Holm	

Blitz • Blitzcat • The Machine Gunners
Size Twelve • Stormsearch • A Time of Fire

E B White Animals · Fantasy

Michael Hoeye
Dick King-Smith
A A Milne
Mary Norton
Ian Ogilvy

Wendy Orr
Philippa Pearce
Dodie Smith
Ursula Moray Williams

Charlotte's Web • Stuart Little

T H White (E) Fantasy · Mythology

Kevin Crossley-Holland
Alan Garner
C S Lewis
Sam Llewellyn

Marcus Sedgwick
Dugald Steer
Rosemary Sutcliff

The Sword in the Stone

Laura Ingalls Wilder Family · Other lands

Louisa May Alcott
Jeanne Birdsall

L M Montgomery
Johanna Spyri

Little House Series

Ursula Moray Williams  Adventure · Animals · Fantasy

Jill Murphy
Laura Owen

Alf Prøysen
E B White

Adventures of the Little Wooden Horse
Gobbolino: the Witch's Cat

Anna Wilson (E) Ballet · Friends · School

5-7

Ann Bryant
Darcey Bussell
Ingrid Lee
Beatrice Masini

Daisy Meadows
Holly Webb
Titania Woods

Kitten Cupid • Kitten Kaboodle • Kitten Smitten
Pup Idol • Puppy Love • Puppy Power
Nina Fairy Ballerina Series

(E) Some titles are available as ebooks

Jacqueline Wilson Ⓔ

Family · Humour · Social issues

5-7
12-14

Ros Asquith
Judy Blume
Meg Cabot
Cathy Cassidy
Narinder Dhami

Fiona Dunbar
Anne Fine
Suzanne LaFleur
Bali Rai
Jean Ure

Cookie • Hetty Feather • Jacky Daydream
Little Darlings • The Longest Whale Song • My Sister Jodie
Tracy Beaker Trilogy

Henry Winkler

Friends · Humour · School

Steve Cole
Louis Sachar

Francesca Simon

Hank Zipzer Series

Titania Woods Ⓔ

Fairy/folk

Linda Chapman
Daisy Meadows

Emily Rodda
Anna Wilson

Glitterwings Academy Series

Jonny Zucker

Adventure · Crime · Sport

5-7

Andy Baxter
Steve Cole
Elizabeth Singer Hunt

H I Larry
Dan Lee
Rex Stone

Striker Boy
Max Flash Series

*Go to back for
lists of:*
Authors by Genre
Graphic novels
Short stories
Prize winners
Further reading

Authors for Ages 12-14

Randa Abdel-Fattah

Family · Friends · Other cultures
Other lands · Social issues
14+

Narinder Dhami
Mary Hooper
Cathy Hopkins
Beverley Naidoo

Bali Rai
Na'ima B Robert
Rosie Rushton

Does My Head Look Big in This?
Ten Things I Hate About Me • *Where the Streets Had a Name*

L J Adlington Ⓔ

Fantasy · Ghost/supernatural
Science fiction · War 1939-45

Malorie Blackman
Sharon Dogar

Gemma Malley

Burning Mountain • *Cherry Heaven* • *Diary of Pelly-D* • *Glittering Eye*

Joan Aiken Ⓔ

Adventure · Fantasy
Ghost/supernatural · Historical
8-11

Paul Bajoria
Linda Buckley-Archer
Ann Halam
Frances Hardinge

Robin Jarvis
Ben Jeapes
Diana Wynne Jones

The Wolves of Willoughby Chase Series

Lloyd Alexander

Fantasy

N M Browne
Susan Cooper
Alison Croggon

Garth Nix
Jonathan Stroud

The Chronicles of Prydain Series

Alison Allen-Gray

Family · Mystery · Science fiction

Stephen Baxter
Patrick Cave
Alan Gibbons
Rhiannon Lassiter
Neal Shusterman

Marc Sumerak
A G Taylor
David Thorpe
Scott Westerfeld
Tim Wynne-Jones

Lifegame • *Unique*

David Almond

Family · Fantasy · Friends
Ghost/supernatural · Social issues

5-7
8-11

Thomas Bloor
Tim Bowler
Sonya Hartnett
Ally Kennen
Nicola Morgan

Sally Nicholls
Susan Price
Louis Sachar
Marcus Sedgwick
Robert Swindells

*Clay • The Fire Eaters • Jackdaw Summer
My Name is Mina • Secret Heart • Skellig*

Laurie Halse Anderson

Historical · Slavery
Social issues

14+

Julie Hearn
Tanya Landman
Anna Perera

Ann Rinaldi
James Riordan
Mildred D Taylor

Chains • Forge

R J Anderson ⬭ Ⓔ

Adventure · Fairy/folk
Fantasy · Magic · Thrillers

8-11

Sarah Rees Brennan
Eoin Colfer
Shannon and Dean Hale
Joanne Harris
Michelle Harrison

Robin Jarvis
Stephenie Meyer
Aprilynne Pike
L J Smith
David Lee Stone

Arrow • Knife • Rebel • Ultraviolet

Gill Arbuthnott

Adventure · Family · Mystery

Marie-Louise Jensen
Suzanne LaFleur

Sally Prue

The Keepers' Daughter • The Keepers' Tattoo

Bernard Ashley ⬭ Ⓔ

Adventure · Slavery · Social issues
Thrillers · War

14+

Anne Cassidy
Pauline Chandler
Jim Eldridge
Alan Gibbons
Keith Gray
Andy McNab and
    Robert Rigby

Catherine MacPhail
Mal Peet
Malcolm Rose
Robert Swindells

*Angel Boy • Flashpoint
No Way to Go • Ronnie's War • Smokescreen BS • Solitaire*

Ros Asquith

Family · Humour · Romance · School

8-11

Meg Cabot
Cathy Cassidy
Rowan Coleman
Sue Limb
Karen McCombie

Chloë Rayban
Louise Rennison
Liz Rettig
Jean Ure

The Teenage Worrier Guide Series

Steve Augarde Ⓔ

Adventure · Dystopia · Environment
Fantasy · Magic · Science fiction

8-11

Suzanne Collins
James Dashner
John Dickinson

Kat Falls
Michael Grant
Trenton Lee Stewart

X Isle
The Touchstone Trilogy

Helen Bailey Ⓔ

Family · Friends · Romance

Ann Brashares
Meg Cabot
Cathy Cassidy
Sarah Dessen

Echo Freer
Cathy Hopkins
Sarah Webb
Jacqueline Wilson

Electra Brown Series

Paul Bajoria

Adventure · Crime · Historical · Mystery · Thrillers

8-11

Joan Aiken
Linda Buckley-Archer
Grace Cavendish

Caroline Lawrence
Chris Priestley
Eleanor Updale

Printer's Devil Trilogy

Lynne Reid Banks Ⓔ

Family · Historical · Other cultures
Other lands · Social issues

8-11

Elizabeth Laird
Beverley Naidoo

Suzanne Fisher Staples
Tim Wynne-Jones

Broken Bridge • The Dungeon
One More River • Stealing Stacey • Tiger, Tiger

Dominic Barker

David Belbin	Anthony Horowitz
Chris Bradford	Terry Pratchett
Charlie Higson	Mark Walden

Adam and the Arkonauts
Blart Series · Mickey Sharp Series

Stephen Baxter

Alison Allen-Gray   Scott Westerfeld

The H-Bomb Girl

Ian Beck

Linda Buckley-Archer	Charlie Higson
James Dashner	Philip Reeve

Pastworld

Tom Becker

Joseph Delaney	Darren Shan
Charlie Fletcher	R L Stine
E E Richardson	G P Taylor

Darkside Series

Frank Beddor

Herbie Brennan	Neil Gaiman
Maite Carranza	Shannon and Dean Hale
Eoin Colfer	Philip Pullman

Looking Glass Wars Series GN

David Belbin

Dominic Barker	Tanya Landman
Malorie Blackman	Nicola Morgan
Charlie Higson	Malcolm Rose
Anthony Horowitz	Robert Swindells

Coma BS · Denial · Festival
Shooting at the Stars · Stray BS

Sophia Bennett

Friends · Social issues

Cathy Cassidy
Chris Higgins
Mary Hogan

Karen McCombie
Hilary McKay
Sarah Webb

Threads Series

T E Berry-Hart

Dystopia · Science fiction

Patrick Cave
John Dickinson
Roderick Gordon and
   Brian Williams

Tim Lott
David Thorpe
Rachel Ward

Genopolis Trilogy

Julie Bertagna

Adventure · Death · Environment
Fantasy · Social issues

Terence Blacker
Patrick Cave
Anne Fine
Adèle Geras

Saci Lloyd
Sophie McKenzie
Catherine MacPhail
Celia Rees

*Exodus • The Opposite of Chocolate
Soundtrack • The Spark Gap • Zenith*

Terence Blacker

Family · Humour · School
Science fiction · Social issues

Julie Bertagna
Malorie Blackman
B R Collins

Pete Johnson
Michael Lawrence
David Walliams

5-7
8-11

*The Angel Factory • Boy 2 Girl
Missing, Believed Crazy • Parent Swap*

Malorie Blackman

Dystopia · Eating disorders · Family
Romance · Social issues · Thrillers

L J Adlington
David Belbin
Terence Blacker
Anne Cassidy
Helena Pielichaty

Chloë Rayban
Nicky Singer
Mildred D Taylor
Kate Thompson

5-7
8-11
14+

*Dead Gorgeous • Tell Me No Lies
Noughts and Crosses Sequence*

GN = Graphic novel

12-14

Thomas Bloor

Fantasy · Horror · War 1939-45
8-11

David Almond
Derek Landy

Robert Swindells

Beast Beneath the Sky • *Bomber Boys* BS
Heart of the Serpent   *Worm in the Blood*

Pseudonymous Bosch

Adventure · Magic · Mystery
8-11

Henry Chancellor
Neil Gaiman
J K Rowling

Ali Sparkes
Trenton Lee Stewart

Secret Series

Tim Bowler

Death · Family · Social issues · Thrillers
14+

David Almond
Lucy Christopher
Gillian Cross
Siobhan Dowd
Catherine Forde

Sonya Hartnett
Ally Kennen
Anthony McGowan
Graham Marks
Sarah Wray

River Boy • *Shadows*
Starseeker • *Walking with the Dead*

Frank Cottrell Boyce

Detective mysteries · Family
Humour · School
8-11

Gennifer Choldenko
Brian Falkner
Anne Fine
Roderick Gordon and
    Brian Williams
Mark Haddon

Eva Ibbotson
Paul Jennings
Jeff Kinney
Louis Sachar
David Walliams

Cosmic • *Desirable* BS
Framed • *Millions*

John Boyne

Death · Illness · Social issues
War 1939-45
8-11

Sharon Dogar
Paul Dowswell
Yanker Glatshteyn
Morris Gleitzman
Damian Kelleher

Suzanne LaFleur
Michael Morpurgo
Sally Nicholls
Suzanne Fisher Staples
Markus Zusak

The Boy in the Striped Pyjamas
Noah Barleywater Runs Away

Jason Bradbury

Science fiction · Thrillers

Andy Briggs
A J Butcher
M G Harris

Anthony Horowitz
Mark Walden

Dot Robot Series

Chris Bradford Ⓔ

Adventure · Historical
Martial Arts · Other lands
8-11

Dominic Barker
Brian Falkner
Alison Goodman
Sam Llewellyn

Joshua Mowll
Jane Prowse
Mark Walden

Virtual Kombat
Young Samurai Series

Ann Brashares

Friends · Social issues

Helen Bailey
Meg Cabot
Cathy Hopkins

Karen McCombie
Hilary McKay
Jean Ure

Girls in Pants · The Second Summer of the Sisterhood
Sisterhood of the Travelling Pants · The Summer That Changed Everything
Summers of the Sisterhood: Forever Blue

Herbie Brennan

Adventure · Humour

Frank Beddor
Eoin Colfer
Michelle Harrison

J K Rowling
David Lee Stone

8-11

Faerie Wars Series

Sarah Rees Brennan

Family · Fantasy
Ghost/supernatural

R J Anderson
Sarwat Chadda
Eoin Colfer

E E Richardson
R L Stine

Demon's Lexicon Series

Go to back for lists of: **Authors by Genre · Graphic novels**
Short stories · Prize winners · Exploring further

12-14

Theresa Breslin

Adventure · Family · Historical
Social issues · War 1914-18
8-11

Berlie Doherty
Adèle Geras
Marie-Louise Jensen

Caroline Lawrence
Michelle Magorian
Meg Rosoff

Alligator BS • *The Medici Seal*
The Nostradamus Prophecy • *Prisoner in Alcatraz* BS
Prisoner of the Inquisition • *Remembrance*

Andy Briggs

Adventure · Bullying · Computers
Science fiction · Social issues

Jason Bradbury
M G Harris
Sophie McKenzie

Will Peterson
Rick Riordan

Hero.com Series • *Vill@in.net Series*

John Brindley Ⓔ

Adventure · Fantasy · Friends
Science fiction · Thrillers

Meg Cabot
James Dashner
Sarah Dessen
John Flanagan

Keith Gray
Catherine MacPhail
Philip Reeve

Blood Crime • *City of Screams* • *The Rule of Claw*
Amy Peppercorn Series

Lauren Brooke

Pony/horse · Romance
8-11

Stacy Gregg
K M Peyton

Jean Ure
Jacqueline Wilson

Heartland Series

Kevin Brooks

Crime · Family · Friends · Social issues
14+

Siobhan Dowd
Catherine Forde
Alan Gibbons
Helen Grant
Keith Gray

Sonya Hartnett
Ally Kennen
Anthony McGowan
Nicky Singer
Sarah Wray

I See You, Baby BS • *Johnny Delgado* BS • *Martyn Pig*

Ⓔ Some titles are available as ebooks

12-14 *(side tab)*

N M Browne

Adventure • Fantasy • Historical: Roman
Mystery • Mythology

Lloyd Alexander
Pauline Chandler
Alison Croggon
Kevin Crossley-Holland

Marianne Curley
Catherine Fisher
William Nicholson
Katherine Roberts

Basilisk • Hunted • Shadow Web
The Spellgrinder's Apprentice • The Story of Stone
Warriors Trilogy

Linda Buckley-Archer

Fantasy • Historical
Time travel
8-11

Joan Aiken
Paul Bajoria
Ian Beck
Chris Priestley

Philip Reeve
Alex Scarrow
Trenton Lee Stewart

Time Quake Trilogy

Jenna Burtenshaw (E)

Fantasy

Trudi Canavan
Joseph Delaney

Sam Osman
J K Rowling

Wintercraft Series

A J Butcher

Adventure • Thrillers

Jason Bradbury
Ally Carter
Carol Hedges
Jack Higgins with
    Justin Richards
Charlie Higson

Anthony Horowitz
Andy McNab and Robert Rigby
Robert Muchamore
Malcolm Rose
Chris Ryan

Spy High Series

Meg Cabot (E)

Detective mysteries • Diaries
Friends • Humour
8-11

Ros Asquith
Helen Bailey
Ann Brashares
John Brindley
Ally Carter

Rowan Coleman
Yvonne Collins and Sandy Rideout
Echo Freer
Jean Ure
Rachel Wright

All American Girl • All American Girl: Ready or Not
Avalon High GN *• How to be Popular When You're a Social Reject Like Me*
Tommy Sullivan is a Freak
Airhead Trilogy • Mediator Series • Missing Series
Princess Diaries Series

Trudi Canavan (E)

Fantasy · Magic
14+

Jenna Burtenshaw	Garth Nix
Alison Croggon	Michelle Paver
Marianne Curley	Katherine Roberts
Stuart Hill	Mark Robson
Stephen R Lawhead	G P Taylor

Magician's Apprentice
Age of Five Series · The Black Magician Trilogy · Traitor Spy Trilogy

Maite Carranza

Family · Fantasy · Ghost/supernatural

Frank Beddor	Tanith Lee
Sarwat Chadda	

War of the Witches Trilogy

Ally Carter (E)

Espionage · Romance · School

A J Butcher	Carol Hedges
Meg Cabot	

Gallager Girls Series

Anne Cassidy

Crime · Death · Detective mysteries
Social issues · Thrillers
5-7
14+

Bernard Ashley	Mark Haddon
Malorie Blackman	Meg Rosoff
Judith Fathallah	Robert Swindells
Catherine Forde	Lee Weatherly
Helen Grant	Tim Wynne-Jones

Careless · The Dead House
Innocent · Looking For JJ · Witness

Cathy Cassidy (E)

Family · Immigration · School
Social issues · Thrillers
8-11

Ros Asquith	Hilary McKay
Helen Bailey	Jean Ure
Sophia Bennett	Sarah Webb
Yvonne Collins and Sandy Rideout	Jacqueline Wilson
Chris Higgins	Kay Woodward

Angel Cake · Cherry Crush
Gingersnaps · Love, Peace and Chocolate · Lucky Star · Sundae Girl

12-14

Some titles are available as Talking books

Patrick Cave Science fiction · Social issues · Thrillers

Alison Allen-Gray
T E Berry-Hart
Julie Bertagna

Gillian Cross
Philip Gross
Malcolm Rose

Blown Away · Last Chance · Number 99 · Sharp North

Grace Cavendish Ⓔ Detective mysteries · Historical: Tudor

Paul Bajoria
Sally Gardner
Julia Golding
Lucy Jago

Caroline Lawrence   8-11
Y S Lee
Carolyn Meyer
Alison Prince

Grace Cavendish Series

Philip Caveney Ⓔ   Adventure · Fantasy · Mystery · Mythology

M G Harris
F E Higgins
David Miller

Rick Riordan   8-11
Michael Scott

Alec Devlin Series · Sebastian Darke Series

Sarwat Chadda Ⓔ   Adventure · Fantasy · Horror

Sarah Rees Brennan
Maite Carranza
Pauline Chandler
Patricia Elliott

Sam Enthoven
Steve Feasey
Helen Grant
Cliff McNish

Devil's Kiss Series

Henry Chancellor Adventure · Fantasy · Historical · Time travel

Pseudonymous Bosch
Eva Ibbotson
David Miller

Christopher Paolini   8-11
Rebecca Promitzer
Trenton Lee Stewart

The Remarkable Adventures of Tom Scatterhorn Series

Pauline Chandler Ⓔ Historical: Roman/Viking · Slavery

Bernard Ashley
N M Browne
Sarwat Chadda
Sally Gardner

Stuart Hill
Marie-Louise Jensen
Carolyn Meyer
Alison Prince

The Mark of Edain · Viking Girl · Warrior Girl

Gennifer Choldenko Ⓔ

Animals · Disability · Family
School · Social issues

Frank Cottrell Boyce
Eoin Colfer
Mark Haddon

Linda Newbery
Louis Sachar
Jerry Spinelli

Al Capone Does My Shirts
Al Capone Shines My Shoes • *If a Tree Falls at Lunch Break*
Notes From a Liar and Her Dog

Lucy Christopher

Fantasy · Friends · Illness
Social issues
8-11

Tim Bowler
Damian Kelleher
Suzanne LaFleur

Michael Morpurgo
Sally Nicholls
Jenny Valentine

Flyaway • *Stolen*

Emma Clayton

Adventure · Dystopia · Science fiction

Suzanne Collins

Michael Grant

Roar Series

Stephen Cole Ⓔ

Horror · Science fiction · Thrillers
8-11

David Gilman
James Patterson
Malcolm Rose
Darren Shan

David Thorpe
Cate Tiernan
Mark Walden
Chris Wooding

The Aztec Code • *The Bloodline Cipher*
Thieves Like Us • *Thieves Till We Die* • *Tripwire*
Dr Who Series • *The Wereling Trilogy*

Rowan Coleman Ⓔ

Family · Friends · Stage

Ros Asquith
Meg Cabot
Yvonne Collins and Sandy Rideout

Echo Freer
Cathy Hopkins
Jean Ure

Ruby Parker Series

Go to back for lists of: Authors by Genre • Graphic novels
Short stories • Prize winners • Exploring further

Eoin Colfer

R J Anderson	Derek Landy
Frank Beddor	Kenneth Oppel
Herbie Brennan	David Lee Stone
Sarah Rees Brennan	Steve Voake
Gennifer Choldenko	Rick Yancey

Airman · *Arctic Incident* GN
Artemis Fowl GN · *Half Moon Investigations*
The Supernaturalist · *The Wish List*
Artemis Fowl Series

B R Collins

Bullying · Fantasy · Friends
Social issues · Thrillers
14+

Terence Blacker	Anthony McGowan
Suzanne Collins	Cliff McNish
Michael Grant	Rachel Ward
Tanith Lee	

Traitor Game · *Trick of the Dark* · *Tyme's End*

Suzanne Collins

Adventure · Dystopia
Mystery · Science fiction
14+

Steve Augarde	Conor Kostick
Emma Clayton	Saci Lloyd
B R Collins	Benjamin J Myers
Kat Falls	James Patterson
Michael Grant	Rachel Ward

Hunger Games Trilogy

Tim Collins

Diaries · Humour · Vampires
14+

Catherine Jinks	Stephenie Meyer
Jeff Kinney	Sue Townsend

Diary of a Wimpy Vampire Series

Yvonne Collins and Sandy Rideout

Friends · Romance
School · Stage

Meg Cabot	Rowan Coleman
Cathy Cassidy	Louise Rennison

Girl v. Boy
Diva Series

GN = Graphic novel

Susan Cooper

Adventure · Fantasy
Historical: Tudor · Time travel
8-11

Lloyd Alexander
Catherine Fisher
Charlie Fletcher
Victoria Hanley
Joanne Harris

Robin Jarvis
Cliff McNish
Sam Osman
Katherine Roberts
J R R Tolkien

King of Shadows
The Dark is Rising Sequence

Zizou Corder

Adventure · Animals · Crime
Fantasy · Mythology
8-11

Michael Ford
Michelle Paver

Ali Sparkes

Boy Thief • Halo
Lionboy Series

D M Cornish

Fantasy

John Flanagan
F E Higgins

Christopher Paolini

Monster Blood Tattoo Series

Joe Craig

Adventure · Thrillers

Jack Higgins with
   Justin Richards
Charlie Higson
Andy McNab and Robert Rigby
Catherine MacPhail
Robert Muchamore

James Patterson
Malcolm Rose
Chris Ryan
Steve Voake
Mark Walden

Jimmy Coates Series

Alison Croggon

Fantasy

Lloyd Alexander
N M Browne
Trudi Canavan
Marianne Curley

Katherine Roberts
G P Taylor
Catherine Webb

Books of Pellinor Series

Some titles are available as Talking books

12-14

Gillian Cross

Adventure · Other cultures
Social issues · Thrillers

Tim Bowler
Patrick Cave
Siobhan Dowd
Helen Grant
Philip Gross

Geraldine McCaughrean   8-11
Michael Morpurgo
Bali Rai
Jean Ure

Calling a Dead Man • *Tightrope* • *Where I Belong*
The Lost Trilogy

Kevin Crossley-Holland

Adventure · Fairy/folk
Historical: Medieval

12-14

N M Browne
John Flanagan
Stephen R Lawhead
Sam Llewellyn

Geraldine McCaughrean   8-11
Michelle Paver
Susan Price
Marcus Sedgwick

Gatty's Tale • *Outsiders* SS
Arthur Series

Marianne Curley

Fantasy · Magic

N M Browne
Trudi Canavan
Alison Croggon
Catherine Fisher

Garth Nix
Katherine Roberts
Jonathan Stroud
Catherine Webb

Guardians of Time Trilogy

Vanessa Curtis

Friends · Humour · Illness · Social issues

Sarah Dessen
Chloë Rayban

Louise Rennison

The Taming of Lilah May
Zelah Green Stories

James Dashner

Adventure · Dystopia · Fantasy
Science fiction · Thrillers

Steve Augarde
Ian Beck
John Brindley

Conor Kostick
Will Peterson
Neal Shusterman

Maze Runner Series

SS = Short stories

Timothee de Fombelle

Adventure · Environment · Fantasy · Friends
8-11

Neil Gaiman
Eva Ibbotson
Brian Jacques

Kenneth Oppel
Terry Pratchett

Toby Alone
Toby and the Secrets of the Tree

Jeremy de Quidt

Fantasy · Thrillers

Joseph Delaney
Neil Gaiman
F E Higgins

Matthew Skelton
A G Taylor

The Toymaker

Joseph Delaney

Ghost/supernatural · Magic
8-11

Tom Becker
Jenna Burtenshaw
Jeremy de Quidt
Steve Feasey
John Flanagan

William Hussey
Robin Jarvis
Derek Landy
Justin Somper
Rick Yancey

Spook's Stories · Wardstone Chronicles

Grace Dent

Friends · Humour
14+

Echo Freer
Sue Limb

Karen McCombie

It's a Girl Thing
Diary of a Chav Series · Diary of a Snob Series

Sarah Dessen

Bullying · Family · Friends
Romance · Social issues
14+

Helen Bailey
John Brindley
Vanessa Curtis
Siobhan Dowd
Jenny Downham

Judith Fathallah
Chris Higgins
Mary Hogan
Sarah Webb

Last Chance
Lock and Key · That Summer

12-14

Go to back for lists of: **Authors by Genre · Graphic novels**
Short stories · Prize winners · Exploring further

Narinder Dhami ⓔ Family · Other cultures · Social issues

8-11

Randa Abdel-Fattah
Anne Fine
Cathy Hopkins
Hilary McKay

Helena Pielichaty
Bali Rai
Na'ima B Robert
Jacqueline Wilson

Bang Bang, You're Dead! • *Bend It Like Beckham*
Bhangra Babes • *Bollywood Babes* • *Sunita's Secret* • *Superstar Babes*
The Beautiful Game Series

John Dickinson ⓔ Dystopia · Fantasy
Historical · Science fiction

14+

Steve Augarde
T E Berry-Hart
Peter Dickinson
Stuart Hill

Susan Price
Marcus Sedgwick
Kate Thompson

The Lightstep • *WE*
Cup of The World Series

Peter Dickinson ⟨ Adventure · Fantasy
Ghost/supernatural · Social issues

John Dickinson
Patricia Elliott
Geraldine McCaughrean
Michelle Paver

Sally Prue
Kate Thompson
Robert Westall

Angel Isle • *The Gift Boat* • *The Ropemaker*

Sharon Dogar ⓔ Family · Friends · Holocaust
War 1939-45

14+

L J Adlington
John Boyne

Yanker Glatshteyn
Morris Gleitzman

Annexed

Berlie Doherty ⓔ Crime · Family · Historical
Social issues · Teen pregnancy

8-11

Theresa Breslin
Jenny Downham
Mary Hooper

Geraldine McCaughrean
Hilary McKay

Abela: The Girl Who Saw Lions
A Beautiful Place for Murder • *Dear Nobody* • *Deep Secret*
Holly Starcross • *Running on Ice* SS

Julia Donaldson Ⓔ

Family · Illness · Mystery
Social issues · Thrillers
5-7

Damian Kelleher
Sophie McKenzie
Benjamin J Myers

Jean Ure
Jenny Valentine

Running on the Cracks

Tommy Donbavand Ⓔ

Horror · Humour
8-11

Sam Enthoven
F E Higgins

Derek Landy
Darren Shan

Scream Street Series

Jennifer Donnelly

Death · Historical · Romance

Siobhan Dowd
Julie Hearn
Linda Newbery

Meg Rosoff
Mildred D Taylor
Karen Wallace

A Gathering Light

Siobhan Dowd Ⓔ Death · Family · Mystery · Social issues

8-11
14+

Tim Bowler
Kevin Brooks
Gillian Cross
Sarah Dessen
Jennifer Donnelly

Anne Fine
Jamila Gavin
Sonya Hartnett
Linda Newbery
Meg Rosoff

Bog Child • *Solace of the Road* • *Swift Pure Cry*

Jenny Downham Ⓔ Death · Family · Friends · Illness

14+

Sarah Dessen
Berlie Doherty

Gayle Forman
Damian Kelleher

Before I Die

Paul Dowswell Ⓔ

Adventure · Historical: C16th/Victorian
Sea/boats · War 1939-45
8-11

John Boyne
Morris Gleitzman
Elizabeth Laird

Michael Molloy
Alison Prince

Auslander • *The Cabinet of Curiosities*
The Adventures of Sam Witchall Series

Helen Dunmore

Cornelia Funke   Eva Ibbotson
Frances Hardinge

Ingo Series

Eve Edwards Ⓔ

Mary Hoffman   Lucy Jago
Mary Hooper   Marie-Louise Jensen

The Other Countess • The Queen's Lady

Jim Eldridge Ⓔ

Bernard Ashley   Chris Ryan
Andy McNab and Robert Rigby   Craig Simpson

Black Ops Series

Patricia Elliott

Sarwat Chadda   Mary Hooper
Peter Dickinson   Lucy Jago
Sally Gardner

Ambergate • Murkmere • The Night Walker
Pimpernelles Series

Deborah Ellis

Nancy Farmer   Beverley Naidoo
Elizabeth Laird   Bali Rai
Adeline Yen Mah   Na'ima B Robert
Henning Mankell   Suzanne Fisher Staples

Beyond the Barricade
The Heaven Shop • The Prison Runner
The Breadwinner Collection

Sam Enthoven ⚪ Ⓔ

Sarwat Chadda   Michael Grant
Tommy Donbavand   Derek Landy
Steve Feasey   Steve Voake
Charlie Fletcher

Black Tattoo • Crawlers
Tim: Defender of the Earth

12-14

Brian Falkner Adventure · Environment · Science fiction · Sport

Frank Cottrell Boyce
Chris Bradford

David Gilman

*Brain Jack • The Flea Thing
The Real Thing • Super Freak • The Tomorrow Code*

Kat Falls Adventure · Dystopia · Science fiction

Steve Augarde
Suzanne Collins

Conor Kostick
Sophie McKenzie

Dark Life • Rip Tide

Nancy Farmer Adventure · Historical: Viking
Mythology · Other lands · Social issues

Deborah Ellis
Ann Halam
Stuart Hill

Marie-Louise Jensen
Beverley Naidoo

*The House of the Scorpion
Sea Trolls Trilogy*

Judith Fathallah Eating disorders · Family

14+

Anne Cassidy
Sarah Dessen

Chris Higgins
Jacqueline Wilson

Monkey Taming

Steve Feasey Fantasy · Ghost/supernatural · Horror

Sarwat Chadda
Joseph Delaney
Sam Enthoven

William Hussey
Chris Priestley
Darren Shan

Changeling Series

Anne Fine Family · Humour · School · Social issues

5-7
8-11

Julie Bertagna
Frank Cottrell Boyce
Narinder Dhami
Siobhan Dowd
Catherine Forde

Cathy Hopkins
Ally Kennen
Helena Pielichaty
Jeremy Strong

*Flour Babies • The Road of Bones
The Tulip Touch • Up on Cloud Nine*

Catherine Fisher

Adventure · Dystopia · Fantasy
Ghost/supernat · Horror · Thrillers

N M Browne
Susan Cooper
Marianne Curley
Stuart Hill
Robin Jarvis

Catherine Jinks
Michael Lawrence
Ursula Le Guin
Gemma Malley
Catherine Webb

8-11

Corbenic • *Crown of Acorns*
Darkhenge • *Incarceron* • *The Pickpocket's Ghost* BS • *Sapphique*
Book of the Crow Series • *The Oracle Trilogy*

Pauline Fisk Ⓔ

Adventure · Death · Family
Fantasy · Social issues

Helen Grant
Sue Limb

Louise Rennison

Flying for Frankie
In the Trees • *The Mrs Marridge Project*
The Children of Plynlimon Series

John Flanagan

Adventure · Fantasy · Historical

John Brindley
D M Cornish
Kevin Crossley-Holland
Joseph Delaney
Charlie Fletcher

Michael Ford
Alison Goodman
K M Grant
Stuart Hill
Alex Scarrow

Ranger's Apprentice Series

Charlie Fletcher

Adventure · Fantasy · Friends

Tom Becker
Susan Cooper
Sam Enthoven
John Flanagan

Kai Meyer
James A Owen
Jonathan Stroud
Robert Westall

8-11

Stone Heart Trilogy

Michael Ford

Adventure · Historical · Mythology

Zizou Corder
John Flanagan

Michelle Harrison
Rick Riordan

8-11

The Poisoned House
Spartan Warrior Series

Catherine Forde Ⓔ

14+

Tim Bowler
Kevin Brooks
Anne Cassidy
Anne Fine

Keith Gray
Catherine MacPhail
Nicola Morgan
Nicky Singer

Dead Men Don't Talk BS • *The Drowning Pond*
Fat Boy Swim • *Firestarter* • *Skarrs* • *Tug of War*

Gayle Forman Ⓔ

Death · Family

14+

Jenny Downham
Damian Kelleher

Meg Rosoff
Jenny Valentine

If I Stay

Echo Freer

Friends · Ghost/supernatural · Humour

Helen Bailey
Meg Cabot
Rowan Coleman
Grace Dent

Cathy Hopkins
Sue Limb
Chloë Rayban
Rosie Rushton

Mimosa Fortune
Magenta Series

Cornelia Funke

Adventure · Fairy/folk · Fantasy

8-11

Helen Dunmore
K M Grant
Mary Hoffman
Eva Ibbotson
Kai Meyer

Philip Pullman
Rick Riordan
Mark Robson
J K Rowling
Matthew Skelton

Reckless • *The Thief Lord*
Inkheart Trilogy

Neil Gaiman Ⓔ

Fantasy · Ghost/supernatural · Humour

5-7
8-11
14+

Frank Beddor
Pseudonymous Bosch
Timothee de Fombelle
Jeremy de Quidt
Roderick Gordon and
    Brian Williams

Armin Greder
Derek Landy
Joanne Owen
Chris Priestley
Shaun Tan

Coraline GN
The Graveyard Book • *M is for Magic* SS

Sally Gardner

Fantasy · Historical: C17th
Magic · Other lands

Grace Cavendish
Pauline Chandler
Patricia Elliott
Frances Hardinge
Michelle Harrison

Mary Hoffman
Mary Hooper
Margaret Mahy
Ann Turnbull

5-7
8-11

I, Coriander • *The Red Necklace* • *The Silver Blade*

Jamila Gavin

Friends · Historical · Other cultures

Siobhan Dowd
Adèle Geras

Nicola Morgan
Suzanne Fisher Staples

The Robber Baron's Daughter
Surya Trilogy

Adèle Geras

Ancient History · Historical · Mythology

Julie Bertagna
Theresa Breslin
Jamila Gavin
Shannon and Dean Hale
Hope Larson

Geraldine McCaughrean
Linda Newbery
Theresa Tomlinson
Ann Turnbull

8-11

Dido • *Ithaka* • *Troy*
Historical House Trilogy

Alan Gibbons

Family · Fantasy · Horror
Social issues · Sport

Alison Allen-Gray
Bernard Ashley
Kevin Brooks

Mal Peet
Bali Rai

8-11
14+

Dark Spaces and Other Stories SS
Julie and Me and Michael Owen Makes Three
Hell's Underground Series • *Legendeer Trilogy* • *Lost Souls Stories*

Maggi Gibson

Friends

Chris Higgins
Saci Lloyd
Louise Rennison

Liz Rettig
Rosie Rushton

Seriously Sassy Series

12-14

SS = Short stories

David Gilman Ⓔ

Adventure · Thrillers

Stephen Cole
Brian Falkner
M G Harris
Jack Higgins with
    Justin Richards

Anthony Horowitz
James Patterson
Chris Ryan
Mark Walden

Danger Zone Series

Yanker Glatshteyn

Friends · Holocaust · War 1939-45

8-11

John Boyne
Sharon Dogar
Morris Gleitzman
James Riordan

Jerry Spinelli
Robert Westall
Markus Zusak

The Storm to Come

Morris Gleitzman Ⓔ

Family · Holocaust · War 1939-45

8-11

John Boyne
Sharon Dogar
Paul Dowswell
Yanker Glatshteyn

Henning Mankell
Louis Sachar
Jerry Spinelli
Markus Zusak

Once • Now • Then

Julia Golding Ⓔ

Adventure · Fantasy · Historical
Stage · Thrillers

8-11

Grace Cavendish
Caroline Lawrence
Michelle Paver

Terry Pratchett
Matthew Skelton

Ship Between the Words • Wolf Cry
Cat Royal Series • Companions Quartet
Darcie Lock Series • Dragonfly Series

Alison Goodman Ⓔ

Fantasy

Chris Bradford
John Flanagan

Michael Grant
Christopher Paolini

Eon Rise of the Dragoneye
Eona the Last Dragoneye

 Some titles are available as **Talking books**

Roderick Gordon & Brian Williams
Adventure · Horror
Science fiction

T E Berry-Hart
Frank Cottrell Boyce
Neil Gaiman

F E Higgins
Will Peterson

Tunnels Series

Candy Gourlay ⓔ
Other lands · Sport

Pete Johnson
Michael Morpurgo

Jacqueline Wilson

8-11

Tall Story

Helen Grant ⓔ
Ghost/supernatural · Horror
Mystery · Thrillers

Kevin Brooks
Anne Cassidy
Sarwat Chadda
Gillian Cross

Pauline Fisk
Ann Halam
Julie Hearn
Sarah Singleton

14+

Glass Demon • Vanishing of Katherina Linden

K M Grant ⓔ
Adventure · Historical

John Flanagan
Cornelia Funke

Mary Hoffman
Christopher Paolini

Belle's Song
De Granville Trilogy • Perfect Fire Trilogy

Michael Grant ⓔ
Dystopia · Fantasy

Steve Augarde
Emma Clayton
B R Collins
Suzanne Collins
Sam Enthoven

Alison Goodman
Conor Kostick
Sophie McKenzie
Neal Shusterman
Rachel Ward

Gone Series • Magnificent 12

Claudia Gray ⓔ
Ghost/supernatural · Vampires

Eden Maguire
Zoë Marriott

Stephenie Meyer
L J Smith

14+

Evernight Series

12-14

Keith Gray 💬 Ⓔ

Friends · Social issues
14+

Bernard Ashley
John Brindley
Kevin Brooks
Catherine Forde
J A Henderson

Pete Johnson
Ally Kennen
Anthony McGowan
Robert Swindells

The Chain BS · *Ghosting* BS
Hoodlum · *Ostrich Boys* · *The Return of Johnny Kemp* BS

Armin Greder

Death · Family · Other cultures · Social issues

Neil Gaiman

Shaun Tan

The City GN · *The Island* GN

Stacy Gregg Ⓔ

Family · Pony/horse
8-11

Lauren Brooke

K M Peyton

Pony Club Rivals Series

Matt Groening

Environment · Family · Humour · Science fiction

Paul Jennings
Terry Pratchett
Jeff Smith

Jeremy Strong
Marc Sumerak
Sue Townsend

Futurama Series GN · *The Simpsons Series* GN

Philip Gross

Other cultures · Thrillers

Patrick Cave
Gillian Cross
Catherine MacPhail

Nicola Morgan
Malcolm Rose

Going for Stone
The Lastling · *The Storm Garden*

Mark Haddon 💬 Ⓔ

Crime · Disability · Family
Humour · Social issues
8-11
14+

Frank Cottrell Boyce
Anne Cassidy
Gennifer Choldenko

Anthony McGowan
Louis Sachar
Jenny Valentine

Boom
The Curious Incident of the Dog in the Night-time

Ann Halam Ghost/supernatural · Horror

Joan Aiken
Nancy Farmer
Helen Grant
Margaret Mahy

Celia Rees
E E Richardson
Chris Wooding

Finders Keepers BS
The Shadow on the Stairs BS · *Siberia* · *Taylor Five* · *The Visitor*

Shannon and Dean Hale Fairy/folk · Fantasy · War

14+

R J Anderson
Frank Beddor
Adèle Geras
Mary Hoffman

Zoë Marriott
Ted Naifeh
Theresa Tomlinson

Calamity Jack GN
Princess Academy · *Rapunzel's Revenge* GN
Books of Bayern Series

Victoria Hanley Fairy/folk · Fantasy · Friends · Magic

Susan Cooper
Ursula Le Guin

Tanith Lee

The Healer's Keep
The Light of the Oracle · *The Seer and the Sword*

Frances Hardinge Fantasy

8-11

Joan Aiken
Helen Dunmore
Sally Gardner
Marie-Louise Jensen

Diana Wynne Jones
Matthew Skelton
Trenton Lee Stewart

Fly By Night · *Gull Struck Island*
Twilight Robbery · *Verdigris Deep*

Joanne Harris Fantasy

14+

R J Anderson
Susan Cooper
Ursula Le Guin

Christopher Paolini
Ali Sparkes
J R R Tolkien

Runemarks

BS = Published by Barrington Stoke
specialists in resources for dyslexic and struggling readers

M G Harris

Adventure

Jason Bradbury
Andy Briggs
Philip Caveney

David Gilman
Rick Riordan
Steve Voake

Joshua Files Series

Michelle Harrison

Fairy/folk · Fantasy

8-11

R J Anderson
Herbie Brennan
Michael Ford

Sally Gardner
Aprilynne Pike
Sarah Singleton

The Thirteen Curses
The Thirteen Secrets • The Thirteen Treasures

Sonya Hartnett

Animals · Social issues · War 1939-45

14+

David Almond
Tim Bowler
Kevin Brooks

Siobhan Dowd
Philip Pullman
Mildred D Taylor

The Ghost's Child • The Midnight Zoo
The Silver Donkey • Stripes of the Sidestep Wolf • Surrender

Julie Hearn

Ghost/supernatural · Historical
Social issues

14+

Laurie Halse Anderson
Jennifer Donnelly
Helen Grant
Michael Molloy

Nicola Morgan
Sarah Singleton
Cate Tiernan

Follow Me Down
The Merrybegot • Rowan the Strange

Carol Hedges

Adventure · Espionage

8-11

A J Butcher
Ally Carter

Sophie McKenzie
Jane Prowse

Spy Girl Series

J A Henderson

Adventure · Thrillers

Keith Gray
Marcus Sedgwick

Chris Wooding

Bunker 10 • Colony • Crash

11-14

Carl Hiaasen Environment · Family · Humour · Social issues

Henning Mankell
Louis Sachar

Jerry Spinelli

Flush • Hoot • Scat

Chris Higgins (E) Adoption · Eating Disorders · Family · Friends

Sophia Bennett
Cathy Cassidy
Sarah Dessen
Judith Fathallah
Maggi Gibson

Cathy Hopkins
Sally Nicholls
Jenny Valentine
Jacqueline Wilson
Kay Woodward

Happy Ever After
It's a 50/50 Thing • Love You Babe • A Perfect Ten
Tapas and Tears • Would You Rather

F E Higgins (E) Adventure · Fantasy
Historical: Vict · Mystery

Philip Caveney
D M Cornish
Jeremy de Quidt
Tommy Donbavand

Roderick Gordon and
   Brian Williams
Will Peterson
Matthew Skelton
David Whitley

Tales From the Sinister City Series

Jack Higgins with Justin Richards  Adventure
Thrillers

A J Butcher
Joe Craig
David Gilman
Anthony Horowitz

Andy McNab and Robert Rigby
James Patterson
Chris Ryan

Death Run • First Strike
Sharp Shot • Sure Fire

Charlie Higson (E) Adventure · Thrillers

Dominic Barker
Ian Beck
David Belbin
A J Butcher
Joe Craig

Anthony Horowitz
Derek Landy
Andy McNab and Robert Rigby
Robert Muchamore
Chris Ryan

8-11
14+

Young Bond Series

Stuart Hill Fantasy

Trudi Canavan
Pauline Chandler
John Dickinson
Nancy Farmer
Catherine Fisher

John Flanagan
William Nicholson
Garth Nix
Michelle Paver
J R R Tolkien

Chronicles of Icemark

Nigel Hinton

Adventure • Family • Historical
Social issues • Thrillers
8-11

S E Hinton
Pete Johnson
Michelle Magorian

Graham Marks
Louis Sachar
Robert Westall

The Road from Home
Time Bomb • Until Proven Guilty BS
The Buddy Series

S E Hinton

Friends • Social issues

Nigel Hinton
Pete Johnson

Catherine MacPhail
Bali Rai

The Outsiders
Rumblefish • Some of Tim's Story

Mary Hoffman

Adventure • Family
Fantasy • Historical
5-7

Eve Edwards
Cornelia Funke
Sally Gardner
K M Grant
Shannon and Dean Hale

Marie-Louise Jensen
Diana Wynne Jones
Kai Meyer
Nicola Morgan

The Falconer's Knot • Troubadour
Stravaganza Series

Mary Hogan

Family • Humour • Social issues

Sophia Bennett
Sarah Dessen
Chloë Rayban

Louise Rennison
Rosie Rushton

The Perfect Girl • The Serious Kiss
Susanna Series

Mary Hooper

Family · Friends · Historical
Social issues
8-11

Randa Abdel-Fattah
Berlie Doherty
Eve Edwards
Patricia Elliott
Sally Gardner

Lucy Jago
Marie-Louise Jensen
Karen McCombie
Dyan Sheldon
Ann Turnbull

*The Betrayal • Fallen Grace
Newes From The Dead • Petals From the Ashes
The Remarkable Life and Times of Eliza Rose
At the House of the Magician Series*

Cathy Hopkins Family · Humour · Romance · Social issues

Randa Abdel-Fattah
Helen Bailey
Ann Brashares
Rowan Coleman
Narinder Dhami

Anne Fine
Echo Freer
Chris Higgins
Karen McCombie
Dyan Sheldon

*Cinnamon Girl Series • Mates Dates Series
Truth, Dare, Kiss or Promise Series • Zodiac Girls Series*

Anthony Horowitz

Adventure · Horror
Humour · Thrillers
8-11

Dominic Barker
David Belbin
Jason Bradbury
A J Butcher
David Gilman

Jack Higgins with
      Justin Richards
Charlie Higson
Andy McNab and Robert Rigby
Sam Osman
Jane Prowse

Killer Camera GN • *More Bloody Horowitz* SS
Point Blanc GN • *Stormbreaker* GN
Alex Rider Series • Power of Five Series

William Hussey

Fantasy · Ghost/supernatural
Historical · Horror
14+

Joseph Delaney
Steve Feasey

Darren Shan
Jonathan Stroud

Witchfinder Series

GN = Graphic novel

135

Eva Ibbotson

Frank Cottrell Boyce
Henry Chancellor
Timothee de Fombelle

Helen Dunmore
Cornelia Funke
Karen Wallace

Journey to the River Sea • The Star of Kazan

Brian Jacques

Timothee de Fombelle
Robin Jarvis
Terry Pratchett

Jonathan Stroud
J R R Tolkien
Clive Woodall

Flying Dutchman Series • Redwall Series

Lucy Jago

Grace Cavendish
Eve Edwards
Patricia Elliott

Mary Hooper
Celia Rees
Ann Turnbull

Montacute House

Robin Jarvis

Joan Aiken
R J Anderson
Susan Cooper
Joseph Delaney
Catherine Fisher

Brian Jacques
Brian Keaney
Terry Pratchett
G P Taylor

Deptford Histories
Tales From the Wyrd Museum Series • Whitby Witches Series

Ben Jeapes

Joan Aiken
Gemma Malley

William Nicholson
Philip Pullman

The New World Order • Time's Chariot

Paul Jennings

Frank Cottrell Boyce
Matt Groening
Pete Johnson

Jeff Kinney
Jeremy Strong
David Walliams

How Hedley Hopkins Did a Dare...
Quirky Tales • Tongue-tied • Unseen

Marie-Louise Jensen Ⓔ

Adventure · Family
Historical · Romance

Gill Arbuthnott
Theresa Breslin
Pauline Chandler
Eve Edwards
Nancy Farmer

Frances Hardinge
Mary Hoffman
Mary Hooper
Carolyn Meyer
Celia Rees

Between Two Seas • Daughter of Fire and Ice
The Lady in the Tower • Sigrun's Secret

Catherine Jinks Ⓔ

Ghost/supernatural
Humour · Vampires

12-14

14+

Tim Collins
Catherine Fisher

Stephenie Meyer

The Abused Werewolf Rescue Group
The Reformed Vampire Support Group

Pete Johnson Ⓔ

Fantasy · Ghost/supernatural
Romance · Social issues

8-11

Terence Blacker
Candy Gourlay
Keith Gray
Nigel Hinton
S E Hinton

Paul Jennings
Jeff Kinney
Louis Sachar
Jeremy Strong
David Walliams

Hero? BS • *How Embarrassing is That* BS
How to Get Famous • Liar BS • *Shut It* BS • *The Vampire Blog*

Diana Wynne Jones Ⓔ

Fantasy · Magic

8-11

Joan Aiken
Frances Hardinge
Mary Hoffman
Michael Lawrence

Ursula Le Guin
Margaret Mahy
J K Rowling
Catherine Webb

Enchanted Glass • The House of Many Ways
Chrestomanci Series

Brian Keaney Ⓔ

Death · Fantasy · Ghost/supernatural
Historical

Robin Jarvis
Linda Newbery
Garth Nix

Darren Shan
Jonathan Stroud
Cate Tiernan

Jacob's Ladder • The Haunting of Nathaniel Wolfe
Nathaniel Wolfe and the Body Snatchers
Promises of Dr Sigmundus Series

Damian Kelleher Ⓔ   Death · Illness · Social issues

John Boyne   Jenny Downham
Lucy Christopher   Gayle Forman
Julia Donaldson

Life Interrupted

Ann Kelley   Adventure · Family · Illness

Saci Lloyd   Mal Peet
Geraldine McCaughrean   Jane Prowse
Linda Newbery

Koh Tabu
Gussie Series

Ally Kennen   Family · Social issues · Thrillers

8-11
14+

David Almond   Anne Fine
Tim Bowler   Keith Gray
Kevin Brooks   Mal Peet

Beast • Bedlam • Quarry

Jeff Kinney Ⓔ   Diaries · Family · Humour

8-11

Frank Cottrell Boyce   Pete Johnson
Tim Collins   Jeff Smith
Paul Jennings   Sue Townsend

Diary of a Wimpy Kid Series

Conor Kostick ◯   Fantasy · Science fiction · Thrillers

14+

Suzanne Collins   Kat Falls
James Dashner   Michael Grant

Epic • Move • Saga

Suzanne LaFleur ◯ Ⓔ   Death · Family · Illness

8-11

Gill Arbuthnott   Lucy Christopher
John Boyne   Sally Nicholls

Love, Aubrey

Ⓔ Some titles are available as ebooks

12-14

Elizabeth Laird Ⓔ

Adventure · Historical · Other cultures
Other lands · Social issues
8-11

Lynne Reid Banks	Michael Molloy
Paul Dowswell	Beverley Naidoo
Deborah Ellis	Anna Perera
Tanya Landman	Suzanne Fisher Staples
Adeline Yen Mah	

Crusade • A Little Piece of Ground
Lost Riders • Oranges in No Man's Land
Secrets of the Fearless • The Witching Hour

Tanya Landman

Detective mysteries · Historical · Other lands

Laurie Halse Anderson	Celia Rees
David Belbin	Ann Rinaldi
Elizabeth Laird	

Apache • I am Apache
Aztec: The Goldsmith's Daughter • The Goldsmith's Daughter
Poppy Fields Mysteries Series

Derek Landy Ⓔ

Fantasy
8-11

Thomas Bloor	Neil Gaiman
Eoin Colfer	Charlie Higson
Joseph Delaney	Terry Pratchett
Tommy Donbavand	Chris Priestley
Sam Enthoven	

Skulduggery Pleasant Series

Hope Larson Ⓔ

Fantasy · Historical · Magic · Pony/horse

Adèle Geras	Ted Naifeh

Gray Horses GN
Mercury GN • Salamander Dream GN

Rhiannon Lassiter Ⓔ

Fantasy · Ghost/supernatural
Horror · Social issues

Alison Allen-Gray	Katherine Roberts
Chloë Rayban	Catherine Webb

Bad Blood • Roundabout
Borderland Trilogy • Rights of Passage Series

GN = Graphic novel

12-14

12-14

Stephen R Lawhead Ⓔ

Fantasy

14+

Trudi Canavan
Kevin Crossley-Holland
Ursula Le Guin

Geraldine McCaughrean
J R R Tolkien

King Raven Series

Caroline Lawrence Ⓔ

Adventure · Detective mysteries
Historical: Roman

8-11

Paul Bajoria
Theresa Breslin
Grace Cavendish

Julia Golding
Katherine Roberts

The Roman Mysteries Series

Michael Lawrence Ⓔ

Family · Fantasy · Mystery
Time travel

5-7

8-11

Terence Blacker
Catherine Fisher

Diana Wynne Jones
Susan Price

Juby's Rock
Aldous Lexicon Series

Ursula Le Guin Ⓔ

Fantasy · Magic

Catherine Fisher
Victoria Hanley
Joanne Harris
Diana Wynne Jones
Stephen R Lawhead

Garth Nix
J R R Tolkien
Beth Webb
Scott Westerfeld

Lavinia
Annals of the Western Shore Series • The Earthsea Series

Tanith Lee Ⓔ

Fantasy

Maite Carranza
B R Collins
Victoria Hanley

Joshua Mowll
Ted Naifeh
Celia Rees

The Claidi Journals (Wolf Tower)
Piratica Series

Y S Lee

Detective mysteries · Historical: Victorian · Thrillers

Grace Cavendish
Philip Pullman

Eleanor Updale
Catherine Webb

The Agency Series

Sue Limb 💬 Ⓔ

Friends · Humour

Ros Asquith	Hilary McKay
Grace Dent	Liz Rettig
Pauline Fisk	Sarah Webb
Echo Freer	Rachel Wright
Karen McCombie	

Girl 15 Series
Girl 16 Series • Zoe and Chloe Series

Sam Llewellyn 💬 Ⓔ

Fairy/folk · Fantasy

8-11

Chris Bradford	Michael Scott
Kevin Crossley-Holland	Marcus Sedgwick

Monsters of Lyonesse Series

Saci Lloyd 💬

Environment · Family

14+

Julie Bertagna	Ann Kelley
Suzanne Collins	Gemma Malley
Maggi Gibson	Neal Shusterman

The Carbon Diaries Series

Tim Lott

Dystopia · Science fiction · Social issues

14+

T E Berry-Hart	Scott Westerfeld
Gemma Malley	

Fearless

Geraldine McCaughrean 💬 Ⓔ

Death · Family · Thrillers

5-7
8-11

Gillian Cross	Ann Kelley
Kevin Crossley-Holland	Stephen R Lawhead
Peter Dickinson	Sally Prue
Berlie Doherty	Theresa Tomlinson
Adèle Geras	Jeanette Winterson

Cyrano • The Death Defying Pepper Roux
Tambulaine's Elephant • The White Darkness

Go to back for lists of: Authors by Genre • Graphic novels
Short stories • Prize winners • Exploring further

Karen McCombie

Family · Friends · Humour
Social issues
8-11

Ros Asquith
Sophia Bennett
Ann Brashares
Grace Dent
Mary Hooper

Cathy Hopkins
Sue Limb
Chloë Rayban
Natsuki Takaya
Rachel Wright

Bliss... Too Good to Be True?
Candy Girl BS • The Seventeen Secrets of the Karma Club
An Urgent Message of Wowness
Ally's World Series • Stella etc Series

12-14

Anthony McGowan

Bullying · Death · Humour
Illness · Social issues
8-11
14+

Tim Bowler
Kevin Brooks
B R Collins
Keith Gray

Mark Haddon
Sally Nicholls
Rebecca Promitzer

Einstein's Underpants and How They Saved the World
Henry Tumour • The Knife that Killed Me

Hilary McKay

Family · Humour · Social issues
5-7
8-11

Sophia Bennett
Ann Brashares
Cathy Cassidy
Narinder Dhami

Berlie Doherty
Sue Limb
Rosie Rushton
Jerry Spinelli

Casson Family Series • The Exiles Series

Sophie McKenzie

Adventure · Science fiction
Thrillers
8-11
14+

Julie Bertagna
Andy Briggs
Julia Donaldson
Kat Falls
Michael Grant

Carol Hedges
James Patterson
Alex Scarrow
A G Taylor
Sarah Wray

Blood Ransom • Blood Ties • Girl Missing
All About Eve Series • The Medusa Project Series

Some titles are available as Talking books

Andy McNab and Robert Rigby

Bernard Ashley
A J Butcher
Joe Craig
Jim Eldridge
Jack Higgins with
   Justin Richards

Charlie Higson
Anthony Horowitz
Chris Ryan
Craig Simpson

Drop Zone
Boy Soldier Series

Cliff McNish Death · Fantasy · Ghost/supernatural
Horror · Magic

Sarwat Chadda
B R Collins
Susan Cooper
William Nicholson
Michelle Paver

Chris Priestley
J K Rowling
Sarah Singleton
G P Taylor

Angel • Breathe: A Ghost Story
Savannah Grey: A Horror Story
The Doomspell Trilogy • Silver Sequence

Catherine MacPhail Adventure · Disability
Fantasy · Social issues
14+

Bernard Ashley
Julie Bertagna
John Brindley
Joe Craig
Catherine Forde

Philip Gross
S E Hinton
Graham Marks
Robert Swindells

Another Me • Grass
Hide and Seek BS *• Out of the Depths*
Sticks and Stones BS *• Under the Skin* BS
Nemesis Series

Michelle Magorian E Family · Historical · War 1939-45
8-11

Theresa Breslin
Nigel Hinton
Linda Newbery

Mal Peet
K M Peyton
James Riordan

Back Home • Goodnight Mister Tom
Just Henry • A Little Love Song • A Spoonful of Jam

12-14

BS = Published by Barrington Stoke
specialists in resources for dyslexic and struggling readers

Eden Maguire Death · Ghost/supernatural · Romance

Claudia Gray
Stephenie Meyer

L J Smith

Beautiful Dead Series

Adeline Yen Mah Family · Other cultures
War 1939-45

Deborah Ellis
Elizabeth Laird

Beverley Naidoo
Jacqueline Wilson

Chinese Cinderella Series

Margaret Mahy Fantasy · Science fiction
Social issues · Thrillers

Sally Gardner
Ann Halam

Diana Wynne Jones
Karen Wallace

The Changeover · Heriot
Maddigan's Fantasia · Organ Music · The Tricksters

Gemma Malley Dystopia · Relationships
Science fiction
14+

L J Adlington
Catherine Fisher
Ben Jeapes
Saci Lloyd

Tim Lott
Neal Shusterman
Scott Westerfeld

The Returners
The Declaration Series

Henning Mankell Family · Other lands · Social issues

Deborah Ellis
Morris Gleitzman

Carl Hiaasen
Beverley Naidoo

Joel Gustafson Series · Sofia Series

Graham Marks  Adventure · Family · Fantasy
Social issues · Thrillers
8-11
14+

Tim Bowler
Nigel Hinton

Catherine MacPhail

Kaï-ro · Omega Place
Snatched! · Takedown
I Spy Series

E Some titles are available as ebooks

Zoë Marriott

Fantasy

Claudia Gray

Shannon and Dean Hale

Daughter of the Flames
The Swan Kingdom

Carolyn Meyer

Historical

Grace Cavendish
Pauline Chandler

Marie-Louise Jensen

Loving Will Shakespeare
In Mozart's Shadow: His Sister's Story
The True Adventures of Charley Darwin
Young Royals Series

Kai Meyer

Fantasy · Magic · Other cultures

Charlie Fletcher
Cornelia Funke
Mary Hoffman

Christopher Paolini
Philip Reeve
Rick Riordan

Dark Reflections Trilogy
The Wave Walkers Series

Stephenie Meyer (E)

Dystopia · Romance
Thrillers · Vampires
14+

R J Anderson
Tim Collins
Claudia Gray
Catherine Jinks
Eden Maguire

Aprilynne Pike
L J Smith
R L Stine
Cate Tiernan

Twilight Saga

David Miller (E)

Adventure
8-11

Philip Caveney
Henry Chancellor

Joshua Mowll
Rebecca Promitzer

Leopards Claw
Sea Wolf • Shark Island

Michael Molloy

Adventure · Historical
8-11

Paul Dowswell
Julie Hearn

Elizabeth Laird
Justin Somper

Peter Raven Series

Nicola Morgan

Adventure · Crime · Family
Historical · Mystery
14+

David Almond
David Belbin
Catherine Forde
Jamila Gavin
Philip Gross

Julie Hearn
Mary Hoffman
Ann Turnbull
Eleanor Updale

Deathwatch · Fleshmarket
The Highwayman's Curse · The Highwayman's Footsteps
Mondays are Red

Michael Morpurgo

Animals · Historical
War 1914-18/1939-45
5-7
8-11

John Boyne
Lucy Christopher
Gillian Cross
Candy Gourlay
Kenneth Oppel

Mal Peet
Anna Perera
James Riordan
Robert Westall
Markus Zusak

Alone on the Wide Wide Sea
An Elephant in the Garden · Private Peaceful · Shadow · War Horse

Joshua Mowll

Adventure · Family · Fantasy · Other cultures
8-11

Chris Bradford
Tanith Lee
David Miller

Rebecca Promitzer
Philip Pullman
Marcus Sedgwick

The Great Space Race
The Guild Trilogy

Robert Muchamore

Adventure · Crime · Friends
Thrillers · War 1939-45

A J Butcher
Joe Craig
Charlie Higson
Benjamin J Myers
Jane Prowse

Malcolm Rose
Chris Ryan
Craig Simpson
Marc Sumerak
Mark Walden

CHERUB Series · Henderson's Boys Series

Benjamin J Myers

Adventure · Family · Fantasy
Science fiction · Social issues

Suzanne Collins
Julia Donaldson

Robert Muchamore

Bad Tuesdays Series

Beverley Naidoo

Other lands · Social issues

Randa Abdel-Fattah	Elizabeth Laird
Lynne Reid Banks	Adeline Yen Mah
Deborah Ellis	Henning Mankell
Nancy Farmer	

Burn My Heart
Journey to Jo'burg · Out of Bounds SS · Web of Lies

Ted Naifeh

Fantasy · Magic

Shannon and Dean Hale	Terry Pratchett
Hope Larson	J K Rowling
Tanith Lee	Natsuki Takaya

Courtney Cumrin Series GN
Polly and the Pirates Series GN

12-14

Linda Newbery

Family · Illness · Social issues
War 1914-18/1939-45

5-7
8-11
14+

Gennifer Choldenko	Ann Kelley
Jennifer Donnelly	Michelle Magorian
Siobhan Dowd	K M Peyton
Adèle Geras	Ann Turnbull
Brian Keaney	Robert Westall

Blitz Boys · Flightsend
Lost Boy · Nevermore · The Sandfather
The Historical House Series

Sally Nicholls

Death · Family · Illness · Mythology

David Almond	Suzanne LaFleur
John Boyne	Anthony McGowan
Lucy Christopher	Jenny Valentine
Chris Higgins	

Season of Secrets · Ways to Live Forever

William Nicholson

Adventure · Dystopia · Fantasy

8-11

N M Browne	Kenneth Oppel
Stuart Hill	Susan Price
Ben Jeapes	Sally Prue
Cliff McNish	Philip Reeve

Wind on Fire Trilogy
Noble Warriors Trilogy

Garth Nix Adventure · Fantasy · Science fiction

Lloyd Alexander
Trudi Canavan
Marianne Curley
Stuart Hill
Brian Keaney

Ursula Le Guin
Beth Webb
Scott Westerfeld
Clive Woodall
Chris Wooding

Keys to the Kingdom Series
Old Kingdom Series • Seventh Tower Series

Kenneth Oppel

Adventure · Animals · Fantasy
Science fiction · Social issues
8-11

Eoin Colfer
Timothee de Fombelle
Michael Morpurgo
William Nicholson

Philip Reeve
Justin Somper
Chris Wooding

Half Brother
Matt Cruse Series • Silverwing Series

Sam Osman

Adventure · Fantasy
8-11

Jenna Burtenshaw
Susan Cooper

Anthony Horowitz
Alex Scarrow

Quick Silver • Serpent's Gold

James A Owen

Fantasy

Charlie Fletcher
Christopher Paolini

Michael Scott
J R R Tolkien

Chronicles of the Imaginarium Geographica

Joanne Owen

Historical · Mystery · Other lands

Neil Gaiman

Chris Priestley

The Alchemist and the Angel
Puppet Master

Christopher Paolini

Fantasy

Henry Chancellor
D M Cornish
Alison Goodman
K M Grant
Joanne Harris

Kai Meyer
James A Owen
Mark Robson
Michael Scott
Matthew Skelton

Inheritance Series

James Patterson Ⓔ

Adventure · Friends · Magic
Science fiction · Social issues

Stephen Cole
Suzanne Collins
Joe Craig
David Gilman
Jack Higgins with
    Justin Richards

Sophie McKenzie
Malcolm Rose
David Lee Stone
Marc Sumerak
David Thorpe

Daniel X Series
Maximum Ride Series • Maximum Ride Manga Series GN
Witch and Wizard Series

Michelle Paver Ⓔ

Fantasy
8-11

Trudi Canavan
Zizou Corder
Kevin Crossley-Holland
Peter Dickinson
Julia Golding

Stuart Hill
Cliff McNish
Susan Price
J R R Tolkien
Beth Webb

Chronicles of Ancient Darkness Series

Mal Peet Ⓔ

Other cultures · Slavery · Social issues
Sport · War 1939-45
14+

Bernard Ashley
Alan Gibbons
Ann Kelley
Ally Kennen

Michelle Magorian
Michael Morpurgo
James Riordan

Keeper • The Penalty • Tamar

Anna Perera Ⓔ

Other lands · Social issues · Thrillers

Laurie Halse Anderson
Elizabeth Laird

Michael Morpurgo

The Glass Collector • Guantanomo Boy

Will Peterson Ⓔ

Adventure · Thrillers

Andy Briggs
James Dashner

Roderick Gordon and
    Brian Williams
F E Higgins

Triskellion Series

K M Peyton

*Adventure · Historical
Pony/horse · Social issues*

Lauren Brooke
Stacy Gregg

Michelle Magorian
Linda Newbery

Blind Beauty • Blue Skies and Gunfire
Flambards Series • Roman Pony Adventures Series

Helena Pielichaty

Family · Social issues

8-11

Malorie Blackman
Narinder Dhami
Anne Fine

Bali Rai
Jerry Spinelli
Jacqueline Wilson

Accidental Friends • Never Ever • Saturday Girl

Aprilynne Pike

Fairy/folk · Magic · Romance

R J Anderson
Michelle Harrison

Stephenie Meyer
L J Smith

Laurel Series

Terry Pratchett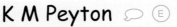

Adventure · Fantasy · Humour

8-11
14+

Dominic Barker
Timothee de Fombelle
Julia Golding
Matt Groening
Brian Jacques

Robin Jarvis
Derek Landy
Ted Naifeh
Paul Stewart
David Lee Stone

Guards! Guards! EN • Nation
Bromeliad Trilogy • The Discworld Series • Johnny Maxwell Stories

Susan Price

*Fairy/folk · Fantasy · Ghost/supernatural
Mythology · Science fiction*

David Almond
Kevin Crossley-Holland
John Dickinson
Michael Lawrence

William Nicholson
Michelle Paver
Sally Prue
Celia Rees

Feasting the Wolf • Hauntings
The King's Head • A Sterkarm Kiss • The Wolf Sisters
Mars Trilogy

⏾ Some titles are available as Talking books

Chris Priestley

Death · Detective mysteries · Ghost/supernat · Historical · Horror

8-11

Paul Bajoria
Linda Buckley-Archer
Steve Feasey
Neil Gaiman

Derek Landy
Cliff McNish
Joanne Owen

The Dead of Winter · *New World*
Tales of Terror Series

Alison Prince

Death · Family · Historical: Vict · Social issues

Grace Cavendish
Pauline Chandler

Paul Dowswell
Mildred D Taylor

Jacoby's Game · *Luck* BS
Speed BS · *Three Blind Eyes* · *Turnaround* · *Web* BS

Rebecca Promitzer

Fantasy · Mystery

Henry Chancellor
Anthony McGowan
David Miller

Joshua Mowll
Ali Sparkes

The Pickle King

Jane Prowse

Adventure · Martial Arts

Chris Bradford
Carol Hedges
Anthony Horowitz

Ann Kelley
Robert Muchamore

Hattori Hachi Series

Sally Prue

Crime · Fantasy · Historical · Humour · Social issues

Gill Arbuthnott
Peter Dickinson
Geraldine McCaughrean

William Nicholson
Susan Price
Kate Thompson

Cold Tom · *The Devil's Toenail*
Goldkeeper · *Ice Maiden* · *Ryland's Footsteps* · *Wheels of War*
Truth Sayer Series

Go to back for lists of: **Authors by Genre** · **Graphic novels**
Short stories · **Prize winners** · **Exploring further**

Philip Pullman

Dystopia · Family · Fantasy · Historical: Vict · Social issues · Thrillers
8-11

Frank Beddor
Cornelia Funke
Sonya Hartnett
Ben Jeapes
Y S Lee

Joshua Mowll
Matthew Skelton
Eleanor Updale
Karen Wallace
Jeanette Winterson

The Broken Bridge • Once Upon a Time in the North
His Dark Materials Trilogy • Sally Lockhart Quartet Series

Bali Rai

Friends · Humour · Other cultures
School · Social issues
8-11
14+

Randa Abdel-Fattah
Gillian Cross
Narinder Dhami
Deborah Ellis
Alan Gibbons

S E Hinton
Helena Pielichaty
Na'ima B Robert
Lee Weatherly

Are you Kidding? BS
Revenge of the Number Two BS • *What's Your Problem?* BS
Tales From Devana High Series

Chloë Rayban

Family · Romance

Ros Asquith
Malorie Blackman
Vanessa Curtis
Echo Freer

Mary Hogan
Rhiannon Lassiter
Keren McCombie
Rosie Rushton

Drama Queen • Hollywood Kiss: My Life So Far
Mwah Mwah • My Life Staring Mom • Wrong Number

Celia Rees

Ghost/supernatural · Historical
Horror · Social issues · Thrillers

Julie Bertagna
Ann Halam
Lucy Jago
Marie-Louise Jensen
Tanya Landman

Tanith Lee
Susan Price
Sarah Singleton
Cate Tiernan

City of Shadows • The Fool's Girl
Pirates! • Sorceress • Sovay • The Vanished

12-14

Philip Reeve

Dystopia · Fantasy · Historical
8-11

Ian Beck	Kenneth Oppel
John Brindley	Paul Stewart
Linda Buckley-Archer	Kate Thompson
Kai Meyer	Chris Wooding
William Nicholson	

Here Lies Arthur • No Such Thing As Dragons
Larklight Series • Mortal Engines (Hungry City) Series

Louise Rennison

Diaries · Friends · Humour · Romance
14+

Ros Asquith	Mary Hogan
Yvonne Collins and Sandy Rideout	Liz Rettig
Vanessa Curtis	Rosie Rushton
Pauline Fisk	Dyan Sheldon
Maggi Gibson	Sue Townsend

Withering Tights
Confessions of Georgia Nicholson Series

Liz Rettig

Diaries · Friends · Romance
14+

Ros Asquith	Louise Rennison
Maggi Gibson	Rosie Rushton
Sue Limb	Sarah Webb

Jumping to Confusions
Kelly Ann Diaries

E E Richardson

Ghost/supernatural · Horror · Magic

Tom Becker	Ann Halam
Sarah Rees Brennan	Darren Shan

Black Bones BS GN
The Devil's Footsteps • Devil For Sale BS
Grave Dirt BS • The Soul Trade • The Summoning

Ann Rinaldi

Historical · Slavery · Thrillers

Laurie Halse Anderson	Mildred D Taylor
Tanya Landman	

Hang a Thousand Trees with Ribbons

GN = Graphic novel

James Riordan

Disability · Friends · Slavery
Social issues · War 1939-45

Laurie Halse Anderson
Yanker Glatshteyn
Michelle Magorian
Michael Morpurgo

Mal Peet
Craig Simpson
Robert Westall

Rebel Cargo • The Sniper • Sweet Clarinet

Rick Riordan

Adventure · Fantasy
Historical · Mythology

8-11

Andy Briggs
Philip Caveney
Michael Ford
Cornelia Funke
M G Harris

Kai Meyer
Alex Scarrow
Michael Scott
David Lee Stone
A G Taylor

*Heroes of Olympus Series
Kane Chronicles • Percy Jackson Series*

Na'ima B Robert (E) Family · Other cultures · Social issues

Randa Abdel-Fattah
Narinder Dhami

Deborah Ellis
Bali Rai

Boys vs. Girls • From Somalia with Love

Katherine Roberts

Fantasy · Mythology

8-11

N M Browne
Trudi Canavan
Susan Cooper
Alison Croggon
Marianne Curley

Rhiannon Lassiter
Caroline Lawrence
Catherine Webb
Rick Yancey

*I Am the Great Horse
Seven Fabulous Wonders Series*

Mark Robson (E)

Fantasy

Trudi Canavan
Cornelia Funke

Christopher Paolini

*Darkweaver Legacy Series
Imperial Trilogy*

Malcolm Rose

Adventure · Historical
Social issues · Thrillers

Bernard Ashley
David Belbin
A J Butcher
Patrick Cave
Stephen Cole

Joe Craig
Philip Gross
Robert Muchamore
James Patterson
Robert Swindells

*Animal Lab • Asteroid • The Death Gene
Forbidden Island • Four Degrees More • Kiss of Death*
Jordan Stryker Series • Traces Series

Meg Rosoff Ⓔ

Adventure · Dystopia · Family
Social issues · War
14+

Theresa Breslin
Anne Cassidy
Jennifer Donnelly
Siobhan Dowd
Gayle Forman

Jenny Valentine
Robert Westall
Scott Westerfeld
Jeanette Winterson

The Bride's Farewell
How I Live Now • Just in Case • What I Was

J K Rowling

Fairy/folk · Fantasy · Magic · School
8-11

Pseudonymous Bosch
Herbie Brennan
Jenna Burtenshaw
Cornelia Funke
Diana Wynne Jones

Cliff McNish
Ted Naifeh
Marcus Sedgwick
Ali Sparkes
G P Taylor

The Tales of Beedle the Bard SS
The Harry Potter Series

Rosie Rushton Ⓔ

Family · Friends · Humour
Romance · Social issues

Randa Abdel-Fattah
Echo Freer
Maggi Gibson
Mary Hogan
Hilary McKay

Chloë Rayban
Louise Rennison
Liz Rettig
Dyan Sheldon
Lee Weatherly

Echoes of Love BS *• Love, Lies and Lizzie*
Secrets of Love • Secret Schemes and Daring Dreams
Summer of Secrets
Leehampton Series • What a Week... Series

Chris Ryan Adventure · Social issues · Thrillers

A J Butcher
Joe Craig
Jim Eldridge
David Gilman
Jack Higgins with
   Justin Richards

Charlie Higson
Andy McNab and Robert Rigby
Robert Muchamore
Craig Simpson
Mark Walden

Alpha Force Series · Code Red Series

Louis Sachar Death · Family · Humour
Illness · Social issues
5-7
8-11

David Almond
Frank Cottrell Boyce
Gennifer Choldenko
Morris Gleitzman
Mark Haddon

Carl Hiaasen
Nigel Hinton
Pete Johnson
Nicky Singer
Jerry Spinelli

The Cardturner · Holes · Small Steps

Alex Scarrow Adventure · Science fiction · Time travel

Linda Buckley-Archer
John Flanagan
Sophie McKenzie

Sam Osman
Rick Riordan
Mark Walden

Time Riders Series

Michael Scott Fantasy · Magic

Philip Caveney
Sam Llewellyn
James A Owen

Christopher Paolini
Rick Riordan
G P Taylor

Secrets of the Immortal Nicholas Flamel Series

Marcus Sedgwick Espionage · Family
Ghost/supernatural · Magic · Mystery
8-11

David Almond
Kevin Crossley-Holland
John Dickinson
J A Henderson
Sam Llewellyn

Joshua Mowll
J K Rowling
Sarah Singleton
G P Taylor
Chris Wooding

Blood Red, Snow White · Book of Dead Days
The Kiss of Death · Revolver · My Swordhand is Singing · White Crow

Darren Shan

Horror · Vampires

14+

Tom Becker	Brian Keaney
Stephen Cole	E E Richardson
Tommy Donbavand	Cate Tiernan
Steve Feasey	Chris Wooding
William Hussey	Rick Yancey

Demonata Series
The Saga of Darren Shan Series GN
The Saga of Larten Crepsley Series

Dyan Sheldon

Friends · Other cultures · Romance
School · Social issues

5-7
8-11

Mary Hooper	Louise Rennison
Cathy Hopkins	Rosie Rushton

And Baby Makes Two • Confessions of a Holiday Star
The Crazy Things Girls Do for Love • My Worst Best Friend
Planet Jane • Sophie Pitt-Turnbull Discovers America

Neal Shusterman

Adventure · Death · Dystopia
Fantasy · Science fiction

Alison Allen-Gray	Saci Lloyd
James Dashner	Gemma Malley
Michael Grant	

Unwind
Skinjacker Trilogy

Craig Simpson (E)

Adventure · Thrillers · War 1939-45

14+

Jim Eldridge	James Riordan
Andy McNab and Robert Rigby	Chris Ryan
Robert Muchamore	

Resistance
Special Operations Series

Nicky Singer

Bullying · Fantasy · Friends · Science fiction

14+

Malorie Blackman	Louis Sachar
Kevin Brooks	Jerry Spinelli
Catherine Forde	

Feather Boy
Gem X • The Innocent's Story

Sarah Singleton

Fantasy · Ghost/supernatural
Historical · Horror · Magic

Helen Grant
Michelle Harrison
Julie Hearn
Cliff McNish

Celia Rees
Marcus Sedgwick
G P Taylor

*Amethyst Child • Century
Heretic • The Poison Garden • Sacrifice*

Matthew Skelton

Fantasy · Historical · Magic

8-11

Jeremy de Quidt
Cornelia Funke
Julia Golding
Frances Hardinge

F E Higgins
Christopher Paolini
Philip Pullman
Eleanor Updale

Endymion Spring • Story of Cirrus Flux

Jeff Smith

Family · Humour · Science fiction

Matt Groening
Jeff Kinney
Jeremy Strong

Marc Sumerak
A G Taylor

*Shazam! The Monster Society of Evil GN
Bone Series GN*

L J Smith

Ghost/supernatural · Romance · Vampires

R J Anderson
Claudia Gray
Eden Maguire

Stephenie Meyer
Aprilynne Pike

14+

Vampire Diaries Series

Justin Somper

Fantasy · Horror

Joseph Delaney
Michael Molloy

Kenneth Oppel
R L Stine

8-11

Vampirates Series

Ali Sparkes

Fantasy · Friends · Ghost/supernatural

Pseudonymous Bosch
Zizou Corder
Joanne Harris

Rebecca Promitzer
J K Rowling

8-11

*Dark Summer • Frozen in Time • Wishful Thinking
Shapeshifter Series*

11-14

Jerry Spinelli Ⓔ

Friends · Holocaust · School
Social issues · War 1939-45

Gennifer Choldenko
Yanker Glatshteyn
Morris Gleitzman
Carl Hiaasen

Hilary McKay
Helena Pielichaty
Louis Sachar
Nicky Singer

Eggs • Loser • Love, Stargirl
The Mighty Crashman • Milkweed • Smiles to Go

Suzanne Fisher Staples

Family · Other cultures
Other lands · Social issues

Lynne Reid Banks
John Boyne
Deborah Ellis

Jamila Gavin
Elizabeth Laird
Tim Wynne-Jones

Daughter of the Wind • House of Djinn • Shiva's Fire
Storm • Under the Persimmon Tree • Under the Same Stars

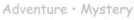

Paul Stewart

Animals · Fantasy

Terry Pratchett
Philip Reeve

David Lee Stone
Steve Voake

5-7
8-11

The Edge Chronicles • Far Flung Adventures Series • Wyrmeweald Series

Trenton Lee Stewart

Adventure · Mystery

Steve Augarde
Pseudonymous Bosch
Linda Buckley-Archer

Henry Chancellor
Frances Hardinge

8-11

The Mysterious Benedict Society Series

R L Stine Ⓔ

Horror · Thrillers

Tom Becker
Sarah Rees Brennan
Stephenie Meyer

Justin Somper
G P Taylor
Robert Westall

8-11

Fear Street Series

David Lee Stone

Fantasy · Humour

R J Anderson
Herbie Brennan
Eoin Colfer
James Patterson

Terry Pratchett
Rick Riordan
Paul Stewart
Jonathan Stroud

8-11

The Illmoor Chronicles

Jeremy Strong

Humour · Social issues

5-7
8-11

Anne Fine
Matt Groening
Paul Jennings

Pete Johnson
Jeff Smith
Sue Townsend

Stuff: The Life of a Cool Demented Dude BS • *Weird*

Jonathan Stroud

Death · Fantasy · Friends
Ghost/supernatural · Social issues

Lloyd Alexander
Marianne Curley
Charlie Fletcher
William Hussey
Brian Jacques

Brian Keaney
David Lee Stone
David Whitley
Jeanette Winterson
Chris Wooding

Buried Fire • *Ghost of Shadow Vale* BS
Heroes of the Valley • *The Last Siege* • *The Leap*
Bartimaeus Sequence Series

Marc Sumerak

Family · Fantasy · School · Science fiction

Alison Allen-Gray
Matt Groening
Robert Muchamore

James Patterson
Jeff Smith
A G Taylor

Hulk Powerpack Series GN
X-Men Powerpack Series GN

Robert Swindells

Adventure · Historical · Social issues
Thrillers · War 1939-45

8-11

David Almond
Bernard Ashley
David Belbin
Thomas Bloor
Anne Cassidy

Keith Gray
Catherine MacPhail
Malcolm Rose
Kate Thompson

Blackout • *Burnout* BS • *Dan's War* BS
Knife Edge BS • *Ruby Tanya* • *Shrapnel*

Natsuki Takaya

Adventure · Fantasy · Friends

Karen McCombie

Ted Naifeh

Fruits Basket Series GN
Phantom Dream Series GN • *Tsubasa Series* GN

Shaun Tan

Environment · Mystery
Other cultures · Social issues
5-7
8-11

Neil Gaiman   Armin Greder

The Arrival GN · *Eric* GN
Tales from Outer Suburbia SS

A G Taylor

Adventure · Science fiction

Alison Allen-Gray   Jeff Smith
Jeremy de Quidt   Marc Sumerak
Sophie McKenzie   David Thorpe
Rick Riordan

Superhumans Series

G P Taylor ⊙ Ⓔ Adventure · Fantasy · Horror · Magic · Vampires

Tom Becker   J K Rowling
Trudi Canavan   Michael Scott
Alison Croggon   Marcus Sedgwick
Robin Jarvis   Sarah Singleton
Cliff McNish   R L Stine

*Maria Mundi Series · Shadowmancer Series
Vampyre Labyrinth Series · Wormwood Series*

Mildred D Taylor ⊙   Historical · Other lands · Social issues

Laurie Halse Anderson   Sonya Hartnett
Malorie Blackman   Alison Prince
Jennifer Donnelly   Ann Rinaldi

The Land · Roll of Thunder, Hear My Cry

Kate Thompson Ⓔ

Animals · Fantasy · Historical
Science fiction · Social issues
8-11
14+

Malorie Blackman   Sally Prue
John Dickinson   Philip Reeve
Peter Dickinson   Robert Swindells

*Alchemist's Apprentice · Annan Water
Beguilers · Creature of the Night · The Fourth Horseman
The Missing Link Trilogy · The New Policeman Trilogy
The Switchers Trilogy*

Go to back for lists of: **Authors by Genre · Graphic novels**
Short stories · Prize winners · Exploring further

David Thorpe

Alison Allen-Gray
T E Berry-Hart
Stephen Cole

James Patterson
A G Taylor

Hybrids

Cate Tiernan

Stephen Cole
Julie Hearn
Brian Keaney
Stephenie Meyer

Celia Rees
Darren Shan
Chris Wooding

Wicca Series

J R R Tolkien

Susan Cooper
Joanne Harris
Stuart Hill
Brian Jacques
Stephen R Lawhead

Ursula Le Guin
James A Owen
Michelle Paver
Clive Woodall

The Hobbit GN
Lord of the Rings Series

Theresa Tomlinson

Adèle Geras
Shannon and Dean Hale

Geraldine McCaughrean

The Moon Riders • Riding the Waves
The Voyage of the Snake Lady • The Wolf Girl
Forestwife Trilogy

Sue Townsend

Tim Collins
Matt Groening
Jeff Kinney

Louise Rennison
Jeremy Strong

Adrian Mole Series

Ann Turnbull

Sally Gardner
Adèle Geras
Mary Hooper

Lucy Jago
Nicola Morgan
Linda Newbery

Alice in Love and War
Forged in the Fire • No Shame No Fear

Eleanor Updale Crime · Family · Historical

Paul Bajoria	Matthew Skelton
Y S Lee	Karen Wallace
Nicola Morgan	Catherine Webb
Philip Pullman	

Johnny Swanson BS · *Saved*
Montmorency Series

Jean Ure Disability · Family · Friends
Romance · Social issues

8-11

Ros Asquith	Cathy Cassidy
Ann Brashares	Rowan Coleman
Lauren Brooke	Gillian Cross
Meg Cabot	Julia Donaldson

Bad Alice · *Boys on the Brain*
Gone Missing · *Love and Kisses* · *Love is Forever* · *Star Crazy Me!*

Jenny Valentine Family · Humour · Mystery
Social issues

5-7
14+

Lucy Christopher	Chris Higgins
Julia Donaldson	Sally Nicholls
Gayle Forman	Meg Rosoff
Mark Haddon	

The Double Life of Cassiel Roadnight
Finding Violet Page

Steve Voake Ⓔ Adventure · Fantasy · Horror
Science fiction · Thrillers

8-11

Eoin Colfer	M G Harris
Joe Craig	Paul Stewart
Sam Enthoven	

Blood Hunters · *The Dreamwalker's Child*
Fightback · *The Starlight Conspiracy* · *Web of Love*

Mark Walden Adventure · Crime · School · Thrillers

8-11

Dominic Barker	David Gilman
Jason Bradbury	Robert Muchamore
Chris Bradford	Chris Ryan
Stephen Cole	Alex Scarrow
Joe Craig	

H.I.V.E. Series

14-21

Karen Wallace

Adventure · Friends · Historical
Other lands · School
5-7
8-11

Jennifer Donnelly
Eva Ibbotson
Margaret Mahy

Philip Pullman
Eleanor Updale

Climbing a Monkey Puzzle Tree
Raspberries on the Yangtze • *The Unrivalled Spangles* • *Wendy*

David Walliams

Friends · Humour · Social issues
8-11

Terence Blacker
Frank Cottrell Boyce

Paul Jennings
Pete Johnson

Billionaire Boy • *The Boy in a Dress* • *Mr Stink*

Rachel Ward

Death · Science fiction
14+

T E Berry-Hart
B R Collins
Suzanne Collins

Michael Grant
Scott Westerfeld

Numbers Series

Lee Weatherly

Family · Friends · Illness · Social issues

Anne Cassidy
Bali Rai

Rosie Rushton

Breakfast at Sadie's • *Child X*
Kat Got Your Tongue • *Missing Abby* • *Them* BS • *Watcher* BS

Beth Webb

Fantasy · Historical · Magic

Ursula Le Guin
Garth Nix

Michelle Paver

Fire Dreamer • *Star Dancer*

Catherine Webb

Detective mysteries · Historical

Alison Croggon
Marianne Curley
Catherine Fisher
Diana Wynne Jones

Rhiannon Lassiter
Y S Lee
Katherine Roberts
Eleanor Updale

The Extraordinary Adventures of Horatio Lyle Series

BS = Published by Barrington Stoke
specialists in resources for dyslexic and struggling readers

Sarah Webb (E)

Helen Bailey
Sophia Bennett
Cathy Cassidy

Sarah Dessen
Sue Limb
Liz Rettig

Ask Amy Green Series

Robert Westall

Adventure · Ghost/supernatural
Historical · Science fiction · War 1939-45

8-11

Peter Dickinson
Charlie Fletcher
Yanker Glatshteyn
Nigel Hinton
Michael Morpurgo

Linda Newbery
James Riordan
Meg Rosoff
R L Stine

Break of Dark • Gulf • The Promise
The Scarecrows • Urn Burial • The Wind Eye

Scott Westerfeld (E)

Dystopia · Historical · Sci-fi
Social issues · Vampires · War

14+

Alison Allen-Gray
Stephen Baxter
Ursula Le Guin
Tim Lott

Gemma Malley
Garth Nix
Meg Rosoff
Rachel Ward

The Last Days • Parasite Positive
Leviathan Series • Midnighters Series • Uglies Quartet Series

David Whitley (E)

Fantasy · Mystery

F E Higgins

Jonathan Stroud

The Children of the Lost • Midnight Charter
The Agora Trilogy

Jacqueline Wilson (E)

Diaries · Family · Humour
Social issues

5-7
8-11

Helen Bailey
Lauren Brooke
Cathy Cassidy
Narinder Dhami
Judith Fathallah

Candy Gourlay
Chris Higgins
Adeline Yen Mah
Helena Pielichaty
Kay Woodward

Girls in Love • Kiss • Little Darlings
Lola Rose • Love Lessons • Vicky Angel

Jeanette Winterson Adventure · Fantasy · Science fiction

Geraldine McCaughrean
Philip Pullman

Meg Rosoff
Jonathan Stroud

The Battle of the Sun • Tanglewreck

Clive Woodall Adventure · Animals · Fantasy

Brian Jacques
Garth Nix

J R R Tolkien

One for Sorrow • Seven for a Secret

Chris Wooding Adventure · Fantasy · Horror
Science fiction

Stephen Cole
Ann Halam
J A Henderson
Garth Nix
Kenneth Oppel

Philip Reeve
Marcus Sedgwick
Darren Shan
Jonathan Stroud
Cate Tiernan

The Haunting of Alaizabel Cray • Havoc • Malice • The Storm Thief
Broken Sky Series

Kay Woodward Family · Humour · Romance

Cathy Cassidy
Chris Higgins

Jacqueline Wilson

Jane Airhead

Sarah Wray Disability · Mystery · Thrillers

Tim Bowler
Kevin Brooks

Sophie McKenzie
Tim Wynne-Jones

Forbidden Room • The Trap

Rachel Wright Adventure · Animals · Family · Humour

Meg Cabot
Sue Limb

Karen McCombie

Get Your Paws Off • You've Got Blackmail

⬭ Some titles are available as Talking books

Tim Wynne-Jones

Bullying · Family · Mystery
Social issues · Thrillers

Alison Allen-Gray
Lynne Reid Banks
Anne Cassidy

Suzanne Fisher Staples
Sarah Wray

The Boy in the Burning House
The Survival Game • *A Thief in the House of Memory* • *The Uninvited*

Rick Yancey

Adventure · Historical: Victorian
Horror · Mythology · Thrillers

Eoin Colfer
Joseph Delaney

Katherine Roberts
Darren Shan

The Adventures of Alfred Kropp Series
Monstrumologist Series

Markus Zusak

Death · Dystopia · Holocaust
Social issues · War 1939-45
14+

John Boyne
Yanker Glatshteyn

Morris Gleitzman
Michael Morpurgo

The Book Thief • *Fighting Ruben Wolfe*
I am the Messenger

12-14

Go to back for
lists of:
Authors by Genre
Graphic novels
Short stories
Prize winners
Further reading

Authors for Ages 14+

Randa Abdel-Fattah Family · Friends · Other cultures · Social issues 12-14

Faïza Guène
Bali Rai

Marjane Satrapi
Gabrielle Zevin

Does My Head Look Big in This?
Ten Things I Hate About Me • *Where the Streets Had a Name*

Sherman Alexie Family · Humour · Social issues

Stephen Emond
Bali Rai

Marjane Satrapi

The Absolutely True Diary of a Part-Time Indian

Laurie Halse Anderson Crime · Eating disorders · Friends · Social issues 12-14

Jay Asher
Judith Fathallah

Kate Morgenroth

Twisted • *Wintergirls*

Kelley Armstrong Ghost/supernatural · Magic

Holly Black
P C & Kristin Cast
Alex Duval
Lauren Kate
Stephenie Meyer

Alyson Noel
Cynthia Leitich Smith
L J Smith
Gabrielle Zevin

Darkest Powers Series

Jay Asher (E) Death · Friends · Social issues

Laurie Halse Anderson
Jenny Downham
Judith Fathallah
Gayle Forman
Joanna Kenrick

Catherine MacPhail
Lauren Oliver
Matt Whyman
Benjamin Zephaniah
Gabrielle Zevin

Thirteen Reasons Why

Bernard Ashley Ⓔ

Adventure · Thrillers

12-14

Suzanne Collins
Jim Eldridge
Andy McNab

Catherine MacPhail
Craig Simpson
Matt Whyman

Down to the Wire • Ten Days to Zero

Sherry Ashworth

Friends · Social issues · Thrillers

Kevin Brooks
Melvin Burgess

Alan Gibbons
Joanna Kenrick

Disconnected • Paralysed • Something Wicked

Clive Barker Ⓔ

Fantasy · Horror

Garth Ennis
Neil Gaiman

Alan Moore
J R R Tolkien

Abarat Series

Nora Raleigh Baskin Ⓔ

Family · Social issues

Jenny Downham

Gayle Forman

All We Know of Love • The Truth About My Bat Mitzvah
What Every Girl (Except Me) Knows

Stephen Baxter Ⓔ

Family · Science fiction

12-14

Melvin Burgess
Gemma Malley

Patrick Ness
Scott Westerfeld

Flood • The H-Bomb Girl

Frank Beddor

Adventure · Dystopia · Fantasy

12-14

Neil Gaiman
Shannon and Dean Hale

Mike Mignola
Bryan Talbot

Hatter M Series GN
Looking Glass Wars Series GN

14+

GN = Graphic novel

169

David Belbin Crime · Family · Immigration · Romance · School

12-14

Malorie Blackman
Anne Cassidy
Monika Feth
Nicola Morgan

Kate Morgenroth
Bali Rai
Benjamin Zephaniah

China Girl BS
Dead Teachers Don't Talk BS • *Love Lessons*

Julia Bell Crime · Friends · Social issues

Melvin Burgess
Graham Marks

Tabitha Suzuma
Benjamin Zephaniah

Dirty Work

Holly Black Fantasy

8-11

Kelley Armstrong
Rachel Caine
Trudi Canavan
Cassandra Clare

Margo Lanagan
Melissa Marr
Deborah Noyes
Maggie Stiefvater

Ironside • *Tithe* • *Valiant*
Good Neighbors Series GN

14+

Malorie Blackman Dystopia · Family · Social issues
Teen pregnancy · Thrillers

David Belbin
Suzanne Collins
Julia Green

Nicky Singer
Kate Thompson
John van de Ruit

5-7
8-11
12-14

Boys Don't Cry • *The Stuff of Nightmares*
Noughts and Crosses Sequence

Tim Bowler Family · Ghost/supernatural
Social issues · Thrillers

12-14

Catherine Forde
Sonya Hartnett
Ally Kennen

Anthony McGowan
Graham Marks
Valerie Mendes

Apocalypse • *Bloodchild*
Buried Thunder • *Frozen Fire*
Blade Series

BS = Published by Barrington Stoke
specialists in resources for dyslexic and struggling readers

Libba Bray

Friends · Historical: Victorian
Magic · School

Becca Fitzpatrick	Lian Hearn
Anna Godbersen	Lauren Kate
Helen Grant	Melissa Marr
Julie Hearn	Lili Wilkinson

A Great and Terrible Beauty • Rebel Angels • The Sweet Far Thing

Kate Brian

School

Grace Dent	Cecily von Ziegesar
Sarah Dessen	Rachel Ward

Lucky T • Sweet 16 • The V Club
Private Series

Kevin Brooks

Crime · Family · Mystery · Social issues

12-14

14+

Sherry Ashworth	Sonya Hartnett
Melvin Burgess	Sam Mills
John Dickinson	Gillian Philip
Sandra Glover	Nicky Singer
Keith Gray	Matt Whyman

Being • Black Rabbit Summer
Bloodline BS • iBoy • I See You, Baby • Killing God

Terry Brooks

Fantasy

Trudi Canavan	Terry Pratchett
Stephen R Lawhead	J R R Tolkien

Landover Series • Shannara Series

Suzanne Bugler

Family · Friends · Romance
Social issues · Teen pregnancy

Anne Cassidy	Catherine MacPhail
Jenny Downham	Lauren Oliver
Monika Feth	

Meet Me at the Boathouse • Staring up at the Sun

Julie Burchill

Friends · Homosexuality · Social issues

Julie Anne Peters	Lili Wilkinson
Cecily von Ziegesar	

Sugar Rush • Sweet

Melvin Burgess

Crime · Social issues

Sherry Ashworth
Stephen Baxter
Julia Bell
Kevin Brooks

B R Collins
Keith Gray
Bryan Talbot
Rachel Ward

Bloodtide • Doing It • Junk
Lady: My Life as a Bitch • Nicholas Dane • Sara's Face

Rachel Caine

Ghost/supernatural · Other lands
School · Vampires

Holly Black
Alex Duval
Claudia Gray
Alyxandra Harvey
Rachel Hawthorne

Richelle Mead
Stephenie Meyer
Alyson Noel
L J Smith

Morganville Vampires Series

Trudi Canavan

Fantasy · Magic
12-14

Holly Black
Terry Brooks

Stephen R Lawhead
J R R Tolkien

The Magician's Apprentice
Age of Five Series • The Black Magician Trilogy
Traitor Spy Trilogy

Kate Cann

Family · Friends · Horror
Social issues · Thrillers

Sarah Dessen
Kate le Vann

Joanna Nadin

Leader of the Pack • Leaving Poppy
Sea Change • Text Game BS
Rayne Series

Dean Vincent Carter

Horror · Thrillers

Charlie Higson
William Hussey
Curtis Jobling

Grant Morrison
Christopher Pike
Darren Shan

Bloodwater
The Hand of the Devil • The Hunting Season

E Some titles are available as ebooks

14+

Anne Cassidy

Crime · Death · Detective mysteries
Social issues · Thrillers
5-7
12-14

David Belbin
Suzanne Bugler
Keren David
Monika Feth
Catherine Forde

Helen Grant
Mark Haddon
Sophie McKenzie
Graham Marks
Kate Morgenroth

Forget Me Not BS · *Getting Away With It*
Guilt Trip · *Heart Burn* · *Just Jealous* · *The Story of My Life*

P C & Kristin Cast

Ghost/supernatural
School · Vampires

Kelley Armstrong
Alex Duval
Becca Fitzpatrick
Alyxandra Harvey
Lauren Kate

Richelle Mead
Stephenie Meyer
Alyson Noel
Christopher Pike
Maggie Stiefvater

Goddess Summoning Series · *House of Night Series*

Aidan Chambers Ⓔ

Family · War 1939-45

Jostein Gaarder

Linda Newbery

Postcards from No Man's Land · *This is All*

Stephen Chbosky

School · Social issues

Stephen Emond
John Green

Mark Haddon
Paul Magrs

The Perks of Being a Wallflower

Cassandra Clare

Fantasy · Ghost/supernatural
Vampires

Holly Black
Becca Fitzpatrick

Melissa Marr
L J Smith

Infernal Devices Series · *The Mortal Instruments Series*

B R Collins

Family · Fantasy · Friends · Social issues
12-14

Melvin Burgess
Siobhan Dowd

Patrick Ness
Rachel Ward

The Traitor Game · *A Trick of the Dark*

14+

Suzanne Collins Ⓔ

Adventure · Dystopia
Mystery · Science fiction
12-14

Bernard Ashley
Malorie Blackman
James Jauncey
Conor Kostick
Saci Lloyd

Gemma Malley
Susan Pfeffer
Laura Powell
Rachel Ward
Scott Westerfeld

Hunger Games Trilogy

Tim Collins Ⓔ

Diaries · Humour · Vampires
12-14

Matt Haig
Catherine Jinks

Terry Pratchett
Sue Townsend

Diary of a Wimpy Vampire Series

Keren David Ⓔ

Crime · Family · Social issues · Thrillers

14+

Anne Cassidy
Catherine Forde
J A Jarman
David Klass

Sam Mills
Nicola Morgan
Jenny Valentine

Almost True • When I was Joe

Melissa de la Cruz Ⓔ

Friends · Social issues

Grace Dent
Anna Godbersen

Carolyn Mackler
Cecily von Ziegesar

The Au Pairs Series

Grace Dent

Family · Friends · Humour
12-14

Kate Brian
Melissa de la Cruz
Sarra Manning
Joanna Nadin

Louise Rennison
Liz Rettig
Helen Salter
Sue Townsend

Diary of a Chav Series
Diary of a Snob Series • LBD Series

Go to back for lists of: Authors by Genre • Graphic novels
Short stories • Prize winners • Exploring further

Sarah Dessen

Death · Family · Relationships
12-14

Kate Brian
Kate Cann
Sharon Dogar
John Green
E Lockhart

Sarra Manning
Jaclyn Moriarty
Julie Anne Peters
Helen Salter
Nicky Singer

*Along for the Ride • Infinity SS • Just Listen
Lock and Key • Someone Like You • The Truth about Forever*

John Dickinson

Dystopia · Science fiction
12-14

Kevin Brooks

Gemma Malley

WE

Sharon Dogar

Family · Romance · Social issues
War 1939-45
12-14

Sarah Dessen
Hilary Freeman
Julia Green
Meg Rosoff

Art Spiegelman
Tabitha Suzuma
Markus Zusak

Annexed • Falling • Waves

14+

Siobhan Dowd

Family · Friends · Social issues
Teen pregnancy
8-11
12-14

B R Collins
Sonya Hartnett
Alice Kuipers
Anthony McGowan
Carolyn Mackler

Meg Rosoff
Tabitha Suzuma
Bryan Talbot
Kate Thompson

*Bog Child
Solace of the Road • Swift Pure Cry*

Jenny Downham

Death · Family · Friends · Illness
12-14

Jay Asher
Nora Raleigh Baskin
Suzanne Bugler
Gayle Forman
Alice Kuipers

Anthony McGowan
Jaclyn Moriarty
Jandy Nelson
Lauren Oliver
Susan Pfeffer

Before I Die • You Against Me

SS = Short stories

Alex Duval

Ghost/supernatural · Vampires

Kelley Armstrong
Rachel Caine
P C & Kristin Cast
Melissa Marr

Richelle Mead
Christopher Pike
L J Smith

Vampire Beach Series

Jim Eldridge Ⓔ

Adventure · War

12-14

Bernard Ashley
Andy McNab

Craig Simpson
Matt Whyman

Black Ops Series

Stephen Emond

Family · Social issues

Sherman Alexie
Stephen Chbosky

John Green
Mark Haddon

Happyface

Garth Ennis   Crime · Fantasy · Horror · Science fiction · Superhero

Clive Barker
Neil Gaiman
Andy McNab
Mike Mignola

Alan Moore
Grant Morrison
Darren Shan

Dan Dare GN

Ghost Rider Series GN · *The Punisher Series* GN

Judith Fathallah

Eating disorders · Social issues

12-14

Laurie Halse Anderson
Jay Asher

Joanna Kenrick
Tabitha Suzuma

Monkey Taming

Monika Feth

Thrillers

David Belbin
Suzanne Bugler

Anne Cassidy
Helen Grant

The Strawberry Ficker

14+

GN = Graphic novel

Becca Fitzpatrick

Fantasy · Ghost/supernatural Romance

Libba Bray	Melissa Marr
P C & Kristin Cast	Stephenie Meyer
Cassandra Clare	Alyson Noel
Lauren Kate	Ann Turnbull

Crescendo • Hush, Hush

Catherine Forde

Friends · Social issues · Thrillers

12-14

Tim Bowler	Catherine MacPhail
Anne Cassidy	Valerie Mendes
Keren David	Benjamin Zephaniah
Keith Gray	

Bad Wedding BS • Fifteen Minute Bob • Sugarcoated

Gayle Forman

Death · Family

12-14

Jay Asher	Lauren Oliver
Nora Raleigh Baskin	Meg Rosoff
Jenny Downham	Maggie Stiefvater
Beth Goobie	Jenny Valentine
Julia Green	

If I Stay Series

Hilary Freeman

Crime · Illness · Relationships · Romance

Sharon Dogar	Paul Magrs
Kate le Vann	Meg Rosoff

Don't Ask • Lifted • Loving Danny • Shades of Love
Camden Town Tales Series

Jostein Gaarder Ⓔ

Death · Fantasy · Philosophy

Aidan Chambers	Gabrielle Zevin
Paul Magrs	

The Christmas Mystery • Orange Girl
The Solitaire Mystery • Sophie's World

14+

Some titles are available as **Talking books**

Neil Gaiman Ⓔ Family · Fantasy · Magic · Superhero

Clive Barker	Mike Mignola	5-7
Frank Beddor	Alan Moore	8-11
Garth Ennis	Grant Morrison	12-14
Jack Gantos	Terry Pratchett	
Joanne Harris	Bryan Talbot	

Batman: Whatever Happened to the Caped Crusader? GN
Coraline GN • *Eternals* GN • *The Graveyard Book*
M is for Magic SS • *Marvel 1602* GN
The Sandman Series GN

Jack Gantos Family · Horror · Humour

Neil Gaiman	Paul Magrs	8-11
Margo Lanagan		

The Love Curse of the Rumbaughs

Alan Gibbons Ⓔ Family · Fantasy · Social issues

Sherry Ashworth	Bali Rai	8-11
Keith Gray	Matt Whyman	12-14
Mal Peet	Benjamin Zephaniah	

Blood Pressure • *The Defender*
Hold On • *Lost Boy's Appreciation Society* • *Night Hunger* BS
Hell's Underground Series • *Lost Souls Stories*

Linzi Glass Ⓔ Apartheid · Family · Friends
Other lands · Social issues

Lian Hearn	Jenny Valentine
Hanna Jansen	Jason Wallace
Meg Rosoff	

Ruby Red • *The Year the Gypsies Came*

Sandra Glover Ⓔ Friends · Ghost/supernatural · Social issues

Kevin Brooks	Catherine MacPhail

Dangerously Close • *Identity*
Somewhere Else • *Spiked* • *You*

Anna Godbersen Ⓔ Historical · Romance

Libba Bray	Melissa Marr
Melissa de la Cruz	Cecily von Ziegesar
Julie Hearn	

Bright Young Things • *The Luxe Series*

 14+

Beth Goobie   School • Social issues

Gayle Forman

Gemma Malley

Joanna Nadin

Scott Westerfeld

Before Wings • The Lottery

Helen Grant   Ghost/supernatural • Horror
Mystery • Other lands • Thrillers

12-14

Libba Bray

Anne Cassidy

Monika Feth

Julie Hearn

Laura Powell

The Vanishing of Katharina Linden
Wish Me Dead

Claudia Gray   Ghost/supernatural • Vampires

12-14

Rachel Caine

Alyxandra Harvey

Rachel Hawthorne

Richelle Mead

Alyson Noel

Cynthia Leitich Smith

Evernight Series

Keith Gray   Friends • Social issues

12-14

Kevin Brooks

Melvin Burgess

Catherine Forde

Alan Gibbons

James Jauncey

Ally Kennen

Bali Rai

Kate Thompson

The Fearful • Ghosting BS
Malarkey • The Ostrich Boys • The Return of Johnny Kemp BS

John Green   Adventure • Death • Friends • Romance

Stephen Chbosky

Sarah Dessen

Stephen Emond

Kate Morgenroth

Gabrielle Zevin

Looking for Alaska • Paper Towns

Julia Green   Death • Family • Friends
Social issues • Teen pregnancy

Malorie Blackman

Sharon Dogar

Gayle Forman

Simmone Howell

Jandy Nelson

Baby Blue • Breathing Underwater
Drawing with Light

Faïza Guène (E)   Family • Other cultures • Other lands

Randa Abdel-Fattah   Marjane Satrapi
Bali Rai
                        Just Like Tomorrow

Mark Haddon 💬 (E)   Crime • Disability • Family • Social issues

Anne Cassidy   Nick Hornby   8-11
Stephen Chbosky   Anthony McGowan   12-14
Stephen Emond   Markus Zusak
           The Curious Incident of the Dog in the Night-time
                    A Spot of Bother

Ben Haggarty   Historical

Alan Moore   Peadar Ó Guilín

               Mezolith GN

Matt Haig 💬 (E)   Family • Vampires

Tim Collins   Sam Mills   8-11
Catherine Jinks
                    The Radleys

Shannon and Dean Hale 💬 (E)   Adventure • Fairy/folk

Frank Beddor   Terry Pratchett   12-14
Joanne Harris   Maggie Stiefvater
Margo Lanagan
               The Book of a Thousand Days
           Calamity Jack GN • *Rapunzel's Revenge* GN

Joanne Harris 💬 (E)   Fantasy • Mythology

Neil Gaiman   Terry Pratchett   12-14
Shannon and Dean Hale   J R R Tolkien
Margo Lanagan
                    Runemarks

Sonya Hartnett 💬   Social issues

Tim Bowler   Siobhan Dowd   12-14
Kevin Brooks
                    The Ghost's Child
         Stripes of the Sidestep Wolf • *Surrender*

Alyxandra Harvey

Family · Fantasy
Friends · Vampires

Rachel Caine
P C & Kristin Cast
Claudia Gray

Richelle Mead
Alyson Noel

Drake Chronicles

Rachel Hawthorne

Ghost/supernatural
Horror · Romance

Rachel Caine
Claudia Gray

Alyson Noel

Dark Guardians Series

Julie Hearn

Historical: Victorian · Social issues
12-14

Libba Bray
Anna Godbersen
Helen Grant

Nicola Morgan
Lili Wilkinson

Hazel · Ivy

Lian Hearn

Fantasy · Historical · Other cultures

Libba Bray
Linzi Glass

Meg Rosoff

Tales of the Otori Series

Charlie Higson

Horror · Science fiction
8-11
12-14

Dean Vincent Carter
William Hussey
Curtis Jobling

Peadar Ó Guilín
Darren Shan

The Dead · The Enemy

Nick Hornby

Sport

Mark Haddon
Graham Marks

Bali Rai

Slam

Simmone Howell

Social issues

Julia Green
Carolyn Mackler
Joyce Carol Oates

Susan Pfeffer
Gabrielle Zevin

Everything Beautiful
Notes from the Teenage Underground

14+

William Hussey

Fantasy · Ghost/supernatural
Historical · Horror
12-14

Dean Vincent Carter
Charlie Higson

Christopher Pike
Darren Shan

Witchfinder Series

Hanna Jansen

Death · Genocide · Other lands

Linzi Glass
Art Spiegelman

Jason Wallace
Markus Zusak

Over a Thousand Hills, I Walk With You

J A Jarman

Crime · Family · Social issues
5-7
8-11

Keren David
David Klass
Catherine MacPhail

Sam Mills
Bali Rai

Inside

James Jauncey

Crime · Detective mysteries · Family
Friends · Thrillers

Suzanne Collins
Keith Gray

Kate le Vann
Patrick Ness

The Reckoning • The Witness

Catherine Jinks

Crusades · Ghost/supernatural
Historical · Humour · Vampires
12-14

Tim Collins
Matt Haig

Stephenie Meyer
Terry Pratchett

The Abused Werewolf Rescue Group
The Reformed Vampire Support Group
Pagan Chronicles

Curtis Jobling

Fantasy · Horror

Dean Vincent Carter
Charlie Higson

Christopher Pike
Darren Shan

Wereworld Series

Lauren Kate

Fantasy · Ghost/supernatural
Romance · Thrillers

Kelley Armstrong
Libba Bray
P C & Kristin Cast

Becca Fitzpatrick
Stephenie Meyer
Maggie Stiefvater

Fallen Series

14+

Ally Kennen Crime · Family · Social issues · Thrillers

Tim Bowler	Bali Rai
Keith Gray	Tabitha Suzuma
Anthony McGowan	Jenny Valentine
Mal Peet	Benjamin Zephaniah

8-11
12-14

Beast · Bedlam · Beserk

Joanna Kenrick

*Friends · Homosexuality
Relationships · Social issues*

Jay Asher	Judith Fathallah
Sherry Ashworth	Tabitha Suzuma

*Mindset BS · Out BS
Red Tears · Screwed · Tears of a Friend*

David Klass

Family · School · Social issues

Keren David	J A Jarman

The Braves · You Don't Know Me

Conor Kostick

Fantasy · Science fiction · Thrillers

Suzanne Collins	Darren Shan

12-14

Epic · Move · Saga

Alice Kuipers ⬭ Ⓔ

Death · Family · Illness

Siobhan Dowd	Joyce Carol Oates
Jenny Downham	Gabrielle Zevin
Jaclyn Moriarty	

Life on the Refrigerator Door

Margo Lanagan Ⓔ

Fairy/folk · Fantasy · Science fiction

Holly Black	Joanne Harris
Jack Gantos	Paul Magrs
Shannon and Dean Hale	Maggie Stiefvater

*Red Spikes SS
Tender Morsels · White Time SS*

Stephen R Lawhead ⬭ Ⓔ

*Adventure · Fantasy
Historical · Mythology*

Terry Brooks	J R R Tolkien
Trudi Canavan	

12-14

King Raven Series

14+

Kate le Vann (E) — Death · Family · Friends · Romance

Kate Cann
Hilary Freeman
James Jauncey
Gemma Malley

Sam Mills
Jenny Valentine
Scott Westerfeld

Rain • Tessa in Love
Things I Know About Love
Two Friends, One Summer • The Worst of Me

Saci Lloyd — Environment · Family · Friends · Science fiction

Suzanne Collins
Gemma Malley

Susan Pfeffer

12-14

The Carbon Diaries 2015 • The Carbon Diaries 2017

E Lockhart — Romance · School

Sarah Dessen

Liz Rettig

The Boy Book
The Boyfriend List • Fly on the Wall

Tim Lott — Dystopia · Science fiction · Social issues

Gemma Malley
Sam Mills

Patrick Ness
Peadar Ó Guilín

12-14

Fearless

Anthony McGowan (E) — Death · Humour · Illness · Social issues

Tim Bowler
Siobhan Dowd
Jenny Downham

Mark Haddon
Ally Kennen
Benjamin Zephaniah

8-11
12-14

Henry Tumour • Hellbent • The Knife that Killed Me

Sophie McKenzie (E) — Crime · Romance · Science fiction

Anne Cassidy

Susan Pfeffer

8-11
12-14

The Fix BS
All About Eve Series • The Medusa Project Series

14+

BS = Published by Barrington Stoke
specialists in resources for dyslexic and struggling readers

Carolyn Mackler

Family · Friends · Relationships
Romance · Social issues

Melissa de la Cruz
Siobhan Dowd
Simmone Howell

Joyce Carol Oates
Louise Rennison
Gabrielle Zevin

The Earth, My Butt and Other Big Round Things
Guyaholic • *Love and Other Four Lettered Words*
Vegan, Virgin, Valentine

Andy McNab

Adventure · Thrillers · War

Bernard Ashley
Jim Eldridge
Garth Ennis

Mike Mignola
Craig Simpson
Matt Whyman

Drop Zone • *Last Night Another Soldier*
Nick Stone Series

Catherine MacPhail

Adventure · School · Social issues
Teen pregnancy · Thrillers
12-14

Jay Asher
Bernard Ashley
Suzanne Bugler
Catherine Forde
Sandra Glover

J A Jarman
Graham Marks
Rachel Ward
Matt Whyman
Benjamin Zephaniah

Bad Company • *Dark Waters*
Grass • *Out of the Depths* • *Roxy's Baby* • *Worse than Boys*
Nemesis Series

Paul Magrs

Relationships · Social issues

Stephen Chbosky
Hilary Freeman
Jostein Gaarder

Jack Gantos
Margo Lanagan

The Diary of a Dr Who Addict
Exchange • *Strange Boy* • *Twin Freaks*

Gemma Malley

Dystopia · Science fiction · Thrillers
12-14

Stephen Baxter
Suzanne Collins
John Dickinson
Beth Goobie
Kate le Vann

Saci Lloyd
Tim Lott
Susan Pfeffer
Meg Rosoff
Scott Westerfeld

Returners
The Declaration Series

Sarra Manning (E)

Family · Romance · Social issues

Grace Dent
Sarah Dessen

Cecily von Ziegesar

Guitar Girl · Let's Get Lost · Nobody's Girl
Diary of a Crush Series · Fashionistas Series

Graham Marks

Family · Historical: Victorian · Other lands
Social issues · Thrillers
8-11
12-14

Julia Bell
Tim Bowler
Anne Cassidy
Nick Hornby

Catherine MacPhail
Susan Pfeffer
Matt Whyman

How it Works · Omega Place
Radio Radio · Tokyo: All Alone in the Big City · Zoo

Melissa Marr (E)

Fairy/folk · Fantasy · Romance

Holly Black
Libba Bray
Cassandra Clare
Alex Duval
Becca Fitzpatrick

Anna Godbersen
Richelle Mead
Alyson Noel
Deborah Noyes
Maggie Stiefvater

Wicked Lovely Series · Wicked Lovely Tokyopop Series GN

14+

Richelle Mead ⬭ (E)

Ghost/supernatural · Romance
School · Vampires

Rachel Caine
P C & Kristin Cast
Alex Duval
Claudia Gray
Alyxandra Harvey

Melissa Marr
Stephenie Meyer
Alyson Noel
Cynthia Leitich Smith
L J Smith

Vampire Academy Series

Valerie Mendes

Bullying · Death · Family · Other lands

Tim Bowler
Catherine Forde

Linda Newbery

Coming of Age
The Drowning · Lost and Found

(E) Some titles are available as ebooks

Stephenie Meyer

Dystopia · Ghost/supernatural
Horror · Romance
12-14

Kelley Armstrong
Rachel Caine
P C & Kristin Cast
Becca Fitzpatrick
Catherine Jinks

Lauren Kate
Richelle Mead
Deborah Noyes
Lauren Oliver
L J Smith

The Host
Twilight Saga

Mike Mignola

Fantasy · Horror · Humour

Frank Beddor
Garth Ennis
Neil Gaiman
Andy McNab

Alan Moore
Grant Morrison
Terry Pratchett

Hellboy Series GN

Sam Mills

Death · Dystopia · Family
Science fiction · Social issues · Thrillers

Kevin Brooks
Keren David
Matt Haig

J A Jarman
Kate le Vann
Tim Lott

Blackout • The Boys Who Saved the World • A Nicer Way To Die

Alan Moore

Dystopia · Fantasy · Science fiction

Clive Barker
Garth Ennis
Neil Gaiman
Ben Haggarty

Mike Mignola
Grant Morrison
Bryan Talbot

Captain Britain GN • V For Vendetta GN • Watchmen GN
Tom Strong Series GN

Nicola Morgan ⓔ

Death · Fantasy · Historical · Social issues
12-14

David Belbin
Keren David
Julie Hearn

Gillian Philip
Tabitha Suzuma
Ann Turnbull

Deathwatch • Fleshmarket
Mondays are Red • The Passionflower Massacre
Sleepwalking • Wasted

Kate Morgenroth (E)

Death · Thrillers

Laurie Halse Anderson
David Belbin

Anne Cassidy
John Green

Echo

Jaclyn Moriarty (E)

Friends · Humour · Letters
School · Social issues

Sarah Dessen
Jenny Downham
Alice Kuipers

Joanna Nadin
Joyce Carol Oates
Gabrielle Zevin

*Becoming Bindy Mackenzie • Dreaming of Amelia
Feeling Sorry for Celia • The Spellbook of Kirsten Taylor*

Grant Morrison

Fantasy · Horror

Dean Vincent Carter
Garth Ennis
Neil Gaiman

Mike Mignola
Alan Moore
Darren Shan

All Star Superman GN *• Arkham Asylum* GN
Emergency Stop GN *• Gothic* GN *• World War III* GN

Joanna Nadin (E)

Humour · Relationships

Kate Cann
Grace Dent
Beth Goobie

Jaclyn Moriarty
Louise Rennison
Helen Salter

Wonderland
Rachel Riley Series

Jandy Nelson

Death · Family

Jenny Downham
Julia Green

Lauren Oliver

The Sky is Everywhere

Patrick Ness (E)

Dystopia · Science fiction
Social issues · War

Stephen Baxter
B R Collins
James Jauncey
Tim Lott
Peadar Ó Guilín

Susan Pfeffer
Gillian Philip
Laura Powell
Kate Thompson
Jason Wallace

Chaos Walking Series

14+

Linda Newbery

Family · Illness · Social issues
War 1914-18/1939-45
5-7
8-11
12-14

Aidan Chambers   Ann Turnbull
Valerie Mendes

*Set in Stone • The Shell House
Sisterland • Some Other War*

Alyson Noel

Ghost/supernatural · Romance

Kelley Armstrong   Alyxandra Harvey
Rachel Caine   Rachel Hawthorne
P C & Kristin Cast   Melissa Marr
Becca Fitzpatrick   Richelle Mead
Claudia Gray   Cynthia Leitich Smith

Immortals Series

Deborah Noyes

Crime · Ghost/supernatural

Holly Black   Stephenie Meyer
Melissa Marr

The Ghosts of Kerfol

Peadar Ó Guilín

Fantasy · Horror · Science fiction

Ben Haggarty   Patrick Ness
Charlie Higson   Darren Shan
Tim Lott

Bone World Trilogy

Joyce Carol Oates

*Family · Friends · School
Social issues*

Simmone Howell   Bali Rai
Alice Kuipers   Benjamin Zephaniah
Carolyn Mackler   Gabrielle Zevin
Jaclyn Moriarty

*Big Mouth & Ugly Girl
Freaky Green Eyes*

Lauren Oliver ⓔ *Death · Dystopia · Romance · Science fiction*

Jay Asher   Stephenie Meyer
Suzanne Bugler   Jandy Nelson
Jenny Downham   Scott Westerfeld
Gayle Forman

Before I Fall • Delirium

14+

Mal Peet (E) Mystery · Social issues · Sport · War 1939-45

Alan Gibbons Matt Whyman 12-14
Ally Kennen

Exposure • The Penalty • Tamar

Julie Anne Peters Family · Friends · Homosexuality
Social issues

Julie Burchill Sarah Dessen

Keeping You a Secret • Luna

Susan Pfeffer   Dystopia · Science fiction

Suzanne Collins Gemma Malley
Jenny Downham Graham Marks
Simmone Howell Patrick Ness
Saci Lloyd Meg Rosoff
Sophie McKenzie Scott Westerfeld

Last Survivors Series

Gillian Philip (E) Family · Fantasy · Social issues

Kevin Brooks Meg Rosoff
Nicola Morgan Rachel Ward
Patrick Ness

Bad Faith • Crossing the Line
Rebel Angels Series

Christopher Pike Horror · Vampires

Dean Vincent Carter William Hussey
P C & Kristin Cast Curtis Jobling
Alex Duval Darren Shan

The Party
The Last Vampire Series

Laura Powell Fantasy · Mystery · Social issues

Suzanne Collins Patrick Ness
Helen Grant

Game of Triumphs Series

Go to back for lists of: Authors by Genre • Graphic novels
Short stories • Prize winners • Exploring further

Terry Pratchett

Fantasy · Humour

8-11
12-14

Terry Brooks
Tim Collins
Neil Gaiman
Shannon and Dean Hale

Joanne Harris
Catherine Jinks
Mike Mignola

Guards! Guards! GN
Discworld Series

Bali Rai

Crime · Friends · Other cultures
School · Social issues

8-11
12-14

Randa Abdel-Fattah
Sherman Alexie
David Belbin
Alan Gibbons
Keith Gray

Faïza Guène
Nick Hornby
J A Jarman
Ally Kennen
Joyce Carol Oates

Angel Collector · City of Ghosts
The Gun BS *· The Last Taboo · Them and Us* BS *· The Whisper*

14+

Louise Rennison

Diaries · Friends · Humour · Romance

12-14

Grace Dent
Carolyn Mackler
Joanna Nadin

Helen Salter
Liz Rettig

Withering Tights
The Confessions of Georgia Nicholson Series

Liz Rettig

Diaries · Family · Romance

12-14

Grace Dent
E Lockhart
Louise Rennison

Helen Salter
Sue Townsend

Jumping to Confusions
Kelly Ann Diaries Series

Meg Rosoff

Adventure · Dystopia · Family
Social issues · War

12-14

Sharon Dogar
Siobhan Dowd
Gayle Forman
Hilary Freeman
Linzi Glass

Lian Hearn
Gemma Malley
Susan Pfeffer
Gillian Philip
Scott Westerfeld

The Bride's Farewell · How I Live Now
Just in Case · What I Was

Helen Salter

Grace Dent
Sarah Dessen
Joanna Nadin

Liz Rettig
Louise Rennison

Do Secrets Count as Sabotage?
Does Glitter Count as Camouflage? • *Does Snogging Count as Exercise?*

Marjane Satrapi

Other cultures • Other lands

Randa Abdel-Fattah
Sherman Alexie
Faïza Guène

Art Spiegelman
Benjamin Zephaniah

Persepolis GN

Darren Shan

Ghost/supernatural • Horror • Vampires

12-14

Dean Vincent Carter
Garth Ennis
Charlie Higson
William Hussey
Curtis Jobling

Conor Kostick
Grant Morrison
Peadar Ó Guilín
Christopher Pike

The Thin Executioner
City Trilogy • *Demonata Series* • *The Saga of Darren Shan Series* GN

Craig Simpson (E)

Adventure • Thrillers • War 1939-45

12-14

Bernard Ashley
Jim Eldridge

Andy McNab
Matt Whyman

Resistance
Special Operations Series

Nicky Singer

Family • Science fiction • Social issues

12-14

Malorie Blackman
Kevin Brooks

Sarah Dessen

Feather Boy • *The Innocent's Story* • *Gem X*

Cynthia Leitich Smith

Romance • Vampires

Kelley Armstrong
Claudia Gray
Richelle Mead

Alyson Noel
Maggie Stiefvater

Tantalize Series

14+

192

L J Smith Vampires

12-14

Kelley Armstrong
Rachel Caine
Cassandra Clare

Alex Duval
Richelle Mead
Stephenie Meyer

Nightworld Series
The Secret Circle Series • Vampire Diaries

Art Spiegelman Holocaust

Sharon Dogar
Hanna Jansen

Marjane Satrapi
Markus Zusak

Maus and Maus II GN

Maggie Stiefvater Fairy/folk • Fantasy
Ghost/supernat • Horror • Romance

Holly Black
P C & Kristin Cast
Gayle Forman
Shannon and Dean Hale

Lauren Kate
Margo Lanagan
Melissa Marr
Cynthia Leitich Smith

Ballard • Lament • Linger • Shiver

Tabitha Suzuma Death • Illness • Social issues • Thrillers

Julia Bell
Sharon Dogar
Siobhan Dowd
Judith Fathallah

Ally Kennen
Joanna Kenrick
Nicola Morgan
Bryan Talbot

Forbidden • From Where I Stand
A Note of Madness • A Voice in the Distance

Bryan Talbot Historical • Social issues

Frank Beddor
Melvin Burgess
Siobhan Dowd

Neil Gaiman
Alan Moore
Tabitha Suzuma

Alice in Sunderland GN
The Tale of One Bad Rat GN

GN = Graphic novel

Kate Thompson

Fantasy · Ghost/supernatural
Social issues
8-11
12-14

| Malorie Blackman | Keith Gray |
| Siobhan Dowd | Patrick Ness |

Creature of the Night

J R R Tolkien

Fantasy
8-11
12-14

Clive Barker	Joanne Harris
Terry Brooks	Stephen R Lawhead
Trudi Canavan	

The Hobbit
Lord of the Rings Series

Sue Townsend

Diaries · Humour
12-14

| Tim Collins | Liz Rettig |
| Grace Dent | John van de Ruit |

Adrian Mole Diaries

Ann Turnbull

Historical · Romance
12-14

| Becca Fitzpatrick | Linda Newbery |
| Nicola Morgan | Lili Wilkinson |

Alice in Love and War
Forged in the Fire • No Shame, No Fear

Jenny Valentine

Romance · Social issues
5-7
12-14

Keren David	Ally Kennen
Gayle Forman	Kate le Vann
Linzi Glass	

The Ant Colony
Broken Soup • Finding Violet Park

John van de Ruit

Apartheid · Family · Humour
Other lands · School

| Malorie Blackman | Jason Wallace |
| Sue Townsend | |

Spud • Spud: Learning to Fly
Spud: The Madness Continues...

Some titles are available as **Talking books**

14+

194

Cecily von Ziegesar Friends · School · Social issues

Kate Brian
Julie Burchill
Melissa de la Cruz

Anna Godbersen
Sarra Manning

Gossip Girl Series

Jason Wallace E

Apartheid · Other cultures
Other lands · School · Social issues

Linzi Glass
Hanna Jansen
Patrick Ness

John van de Ruit
Markus Zusak

Out of the Shadows

Rachel Ward

Adventure · Death · Science fiction · Thrillers

Kate Brian
Melvin Burgess
B R Collins
Suzanne Collins

Catherine MacPhail
Gillian Philip
Scott Westerfeld

12-14

Numbers Series

Scott Westerfeld E

Dystopia · Ghost/supernatural ·
Sci-fi · Social issues · Vampires

Stephen Baxter
Suzanne Collins
Beth Goobie
Kate le Vann
Gemma Malley

Lauren Oliver
Susan Pfeffer
Meg Rosoff
Rachel Ward

12-14

Midnighters Series
Peeps Series • Uglies Series

Matt Whyman E

Crime · Family · Other cultures
Social issues · Thrillers

Jay Asher
Bernard Ashley
Kevin Brooks
Jim Eldridge
Alan Gibbons

Andy McNab
Catherine MacPhail
Graham Marks
Mal Peet
Craig Simpson

Boy Kills Man • Gold Strike
Inside the Cage • Street Runners • The Wild

E Some titles are available as ebooks

14+

Lili Wilkinson

Historical · Homosexuality
Other lands · Social issues

Libba Bray
Julie Burchill

Julie Hearn
Ann Turnbull

Pink · Scatterheart

Benjamin Zephaniah

Other cultures · Social issues · War

Jay Asher
David Belbin
Julia Bell
Catherine Forde
Alan Gibbons

Ally Kennen
Anthony McGowan
Catherine MacPhail
Joyce Carol Oates
Marjane Satrapi

Face · Gangsta Rap
Refugee Boy · Teacher's Dead

14+

Gabrielle Zevin

Death · Family · Friends

Randa Abdel-Fattah
Kelley Armstrong
Jay Asher
Jostein Gaarder
John Green

Simmone Howell
Alice Kuipers
Carolyn Mackler
Jaclyn Moriarty
Joyce Carol Oates

Elsewhere
Memoirs of a Teenage Amnesiac

Markus Zusak

Death · Dystopia · Family
Sport · War 1939-45
12-14

Sharon Dogar
Mark Haddon
Hanna Jansen

Art Spiegelman
Jason Wallace

The Book Thief · Fighting Ruben Wolfe

Go to back for
lists of:
Authors by Genre
Graphic novels
Short stories
Prize winners
Further reading

Genres and Themes

8-11
Pippa Funnell

12-14
Chris Higgins
Theresa Tomlinson

5-7

Jenny Alexander
Simon Bartram
Martyn Beardsley
Emily Bearn
Ben 10
Sue Bentley
Malorie Blackman
Jon Blake
Benedict Blathwayt
Michael Broad
Jeff Brown
Judy Brown
Nick Butterworth
Alex Cliff
Andrew Cope
Jonathan Emmett
Joe Friedman
Mick Gowar
John Grant
Sally Grindley

Stella Gurney
Mary Hoffman
Harry Horse
Elizabeth Singer Hunt
Julia Jarman
Ann Jungman
Diana Kimpton
Timothy Knapman
H I Larry
Michael Lawrence
Neal Layton
Astrid Lindgren
Elizabeth Lindsay
Colin McNaughton
Martine Murray
Hilda Offen
Hiawyn Oram
David Orme
Laura Owen

Daniel Postgate
Chris Powling
Alf Prøysen
Shoo Rayner
Margaret Ryan
Dyan Sheldon
Dee Shulman
Sophie Smiley
Geronimo Stilton
Rex Stone
Jeremy Strong
Martin Waddell
Summer Waters
Holly Webb
Ian Whybrow
David Henry Wilson
Jacqueline Wilson
Philip Wooderson
Jonny Zucker

8-11

Deborah Abela
Joan Aiken
Roy Apps
Philip Ardagh
Paul Bajoria
Blue Balliett
Dominic Barker
Betty G Birney
Terence Blacker
Malorie Blackman
Adam Blade

Enid Blyton
Pseudonymous Bosch
Lucy M Boston
Frank Cottrell Boyce
Chris Bradford
Tony Bradman
Herbie Brennan
Linda Buckley-Archer
Annette Butterworth
Georgia Byng
Philip Caveney

Henry Chancellor
Simon Cheshire
Michael Coleman
Eoin Colfer
Susan Cooper
Zizou Corder
Gillian Cross
Kevin Crossley-Holland
Chris d'Lacey
Anna Dale
Colin Dann

Genres

Adventure (cont)

8-11 (cont)

Timothee de Fombelle
Kate di Camillo
Joshua Doder
Berlie Doherty
Siobhan Dowd
Helen Dunmore
John Fardell
Michael Ford
Cornelia Funke
Alan Garner
Alan Gibbons
Julia Golding
Harriet Goodwin
Mark Haddon
Geri Halliwell
Paul Haven
Carol Hedges
Hergé
Jason Hightman
Charlie Higson
Nigel Hinton
Michael Hoeye
Anthony Horowitz
Elizabeth Singer Hunt
Erin Hunter
Eva Ibbotson
Steve Jackson and
    Ian Livingstone
Brian Jacques

Ceci Jenkinson
Pete Johnson
Allan Frewin Jones
P B Kerr
Garry Kilworth
Clive King
Elizabeth Laird
H I Larry
Joan Lennon
Penelope Lively
Sam Llewellyn
Graham Marks
Jill Marshall
Anna Maxted
David Miller
Michael Molloy
Michael Morpurgo
Chris Mould
Joshua Mowll
Andrew Newbound
William Nicholson
Mary Norton
Kenneth Oppel
Wendy Orr
Sam Osman
Philippa Pearce
Chris Powling
Chris Priestley

Philip Pullman
Arthur Ransome
Shoo Rayner
Philip Reeve
Ellen Renner
Justin Richards
Rick Riordan
Katherine Roberts
Emily Rodda
Sebastian Rook
S F Said
Dyan Sheldon
Charlie Small
Dodie Smith
Ali Sparkes
Lauren St John
Dugald Steer
Trenton Lee Stewart
Jeff Stone
Rex Stone
Robert Swindells
J R R Tolkien
Mark Walden
Karen Wallace
Cat Weatherill
Robert Westall
Ursula Moray Williams
Jonny Zucker

12-14

Joan Aiken
R J Anderson
Gill Arbuthnott
Bernard Ashley
Steve Augarde
Paul Bajoria
Frank Beddor
David Belbin
Julie Bertagna
Pseudonymous Bosch
Chris Bradford
Herbie Brennan

Theresa Breslin
Andy Briggs
John Brindley
N M Browne
A J Butcher
Philip Caveney
Sarwat Chadda
Henry Chancellor
Emma Clayton
Suzanne Collins
Susan Cooper
Zizou Corder

Joe Craig
Gillian Cross
Kevin Crossley-Holland
James Dashner
Timothee de Fombelle
Peter Dickinson
Paul Dowswell
Jim Eldridge
Deborah Ellis
Brian Falkner
Kat Falls
Nancy Farmer

Genres

12-14 (cont)

Catherine Fisher
Pauline Fisk
John Flanagan
Charlie Fletcher
Michael Ford
Cornelia Funke
David Gilman
Julia Golding
Roderick Gordon and
  Brian Williams
K M Grant
M G Harris
Carol Hedges
J A Henderson
F E Higgins
Jack Higgins with
  Justin Richards
Charlie Higson
Nigel Hinton
Mary Hoffman
Anthony Horowitz
Eva Ibbotson
Brian Jacques

Marie-Louise Jensen
Ann Kelley
Elizabeth Laird
Caroline Lawrence
Sophie McKenzie
Andy McNab and
  Robert Rigby
Catherine MacPhail
Graham Marks
David Miller
Michael Molloy
Nicola Morgan
Joshua Mowll
Robert Muchamore
Benjamin J Myers
William Nicholson
Garth Nix
Kenneth Oppel
Sam Osman
James Patterson
Will Peterson
K M Peyton
Terry Pratchett

Jane Prowse
Rick Riordan
Malcolm Rose
Meg Rosoff
Chris Ryan
Alex Scarrow
Neal Shusterman
Craig Simpson
Trenton Lee Stewart
Robert Swindells
Natsuki Takaya
A G Taylor
G P Taylor
Ann Turnbull
Steve Voake
Mark Walden
Karen Wallace
Robert Westall
Jeanette Winterson
Clive Woodall
Chris Wooding
Rachel Wright
Rick Yancey

14+

Bernard Ashley
Frank Beddor
Suzanne Collins
Jim Eldridge

John Green
Shannon and Dean Hale
Stephen R Lawhead
Andy McNab

Catherine MacPhail
Meg Rosoff
Craig Simpson
Rachel Ward

Ancient history

AG is Ancient Greece • AE is Ancient Egypt

8-11

Zizou Corder AG
Michael Ford
Jill Marshall AE

12-14

Adèle Geras

Genres

Animals

5-7

Anne Adeney
Allan Ahlberg
Scoular Anderson
Sorrel Anderson
Giles Andreae
Dosh Archer
Antonia Barber
Emily Bearn
Sue Bentley
Michael Broad
Marc Brown
Anthony Browne
John Burningham
Nick Butterworth
Anne Cassidy
Emma Chichester Clark
Helen Cooper
Paul Cooper
Andrew Cope
Chris d'Lacey
Lucy Daniels
Hayley Daze
Ted Dewan
Lynley Dodd
Penny Dolan
Julia Donaldson
Malachy Doyle
Ian Falconer
Jan Fearnley
Vivian French

Joe Friedman
Neil Gaiman
Pippa Goodhart
Bob Graham
Emily Gravett
Kes Gray
Sally Grindley
Harry Horse
Rose Impey
Mick Inkpen
Julia Jarman
Diana Kimpton
Daren King
Dick King-Smith
Satoshi Kitamura
Neal Layton
Elizabeth Lindsay
Sam Lloyd
David McKee
Colin McNaughton
James Marshall
David Melling
Tony Mitton
Sue Mongredien
Bel Mooney
Michael Morpurgo
Margaret Nash
Linda Newbery
Jenny Nimmo

Hiawyn Oram
Mal Peet and
   Elspeth Graham
Daniel Postgate
Beatrix Potter
Jillian Powell
Simon Puttock
Shoo Rayner
Chris Riddell
Hilary Robinson
Frank Rodgers
Tony Ross
Alan Rusbridger
Hannah Shaw
Jane Simmons
Mark Skelton
Geronimo Stilton
Joan Stimson
Julie Sykes
Jill Tomlinson
Alison Uttley
Summer Waters
Holly Webb
Colin West
Ian Whybrow
Mo Willems
Jeanne Willis
Anna Wilson
Jane Yolen

8-11

Richard Adams
Michelle Bates
Betty G Birney
Malorie Blackman
Michael Bond
Annette Butterworth
Betsy Byars
Linda Chapman
Lucy Christopher
David Clement-Davies
Louise Cooper

Andrew Cope
Zizou Corder
Jenny Dale
Lucy Daniels
Colin Dann
Katie Davies
Narinder Dhami
Kate di Camillo
Joshua Doder
Roddy Doyle
Morris Gleitzman

Kenneth Grahame
Michael Hoeye
Mary Hooper
Erin Hunter
Brian Jacques
Allan Frewin Jones
Deborah Kent
Garry Kilworth
Diana Kimpton
Daren King
Dick King-Smith

8-11 (cont)

Ingrid Lee
Elizabeth Lindsay
Livi Michael
A A Milne
Linda Newbery
Jenny Oldfield
Kenneth Oppel
Wendy Orr
Michelle Paver

Philippa Pearce
Mal Peet and
   Elspeth Graham
Daniel Pennac
Angie Sage
S F Said
Anna Sewell
Mark Skelton

Dodie Smith
Lauren St John
Paul Stewart
Geronimo Stilton
Rex Stone
Jeremy Strong
E B White
Ursula Moray Williams

12-14

Dominic Barker
Gennifer Choldenko
Zizou Corder
Sonya Hartnett

Michael Morpurgo
Kenneth Oppel
Paul Stewart

Kate Thompson
Clive Woodall
Rachel Wright

Apartheid

14+

Linzi Glass

John van de Ruit

Jason Wallace

Ballet

Genres

5-7

Ann Bryant
Darcey Bussell
Harriet Castor
Beatrice Masini
Natasha May
James Mayhew
Anna Wilson

8-11

Darcey Bussell
Adèle Geras
Beatrice Masini
Noel Streatfeild
Anna Wilson

Bullying

8-11

Jeff Kinney

12-14

Andy Briggs
B R Collins
Sarah Dessen
Anthony McGowan
Nicky Singer
Tim Wynne-Jones

14+

Valerie Mendes

Computers

8-11
Terence Blacker   Michael Coleman   Charlie Higson
Malorie Blackman   Alan Gibbons

12-14
Andy Briggs

Crime

8-11
Frank Cottrell Boyce   Paul Haven   Andrew Lane
Zizou Corder   Pete Johnson   Jonny Zucker

12-14
Paul Bajoria   Zizou Corder   Robert Muchamore
Ian Beck   Berlie Doherty   Sally Prue
Kevin Brooks   Mark Haddon   Eleanor Updale
Anne Cassidy   Nicola Morgan   Mark Walden

14+
Laurie Halse Anderson   Keren David   Ally Kennen
David Belbin   Garth Ennis   Sophie McKenzie
Julia Bell   Hilary Freeman   Deborah Noyes
Kevin Brooks   Mark Haddon   Bali Rai
Melvin Burgess   J A Jarman   Matt Whyman
Anne Cassidy   James Jauncey

Crusades

14+
Catherine Jinks

Death

5-7
Oliver Jeffers   Michael Rosen

8-11
David Almond   Sally Grindley   Ally Kennen
John Boyne   Oliver Jeffers   Suzanne LaFleur
Harriet Goodwin

12-14

Julie Bertagna	Armin Greder	Sally Nicholls
Tim Bowler	Brian Keaney	Chris Priestley
John Boyne	Damian Kelleher	Alison Prince
Anne Cassidy	Suzanne LaFleur	Louis Sachar
Jennifer Donnelly	Geraldine McCaughrean	Neal Shusterman
Siobhan Dowd	Anthony McGowan	Jonathan Stroud
Jenny Downham	Cliff McNish	Rachel Ward
Pauline Fisk	Eden Maguire	Markus Zusak
Gayle Forman		

14+

Jay Asher	Hanna Jansen	Kate Morgenroth
Anne Cassidy	Alice Kuipers	Jandy Nelson
Sarah Dessen	Kate le Vann	Lauren Oliver
Jenny Downham	Anthony McGowan	Tabitha Suzuma
Gayle Forman	Valerie Mendes	Rachel Ward
Jostein Gaarder	Sam Mills	Gabrielle Zevin
John Green	Nicola Morgan	Markus Zusak
Julia Green		

Detective mysteries

Genres

5-7

Barbara Mitchelhill	Kaye Umansky

8-11

Deborah Abela	Eoin Colfer	Tom Palmer
Blue Balliett	Siobhan Dowd	Chris Priestley
Dominic Barker	Garry Kilworth	Anthony Read
Malorie Blackman	Andrew Lane	Ellen Renner
Thomas Bloor	Caroline Lawrence	Justin Richards
Enid Blyton	Joan Lennon	Emily Rodda
Grace Cavendish	Barbara Mitchelhill	Lauren St John
Simon Cheshire		

12-14

Dominic Barker	Grace Cavendish	Y S Lee
Frank Cottrell Boyce	Eoin Colfer	Chris Priestley
Meg Cabot	Tanya Landman	Catherine Webb
Anne Cassidy	Caroline Lawrence	

14+

Anne Cassidy	James Jauncey

Diaries

5-7
Simon Bartram

8-11

Sharon Creech	Dennis Hamley	Richard Platt
Lucy Daniels	Jeff Kinney	Jamie Rix
Anne Fine	Kelly McKain	Charlie Small
Adèle Geras	Helena Pielichaty	Jean Ure

12-14

Meg Cabot	Jeff Kinney	Sue Townsend
Tim Collins	Louise Rennison	Jacqueline Wilson
Adèle Geras	Liz Rettig	

14+

Tim Collins	Liz Rettig
Louise Rennison	Sue Townsend

Disability

5-7	**12-14**	**14+**
Sophie Smiley	Gennifer Choldenko	Mark Haddon
	Mark Haddon	
	Catherine MacPhail	
	James Riordan	
	Jean Ure	
	Sarah Wray	

Dystopia

8-11
William Nicholson

12-14

Steve Augarde	John Dickinson	William Nicholson
Frank Beddor	Kat Falls	Philip Pullman
T E Berry-Hart	Catherine Fisher	Philip Reeve
Malorie Blackman	Michael Grant	Meg Rosoff
Emma Clayton	Tim Lott	Neal Shusterman
Suzanne Collins	Gemma Malley	Scott Westerfeld
James Dashner	Stephenie Meyer	Marcus Zusak

Dystopia (cont)

14+

Frank Beddor
Malorie Blackman
Suzanne Collins
John Dickinson
Tim Lott

Gemma Malley
Stephenie Meyer
Sam Mills
Alan Moore
Patrick Ness

Lauren Oliver
Susan Pfeffer
Meg Rosoff
Scott Westerfeld
Markus Zusak

Easy reader

5-7

Anne Adeney
Allan Ahlberg
Jenny Alexander
Scoular Anderson
Laurence Anholt
Stan and
   Jan Berenstain
Andy Blackford
Marc Brown

Ann Bryant
Anne Cassidy
Penny Dolan
Malachy Doyle
Alan Durant
P D Eastman
Vivian French
Pippa Goodhart
Mick Gowar

Sue Graves
Stella Gurney
James Marshall
Margaret Nash
David Orme
Jillian Powell
Russell Punter
Dr Seuss
Joan Stimson

Eating disorders

12-14

Malorie Blackman
Judith Fathallah
Chris Higgins

14+

Laurie Halse Anderson
Judith Fathallah

Environment

5-7

Harry Horse

Dr Seuss

Colin Thompson

8-11

Richard Adams
Tony Bradman

Timothee de Fombelle
Ted Hughes

Clive King
Robert C O'Brien

12-14

Steve Augarde
Julie Bertagna
Timothee de Fombelle

Brian Falkner
Matt Groening
Carl Hiaasen

Saci Lloyd
Shaun Tan
David Thorpe

14+

Saci Lloyd

205

Espionage

12-14

Ally Carter	Carol Hedges	Marcus Sedgwick

Fairy/folk

5-7

Anne Adeney	Mini Grey	Laura North
Laurence Anholt	Karina Law	Russell Punter
Tony Bradman	Margaret Mayo	Martin Waddell
Anne Cassidy	Tony Mitton	Barrie Wade
Lauren Child	Maggie Moore	Karen Wallace
Malachy Doyle	Michael Morpurgo	Chris Wormell

8-11

R J Anderson	Katherine Langrish	Gwyneth Rees
E D Baker	Geraldine McCaughrean	Emily Rodda
Ian Beck	Philip Pullman	Titania Woods
Michelle Harrison		

12-14

R J Anderson	Victoria Hanley	Aprilynne Pike
Kevin Crossley-Holland	Michelle Harrison	Susan Price
Cornelia Funke	Sam Llewellyn	J K Rowling
Shannon and Dean Hale		

14+

Shannon and Dean Hale	Melissa Marr
Margo Lanagan	Maggie Stiefvater

Family

5-7

Allan Ahlberg	Nick Butterworth	Mary Hoffman
David Almond	Ann Cameron	Shirley Hughes
Ronda and	Lauren Child	Rose Impey
David Armitage	Chris d'Lacey	Dick King-Smith
Atinuke	Dorothy Edwards	Karina Law
Martyn Beardsley	Jan Fearnley	Paeony Lewis
Stan and	Anne Fine	Alan MacDonald
Jan Berenstain	Joe Friedman	Hilary McKay
Jon Blake	Maeve Friel	David Melling
Joyce Lankester Brisley	Neil Gaiman	Barbara Mitchelhill
Marc Brown	Bob Graham	Sue Mongredien
Anthony Browne	Kes Gray	Bel Mooney
John Burningham	Mairi Hedderwick	Michael Morpurgo

Genres

5-7 (cont)

Martine Murray
Margaret Nash
Jenny Nimmo
Hilda Offen
Daniel Postgate
Beatrix Potter
Jillian Powell
Chris Powling

Tony Ross
Margaret Ryan
Dyan Sheldon
Francesca Simon
Sophie Smiley
Wendy Smith
Paul Stewart
Jeremy Strong

Kaye Umansky
Jenny Valentine
Karen Wallace
Colin West
David Henry Wilson
Jacqueline Wilson
Jonny Zucker

8-11

Allan Ahlberg
Joan Aiken
Louisa May Alcott
David Almond
Lynne Reid Banks
Nina Bawden
Ian Beck
Jeanne Birdsall
Betty G Birney
Thomas Bloor
Judy Blume
Michael Bond
Lucy M Boston
Frank Cottrell Boyce
John Boyne
Christiana Brand
Frances
   Hodgson Burnett
Betsy Byars
Meg Cabot
Cathy Cassidy
Linda Chapman
Lucy Christopher
Sharon Creech
Richmal Crompton
Chris d'Lacey
Annie Dalton

Katie Davies
Kate di Camillo
Berlie Doherty
Fiona Dunbar
Helen Dunmore
Anne Fine
Jackie French
Neil Gaiman
Jack Gantos
Adèle Geras
Morris Gleitzman
Debi Gliori
Candy Gourlay
Sally Grindley
Dennis Hamley
Diana Hendry
Rose Impey
Julia Jarman
Ally Kennen
Liz Kessler
Dick King-Smith
Suzanne LaFleur
Elizabeth Laird
Lois Lowry
Karen McCombie
Megan McDonald
Hilary McKay

Michelle Magorian
Anna Maxted
Livi Michael
Barbara Mitchelhill
L M Montgomery
Joshua Mowll
E Nesbit
Linda Newbery
Jenny Nimmo
Andrew Norriss
Mary Norton
Jenny Oldfield
Wendy Orr
Philippa Pearce
Sara Pennypacker
Arthur Ransome
Philip Ridley
Margaret Ryan
Marcus Sedgwick
Francesca Simon
Ali Sparkes
Johanna Spyri
Noel Streatfeild
Jeremy Strong
P L Travers
Laura Ingalls Wilder
Jacqueline Wilson

12-14

Randa Abdel-Fattah
Alison Allen-Gray
David Almond
Gill Arbuthnott
Ros Asquith

Helen Bailey
Lynne Reid Banks
Stephen Baxter
Terence Blacker
Malorie Blackman

Tim Bowler
Frank Cottrell Boyce
Sarah Rees Brennan
Theresa Breslin
Kevin Brooks

12-14 (cont)

Maite Carranza
Cathy Cassidy
Gennifer Choldenko
Rowan Coleman
Sarah Dessen
Narinder Dhami
Sharon Dogar
Berlie Doherty
Julia Donaldson
Siobhan Dowd
Jenny Downham
Helen Dunmore
Deborah Ellis
Judith Fathallah
Anne Fine
Pauline Fisk
Gayle Forman
Alan Gibbons
Morris Gleitzman
Armin Greder
Stacy Gregg
Matt Groening
Mark Haddon
Carl Hiaasen

Chris Higgins
Nigel Hintor
Mary Hoffman
Mary Hogan
Mary Hooper
Cathy Hopkins
Marie-Louise Jensen
Ann Kelley
Ally Kennen
Jeff Kinney
Suzanne LaFleur
Michael Lawrence
Saci Lloyd
Geraldine McCaughrean
Karen McCombie
Hilary McKay
Michelle Magorian
Adeline Yen Mah
Henning Mankell
Graham Marks
Nicola Morgan
Joshua Mowll
Benjamin J Myers
Linda Newbery

Sally Nicholls
Helena Pielichaty
Alison Prince
Philip Pullman
Chloë Rayban
Na'ima B Robert
Meg Rosoff
Rosie Rushton
Louis Sachar
Marcus Sedgwick
Jeff Smith
Suzanne Fisher Staples
Marc Sumerak
Theresa Tomlinson
Eleanor Updale
Jean Ure
Jenny Valentine
Lee Weatherly
Sarah Webb
Jacqueline Wilson
Kay Woodward
Rachel Wright
Tim Wynne-Jones

Genres

14+

Randa Abdel-Fattah
Sherman Alexie
Nora Raleigh Baskin
Stephen Baxter
David Belbin
Malorie Blackman
Tim Bowler
Kevin Brooks
Suzanne Bugler
Kate Cann
Aidan Chambers
B R Collins
Keren David
Grace Dent
Sarah Dessen
Sharon Dogar
Siobhan Dowd
Jenny Downham

Stephen Emond
Gayle Forman
Neil Gaiman
Jack Gantos
Alan Gibbons
Linzi Glass
Julia Green
Faïza Guène
Mark Haddon
Matt Haig
Alyxandra Harvey
J A Jarman
James Jauncey
Ally Kennen
David Klass
Alice Kuipers
Kate le Vann
Saci Lloyd

Carolyn Mackler
Sarra Manning
Graham Marks
Valerie Mendes
Sam Mills
Jandy Nelson
Linda Newbery
Joyce Carol Oates
Julie Anne Peters
Gillian Philip
Liz Rettig
Meg Rosoff
Nicky Singer
John van de Ruit
Matt Whyman
Gabrielle Zevin
Markus Zusak

5-7

David Almond
Giles Andreae
Simon Bartram
Ben 10
Tony Bradman
Michael Broad
Jeff Brown
Judy Brown
Keith Brumpton
John Burningham
Linda Chapman
Alex Cliff
June Crebbin

Chris d'Lacey
Roald Dahl
Julia Donaldson
Anne Fine
Neil Gaiman
Sally Gardner
Pippa Goodhart
Mini Grey
Oliver Jeffers
Ann Jungman
Dick King-Smith
Timothy Knapman
Megan McDonald

Kelly McKain
Tiffany Mandrake
Jenny Nimmo
Alf Prøysen
Chris Riddell
Rex Stone
Jeremy Strong
Shaun Tan
Colin Thompson
Kaye Umansky
Jacqueline Wilson
Chris Wormell

8-11

Richard Adams
Allan Ahlberg
Joan Aiken
David Almond
R J Anderson
Roy Apps
Steve Augarde
Lynne Reid Banks
Dominic Barker
J M Barrie
Guy Bass
Frank L Baum
Holly Black
Adam Blade
Lucy M Boston
Theresa Breslin
Raymond Briggs
Georgia Byng
Lewis Carroll
Philip Caveney
Henry Chancellor
Linda Chapman
David Clement-Davies
Alex Cliff
Eoin Colfer
Louise Cooper
Susan Cooper
Zizou Corder

Cressida Cowell
Sharon Creech
Chris d'Lacey
Roald Dahl
Annie Dalton
Timothee de Fombelle
Berlie Doherty
Jeanne DuPrau
Catherine Fisher
Charlie Fletcher
Cornelia Funke
Neil Gaiman
Sally Gardner
Alan Garner
Alan Gibbons
Debi Gliori
Julia Golding
Harriet Goodwin
John Gordon
Elizabeth Goudge
Kenneth Grahame
Kes Gray
Matt Haig
Frances Hardinge
Lucinda Hare
Michelle Harrison
Diana Hendry
Jason Hightman

Nigel Hinton
Michael Hoeye
Ted Hughes
Erin Hunter
Barry Hutchison
Eva Ibbotson
Steve Jackson and
    Ian Livingstone
Brian Jacques
Robin Jarvis
Oliver Jeffers
Paul Jennings
Allan Frewin Jones
Diana Wynne Jones
Elizabeth Kay
P B Kerr
Liz Kessler
Garry Kilworth
Caro King
Derek Landy
Katherine Langrish
Michael Lawrence
Joan Lennon
C S Lewis
Penelope Lively
Sam Llewellyn
Geraldine McCaughrean
Anthony McGowan

8-11 (cont)

Ross Mackenzie
Graham Marks
Hazel Marshall
Livi Michael
Michael Molloy
Joshua Mowll
Jill Murphy
E Nesbit
Andrew Newbound
William Nicholson
Jenny Nimmo
Andrew Norriss
Mary Norton
Robert C O'Brien
Ian Ogilvy
Kenneth Oppel

Sam Osman
Michelle Paver
Philippa Pearce
Terry Pratchett
Sarah Prineas
Philip Pullman
Ellen Renner
Philip Ridley
Katherine Roberts
Emily Rodda
J K Rowling
Kate Saunders
Matthew Skelton
Lemony Snicket
Justin Somper

Ali Sparkes
Paul Stewart
David Lee Stone
Shaun Tan
Kate Thompson
Di Toft
J R R Tolkien
P L Travers
Steve Voake
John Vornholt
Pat Walsh
Cat Weatherill
E B White
T H White
Ursula Moray Williams

12-14

L J Adlington
Joan Aiken
Lloyd Alexander
David Almond
R J Anderson
Steve Augarde
Dominic Barker
Frank Beddor
Julie Bertagna
Thomas Bloor
Sarah Rees Brennan
John Brindley
N M Browne
Linda Buckley-Archer
Jenna Burtenshaw
Trudi Canavan
Maite Carranza
Philip Caveney
Sarwat Chadda
Henry Chancellor
Lucy Christopher
Eoin Colfer
B R Collins
Susan Cooper
Zizou Corder
D M Cornish

Alison Croggor
Marianne Curley
James Dashner
Timothee de Fombelle
Jeremy de Quidt
John Dickinson
Peter Dickinson
Helen Dunmore
Patricia Elliot
Sam Enthoven
Steve Feasey
Catherine Fisher
Pauline Fisk
John Flanagan
Charlie Fletcher
Cornelia Funke
Neil Gaiman
Sally Gardner
Alan Gibbons
Julia Golding
Alison Goodman
Michael Grant
Shannon and Dean Hale
Victoria Hanley
Frances Hardinge
Joanne Harris

Michelle Harrison
F E Higgins
Stuart Hill
Mary Hoffman
William Hussey
Brian Jacques
Robin Jarvis
Pete Johnson
Diana Wynne Jones
Brian Keaney
Conor Kostick
Derek Landy
Hope Larson
Rhiannon Lassiter
Stephen R Lawhead
Michael Lawrence
Ursula Le Guin
Tanith Lee
Sam Llewellyn
Cliff McNish
Catherine MacPhail
Margaret Mahy
Graham Marks
Zoë Marriott
Kai Meyer
Joshua Mowll

Genres

12-14 (cont)

Benjamin J Myers
Ted Naifeh
William Nicholson
Garth Nix
Kenneth Oppel
Sam Osman
James A Owen
Christopher Paolini
Michelle Paver
Terry Pratchett
Susan Price
Rebecca Promitzer
Sally Prue
Philip Pullman

Philip Reeve
Rick Riordan
Katherine Roberts
Mark Robson
J K Rowling
Michael Scott
Neal Shusterman
Nicky Singer
Sarah Singleton
Matthew Skelton
Justin Somper
Ali Sparkes
Paul Stewart

David Lee Stone
Jonathan Stroud
Marc Sumerak
Natsuki Takaya
G P Taylor
Kate Thompson
J R R Tolkien
Steve Voake
Beth Webb
David Whitley
Jeanette Winterson
Clive Woodall
Chris Wooding

14+

Clive Barker
Frank Beddor
Holly Black
Terry Brooks
Trudi Canavan
Cassandra Clare
B R Collins
Garth Ennis
Becca Fitzpatrick
Jostein Gaarder
Neil Gaiman

Alan Gibbons
Joanne Harris
Alyxandra Harvey
Lian Hearn
William Hussey
Curtis Jobling
Lauren Kate
Conor Kostick
Margo Lanagan
Stephen R Lawhead
Melissa Marr

Mike Mignola
Alan Moore
Nicola Morgan
Grant Morrison
Peadar Ó Guilín
Gillian Philip
Laura Powell
Terry Pratchett
Maggie Stiefvater
Kate Thompson
J R R Tolkien

Genres

5-7

Giles Andreae
Klaus Baumgart
Marc Brown
Ann Bryant
Ann Cameron
Harriet Castor
Emma Chichester Clark
Helen Cooper
John Cunliffe
Lucy Daniels
Alan Durant
Dorothy Edwards
Jonathan Emmett

Jan Fearnley
Anne Fine
Paul Fleischman
Joe Friedman
Maeve Friel
Mick Gowar
Bob Graham
Sally Grindley
Mary Hoffman
Oliver Jeffers
Neal Layton
Paeony Lewis
Astrid Lindgren

Hilary McKay
David McKee
Tiffany Mandrake
Beatrice Masini
Anna Maxted
Natasha May
Sue Mongredien
Jenny Oldfield
Tony Ross
Wendy Smith
Anna Wilson
Bob Wilson
Jane Yolen

Genres

8-11

Louise Arnold
Ros Asquith
David Bedford
Ann Bryant
Meg Cabot
Katie Davies
Helen Dunmore
Catherine Fisher
Charlie Fletcher
Yanker Glatshteyn
David Grimstone

Geri Halliwell
Meg Harper
Rose Impey
Cindy Jefferies
Liz Kessler
Clive King
Dick King-Smith
Jeff Kinney
Karen McCombie
Anthony McGowan
Kelly McKain

Beatrice Masini
Daisy Meadows
Tom Palmer
Sara Pennypacker
Helena Pielichaty
Caroline Plaisted
Bali Rai
David Walliams
Holly Webb
Anna Wilson
Henry Winkler

12-14

Randa Abdel-Fattah
David Almond
Helen Bailey
Sophia Bennett
Ann Brashares
John Brindley
Kevin Brooks
Meg Cabot
Lucy Christopher
Rowan Coleman
B R Collins
Yvonne Collins and
    Sandy Rideout
Vanessa Curtis
Timothee de Fombelle
Grace Dent
Sarah Dessen

Sharon Dogar
Jenny Downham
Charlie Fletcher
Catherine Forde
Echo Freer
Jamila Gavin
Maggi Gibson
Yanker Glatshteyn
Keith Gray
Victoria Hanley
Chris Higgins
S E Hinton
Mary Hooper
Paul Jennings
Sue Limb
Karen McCombie
Robert Muchamore

James Patterson
Bali Rai
Louise Rennison
Liz Rettig
James Riordan
Rosie Rushton
Dyan Sheldon
Nicky Singer
Ali Sparkes
Jerry Spinelli
Jonathan Stroud
Natsuki Takaya
Jean Ure
Karen Wallace
David Walliams
Lee Weatherly
Sarah Webb

14+

Randa Abdel-Fattah
Laurie Halse Anderson
Jay Asher
Sherry Ashworth
Julia Bell
Libba Bray
Suzanne Bugler
Julie Burchill
Kate Cann
B R Collins
Melissa de la Cruz

Grace Dent
Siobhan Dowd
Jenny Downham
Catherine Forde
Linzi Glass
Sandra Glover
Keith Gray
John Green
Julia Green
Alyxandra Harvey
James Jauncey

Joanna Kenrick
Kate le Vann
Saci Lloyd
Carolyn Mackler
Jaclyn Moriarty
Joyce Carol Oates
Julie Anne Peters
Bali Rai
Louise Rennison
Cecily von Ziegesar
Gabrielle Zevin

14+

Hanna Jansen

5-7

Tony Bradman
Penny Dolan
David Melling

Hilda Offen
Daniel Postgate

Chris Powling
Dee Shulman

8-11

Joan Aiken
R J Anderson
Louise Arnold
Matt Crossick
Joseph Delaney
Neil Gaiman
Harriet Goodwin
John Gordon
Mary Hooper

Eva Ibbotson
Julia Jarman
Pete Johnson
Diana Wynne Jones
Daren King
Derek Landy
Penelope Lively
David Melling
Chris Mould

Andrew Newbound
Jenny Nimmo
Chris Powling
Chris Priestley
Justin Richards
Robert Swindells
Kate Thompson
Jean Ure
Robert Westall

12-14

L J Adlington
Joan Aiken
David Almond
Tom Becker
Sarah Rees Brennan
Maite Carranza
Joseph Delaney
Peter Dickinson
Patricia Elliott
Steve Feasey
Catherine Fisher
Echo Freer

Neil Gaiman
Helen Grant
Claudia Gray
Ann Halam
Julie Hearn
William Hussey
Paul Jennings
Catherine Jinks
Pete Johnson
Brian Keaney
Rhiannon Lassiter
Cliff McNish

Eden Maguire
Susan Price
Chris Priestley
Celia Rees
E E Richardson
Marcus Sedgwick
Sarah Singleton
L J Smith
Ali Sparkes
Jonathan Stroud
Robert Westall

14+

Kelley Armstrong
Tim Bowler
Rachel Caine
P C & Kristin Cast
Cassandra Clare
Alex Duval
Becca Fitzpatrick
Sandra Glover

Helen Grant
Claudia Gray
Rachel Hawthorne
William Hussey
Catherine Jinks
Lauren Kate
Richelle Mead

Stephenie Meyer
Alyson Noel
Deborah Noyes
Darren Shan
Maggie Stiefvater
Kate Thompson
Scott Westerfeld

Genres

Historical

C is Century • M is Medieval • R is Roman
T is Tudor • V is Victorian • Vk is Viking

5-7

Laurence Anholt
John Grant
Damian Harvey

Julia Jarman T
Ann Jungman R
James Mayhew

Colin Thompson
Philip Wooderson

8-11

Paul Bajoria
Theresa Breslin
Linda Buckley-Archer
Frances
   Hodgson Burnett V
Grace Cavendish T
Susan Cooper
Cressida Cowell
Gillian Cross R
Kevin Crossley-Holland M
Terry Deary
Berlie Doherty
Paul Dowswell V
Sally Gardner
Adèle Geras

Julia Golding
René Goscinny R
David Grimstone R
Hergé
Mary Hooper
Julia Jarman
Deborah Kent
Elizabeth Laird
Katherine Langrish Vk
Caroline Lawrence R
Joan Lennon
Geraldine McCaughrean
Hazel Marshall
Michael Molloy V

Michael Morpurgo
Richard Platt
Chris Priestley
Philip Pullman V
Anthony Read V
Katherine Roberts
Paul Shipton
Dugald Steer
Paul Stewart
David Lee Stone R
Rosemary Sutcliff M R
Kate Thompson R
Karen Wallace
Pat Walsh

Genres

12-14

Joan Aiken
Laurie Halse Anderson
Paul Bajoria
Lynne Reid Banks
Ian Beck V
Chris Bradford
Theresa Breslin
N M Browne R
Linda Buckley-Archer
Grace Cavendish T
Henry Chancellor
Pauline Chandler R Vk
Susan Cooper T
Kevin Crossley-Holland M
John Dickinson
Berlie Doherty
Jennifer Donnelly
Paul Dowswell C16th V
Eve Edwards T
Patricia Elliott C18th

Nancy Farmer Vk
John Flanagan
Michael Ford
Sally Gardner C17th
Jamila Gavin
Adèle Geras
Julia Golding
K M Grant
Julie Hearn
F E Higgins V
Nigel Hinton
Mary Hoffman
Mary Hooper
William Hussey
Eva Ibbotson
Lucy Jago T
Ben Jeapes
Marie-Louise Jensen
Brian Keaney
Elizabeth Laird

Tanya Landman
Hope Larson
Caroline Lawrence R
Y S Lee V
Michelle Magorian
Carolyn Meyer
Michael Molloy
Nicola Morgan
Michael Morpurgo
Joanne Owen
K M Peyton
Chris Priestley
Alison Prince V
Sally Prue
Philip Pullman V
Celia Rees
Philip Reeve
Ann Rinaldi
Rick Riordan
Malcolm Rose

12-14 (cont)

Sarah Singleton
Matthew Skelton
Robert Swindells
Mildred D Taylor
Kate Thompson

Theresa Tomlinson
Ann Turnbull C17th
Eleanor Updale
Karen Wallace
Beth Webb

Catherine Webb
Robert Westall
Scott Westerfeld
Rick Yancey V

14+

Libba Bray V
Anna Godbersen
Ben Haggarty
Julie Hearn V
Lian Hearn

William Hussey
Catherine Jinks
Stephen R Lawhead
Graham Marks V

Nicola Morgan
Bryan Talbot
Ann Turnbull
Lili Wilkinson

Holocaust

8-11

Yanker Glatshteyn

12-14

Sharon Dogar
Yanker Glatshteyn
Morris Gleitzman
Jerry Spinelli
Markus Zusak

14+

Art Spiegelman

Homosexuality

14+

Julie Burchill
Joanna Kenrick

Julie Anne Peters
Lili Wilkinson

Horror

8-11

Tommy Donbavand
Barry Hutchison
Derek Landy
Sam Llewellyn

Sebastian Rook
Nick Shadow
Justin Somper

Paul Stewart
R L Stine
Di Toft

12-14

Tom Becker
Thomas Bloor
Sarwat Chadda
Stephen Cole
Tommy Donbavand

Steve Feasey
Catherine Fisher
Alan Gibbons
Roderick Gordon and
    Brian Williams

Helen Grant
Ann Halam
Anthony Horowitz
William Hussey
Rhiannon Lassiter

Genres

12-14 (cont)

Cliff McNish
Chris Priestley
Celia Rees
E E Richardson

Darren Shan
Sarah Singleton
Justin Somper
R L Stine

G P Taylor
Steve Voake
Chris Wooding
Rick Yancey

14+

Clive Barker
Kate Cann
Dean Vincent Carter
Garth Ennis
Jack Gantos
Helen Grant

Rachel Hawthorne
Charlie Higson
William Hussey
Curtis Jobling
Stephenie Meyer
Mike Mignola

Grant Morrison
Peadar Ó Guilín
Christopher Pike
Darren Shan
Maggie Stiefvater

Humour

5-7

Anne Adeney
Allan Ahlberg
Jenny Alexander
Jonathan Allen
Scoular Anderson
Sorrel Anderson
Giles Andreae
Laurence Anholt
Dosh Archer
Philip Ardagh
Ronda and
    David Armitage
Atinuke
Simon Bartram
Martyn Beardsley
Emily Bearn
David Bedford
Stan and
    Jan Berenstain
Terence Blacker
Andy Blackford
Jon Blake
Tony Bradman
Raymond Briggs
Joyce Lankester Brisley
Michael Broad
Marc Brown

Keith Brumpton
Ann Bryant
Janet Burchett and
    Sara Vogler
Nick Butterworth
Ann Cameron
Humphrey Carpenter
Anne Cassidy
Lauren Child
Emma Chichester Clark
Helen Cooper
Paul Cooper
Andrew Cope
June Crebbin
John Cunliffe
Chris d'Lacey
Roald Dahl
Ted Dewan
Lynley Dodd
Penny Dolan
Malachy Doyle
Alan Durant
P D Eastman
Dorothy Edwards
Jonathan Emmett
Ian Falconer
Jan Fearnley

Paul Fleischman
Vivian French
Maeve Friel
Mick Gowar
Bob Graham
Sue Graves
Emily Gravett
Kes Gray
Mini Grey
Stella Gurney
Damian Harvey
Mary Hoffman
Shirley Hughes
Rose Impey
Mick Inkpen
Oliver Jeffers
Ann Jungman
Daren King
Dick King-Smith
Satoshi Kitamura
Karina Law
Michael Lawrence
Astrid Lindgren
Sam Lloyd
Alan MacDonald
Megan McDonald
Hilary McKay

Genres

5-7 (cont)

David McKee
Colin McNaughton
Tiffany Mandrake
James Marshall
Anna Maxted
David Melling
Barbara Mitchelhill
Tony Mitton
Sue Mongredien
Bel Mooney
Maggie Moore
Jill Murphy
Martine Murray
Margaret Nash
Laura North
Hilda Offen
Jenny Oldfield
Hiawyn Oram
David Orme
Laura Owen
Dav Pilkey

Daniel Postgate
Jillian Powell
Chris Powling
Alf Prøysen
Russell Punter
Simon Puttock
Shoo Rayner
Chris Riddell
Hilary Robinson
Frank Rodgers
Alan Rusbridger
Margaret Ryan
Louis Sachar
Dr Seuss
Nick Sharratt
Hannah Shaw
Dyan Sheldon
Dee Shulman
Francesca Simon
Mark Skelton
Sophie Smiley

Wendy Smith
Andy Stanton
Paul Stewart
Joan Stimson
Jeremy Strong
Julie Sykes
Valerie Thomas
Jill Tomlinson
Kaye Umansky
Jenny Valentine
Barrie Wade
Karen Wallace
Colin West
Ian Whybrow
Jeanne Willis
Bob Wilson
David Henry Wilson
Jacqueline Wilson
Philip Wooderson
Jane Yolen

8-11

Allan Ahlberg
Giles Andreae
Laurence Anholt
Roy Apps
Philip Ardagh
Ros Asquith
E D Baker
Dominic Barker
Steve Barlow and
    Steve Skidmore
Guy Bass
Martyn Beardsley
Betty G Birney
Terence Blacker
Judy Blume
Frank Cottrell Boyce
Tony Bradman
Christiana Brand
Herbie Brennan
Theresa Breslin
Raymond Briggs

Ann Bryant
Annette Butterworth
Betsy Byars
Georgia Byng
Simon Cheshire
Lauren Child
Steve Cole
Eoin Colfer
Andrew Cope
Cressida Cowell
Sharon Creech
Richmal Crompton
Gillian Cross
Matt Crossick
Roald Dahl
Katie Davies
Terry Deary
Joshua Doder
Tommy Donbavand
Roddy Doyle
Heather Dyer

John Fardell
Anne Fine
Neil Gaiman
Jack Gantos
Morris Gleitzman
Debi Gliori
René Goscinny
Kes Gray
Andy Griffiths
Mark Haddon
Meg Harper
Charlie Higson
Michael Hoeye
Mary Hooper
Anthony Horowitz
Eva Ibbotson
Rose Impey
Oliver Jeffers
Ceci Jenkinson
Paul Jennings
Pete Johnson

Genres

8-11 (cont)

Gene Kemp
Daren King
Dick King-Smith
Jeff Kinney
Michael Lawrence
Sam Llewellyn
Lois Lowry
Karen McCombie
Alan MacDonald
Megan McDonald
Anthony McGowan
Kelly McKain
Hilary McKay
Jill Marshall
Anna Maxted
David Melling
Livi Michael

Barbara Mitche hill
Chris Mould
Jill Murphy
Andrew Norriss
Ian Ogilvy
Jenny Oldfield
Wendy Orr
Dav Pilkey
Chris Powling
Terry Pratchett
Shoo Rayner
Philip Reeve
Philip Ridley
Rick Riordan
Jamie Rix
Margaret Rycn
Louis Sachar

Marcus Sedgwick
Dyan Sheldon
Paul Shipton
Francesca Simon
Mark Skelton
Charlie Small
Lemony Snicket
Andy Stanton
Geronimo Stilton
Jeremy Strong
Shaun Tan
Di Toft
P L Travers
Kaye Umansky
David Walliams
Jacqueline Wilson
Henry Winkler

12-14

Ros Asquith
Dominic Barker
Terence Blacker
Frank Cottrell Boyce
Herbie Brennan
Meg Cabot
Eoin Colfer
Tim Collins
Vanessa Curtis
Grace Dent
Tommy Donbavand
Anne Fine
Echo Freer
Neil Gaiman

Matt Groening
Mark Haddon
Carl Hiaasen
Mary Hogan
Cathy Hopkins
Anthony Horowitz
Paul Jennings
Catherine Jirks
Jeff Kinney
Sue Limb
Karen McCombie
Anthony McGowan
Hilary McKay
Terry Pratchett

Sally Prue
Bali Rai
Louise Rennison
Rosie Rushton
Louis Sachar
Jeff Smith
David Lee Stone
Jeremy Strong
Sue Townsend
Jenny Valentine
David Walliams
Jacqueline Wilson
Kay Woodward
Rachel Wright

14+

Sherman Alexie
Tim Collins
Grace Dent
Jack Gantos
Catherine Jinks

Anthony McGowan
Mike Mignola
Jaclyn Moriarty
Joanna Nadin

Terry Pratchett
Louise Rennison
Sue Townsend
John van de Ruit

Genres

8-11

John Boyne	Candy Gourlay
Lucy Christopher	Suzanne LaFleur

12-14

John Boyne	Damian Kelleher	Linda Newbery
Lucy Christopher	Ann Kelley	Sally Nicholls
Vanessa Curtis	Suzanne LaFleur	Louis Sachar
Julia Donaldson	Anthony McGowan	Lee Weatherly
Jenny Downham		

14+

Jenny Downham	Alice Kuipers	Linda Newbery
Hilary Freeman	Anthony McGowan	Tabitha Suzuma

Immigration

12-14
Cathy Cassidy

14+
David Belbin

Letters

5-7
Ian Whybrow

8-11
Herbie Brennan
Sally Grindley
Helena Pielichaty
Jean Ure

14+
Jaclyn Moriarty

Genres

Magic

5-7

Jonathan Allen	Maeve Friel	Sue Mongredien
Scoular Anderson	Bob Graham	Jill Murphy
Terence Blacker	Emily Gravett	Jenny Nimmo
Malorie Blackman	Damian Harvey	Hilda Offen
Ann Bryant	Julia Jarman	Jenny Oldfield
Janet Burchett and	Ann Jungman	Hiawyn Oram
Sara Vogler	Elizabeth Lindsay	Laura Owen
Darcey Bussell	Alan MacDonald	Alf Prøysen
Humphrey Carpenter	Kelly McKain	Gwyneth Rees
Linda Chapman	Tiffany Mandrake	Frank Rodgers
Hayley Daze	Daisy Meadows	Michael Rosen
Jonathan Emmett	David Melling	Margaret Ryan

5-7 (cont)

Dyan Sheldon
Wendy Smith
Shaun Tan

Valerie Thomas
Jill Tomlinson
Kaye Umansky

Summer Waters
Holly Webb

8-11

R J Anderson
E D Baker
Pseudonymous Bosch
Theresa Breslin
Darcey Bussell
Linda Chapman
Louise Cooper
Anna Dale
Joseph Delaney
Kate di Camillo
Fiona Dunbar
Heather Dyer
Jackie French
Maeve Friel
Sally Gardner

Alan Garner
Debi Gliori
Matt Haig
Erin Hunter
Ceci Jenkinson
Diana Wynne Jones
Elizabeth Kay
Liz Kessler
Elizabeth Lindsay
Alan MacDonald
Ross Mackenzie
Daisy Meadows
David Melling
Chris Mould
Jill Murphy

Laura Owen
Sarah Prineas
Alf Prøysen
Gwyneth Rees
Philip Ridley
J K Rowling
Angie Sage
Kate Saunders
Marcus Sedgwick
Dyan Sheldon
Dugald Steer
P L Travers
Kaye Umansky
Pat Walsh
Cat Weatherill

12-14

R J Anderson
Steve Augarde
Pseudonymous Bosch
Trudi Canavan
Marianne Curley
Joseph Delaney
Sally Gardner
Victoria Hanley
Diana Wynne Jones

Hope Larson
Ursula Le Guin
Cliff McNish
Kai Meyer
Ted Naifeh
James Patterson
Aprilynne Pike
E E Richardson

J K Rowling
Michael Scott
Marcus Sedgwick
Sarah Singleton
Matthew Skelton
G P Taylor
Cate Tiernan
Beth Webb

14+

Kelley Armstrong
Libba Bray

Trudi Canavan
Neil Gaiman

8-11

Jeff Stone

12-14

Chris Bradford
Sam Enthoven
Jane Prowse

Genres

8-11

Pseudonymous Bosch
John Fardell

Catherine Fisher
Paul Haven

Sam Osman
Trenton Lee Stewart

12-14

Alison Allen-Gray
Gill Arbuthnott
Paul Bajoria
Pseudonymous Bosch
N M Browne
Philip Caveney
Suzanne Collins
Julia Donaldson

Siobhan Dowd
Helen Grant
F E Higgins
Lucy Jago
Michael Lawrence
Nicola Morgan
Joanne Owen
Rebecca Promitzer

Marcus Sedgwick
Trenton Lee Stewart
Shaun Tan
Jenny Valentine
David Whitley
Sarah Wray
Tim Wynne-Jones

14+

Kevin Brooks
Suzanne Collins

Helen Grant
Mal Peet

Laura Powell

5-7

Damian Harvey
Maggie Moore
Laura North

Saviour Pirotta
Martin Waddell

Barrie Wade
Karen Wallace

8-11

Steve Barlow and
   Steve Skidmore
Kevin Crossley-Holland
Terry Deary

Harriet Goodwin
Ted Hughes
Rick Riordan
Katherine Roberts

Paul Shipton
Rosemary Sutcliff
T H White

12-14

N M Browne
Philip Caveney
Zizou Corder
Nancy Farmer

Michael Ford
Sally Nicholls
Susan Price

Rick Riordan
Katherine Roberts
Rick Yancey

14+

Joanne Harris

Stephen R Lawhead

Other cultures

5-7
Atinuke
Ann Cameron
Stella Gurney

Mary Hoffman
Julia Jarman
Astrid Lindgren

Margaret Nash
Shaun Tan

8-11
Bob Cattell
Narinder Dhami
Sally Grindley

Elizabeth Laird
Joshua Mowll

Bali Rai
Sandi Toksvig

12-14
Randa Abdel-Fattah
Lynne Reid Banks
Gillian Cross
Narinder Dhami
Deborah Ellis
Jamila Gavin

Armin Greder
Philip Gross
Elizabeth Laird
Adeline Yen Mah
Kai Meyer
Joshua Mowll

Mal Peet
Bali Rai
Na'ima B Robert
Dyan Sheldon
Suzanne Fisher Staples
Shaun Tan

14+
Randa Abdel-Fattah
Faïza Guène
Lian Hearn

Bali Rai
Marjane Satrapi
Jason Wallace

Matt Whyman
Benjamin Zephaniah

Other lands

5-7
Malorie Blackman
Elizabeth Singer Hunt

Mal Peet and
    Elspeth Graham

8-11
Chris Bradford
Kate di Camillo
Sally Gardner
Candy Gourlay

Paul Haven
Geraldine McCaughrean
Sam Osman

Mal Peet and
    Elspeth Graham
Lauren St John
Laura Ingalls Wilder

12-14
Randa Abdel-Fattah
Lynne Reid Banks
Chris Bradford
Deborah Ellis
Nancy Farmer
Sally Gardner

Candy Gourlay
Elizabeth Laird
Tanya Landman
Henning Mankell
Beverley Naidoo

Joanne Owen
Anna Perera
Suzanne Fisher Staples
Mildred D Taylor
Karen Wallace

14+

Rachel Caine
Linzi Glass
Helen Grant
Faïza Guène

Hanna Jansen
Graham Marks
Valerie Mendes
Marjane Satrapi

John van de Ruit
Jason Wallace
Lili Wilkinson

Philosophy

14+

Jostein Gaarder

Pony/horse

5-7	8-11	12-14
Linda Chapman	Lauren Brooke	Lauren Brooke
June Crebbin	Pippa Funnell	Stacy Gregg
Pippa Funnell	Stacy Gregg	Hope Larson
Elizabeth Lindsay	Jenny Oldfield	K M Peyton
Kelly McKain	Katherine Roberts	
	Anna Sewell	

Relationships

12-14

Gemma Malley

14+

Sarah Dessen
Hilary Freeman

Joanna Kenrick
Carolyn Mackler

Paul Magrs
Joanna Nadin

Romance

12-14

Ros Asquith
Helen Bailey
Malorie Blackman
Lauren Brooke
Ally Carter
Yvonne Collins and
  Sandy Rideout
Sarah Dessen
Jennifer Donnelly

Eve Edwards
Cathy Hopkins
Marie-Louise Jensen
Pete Johnson
Eden Maguire
Stephenie Meyer
Aprilynne Pike
Chloë Rayban

Louise Rennison
Liz Rettig
Rosie Rushton
Dyan Sheldon
L J Smith
Ann Turnbull
Jean Ure
Kay Woodward

Genres

Romance (cont)

14+

David Belbin
Suzanne Bugler
Sharon Dogar
Becca Fitzpatrick
Hilary Freeman
Anna Godbersen
John Green
Rachel Hawthorne
Lauren Kate

Kate le Vann
E Lockhart
Sophie McKenzie
Carolyn Mackler
Sarra Manning
Melissa Marr
Richelle Mead
Stephenie Meyer
Alyson Noel

Lauren Oliver
Louise Rennison
Liz Rettig
Helen Salter
Cynthia Leitich Smith
Maggie Stiefvater
Ann Turnbull
Jenny Valentine

School

5-7

Klaus Baumgart
Terence Blacker
Humphrey Carpenter
Rob Childs
Alan Durant
Anne Fine

Paul Fleischman
Pippa Goodhart
Stella Gurney
Neal Layton
Alan MacDonald
Tiffany Mandrake

Jenny Oldfield
Jillian Powell
Dyan Sheldon
Francesca Simon
Anna Wilson

8-11

Roy Apps
Blue Balliett
Betty G Birney
Judy Blume
Enid Blyton
Ann Bryant
Betsy Byars
Simon Cheshire
Lauren Child
Richmal Crompton
Gillian Cross
Matt Crossick

Narinder Dhami
Helen Dunmore
Anne Fine
Jack Gantos
Andy Griffiths
Geri Halliwell
Cindy Jefferies
Ceci Jenkinson
Gene Kemp
Jeff Kinney
Sam Llewellyn
Kelly McKair

Beatrice Masini
Jill Murphy
Helena Pielichaty
Bali Rai
Justin Richards
J K Rowling
Louis Sachar
Kate Saunders
Jean Ure
Anna Wilson
Henry Winkler

12-14

Ros Asquith
Terence Blacker
Frank Cottrell Boyce
Ally Carter
Cathy Cassidy
Gennifer Choldenko

Yvonne Collins and
   Sandy Rideout
Anne Fine
Bali Rai
J K Rowling

Dyan Sheldon
Jerry Spinelli
Marc Sumerak
Mark Walden
Karen Wallace

Genres

14+

David Belbin
Libba Bray
Kate Brian
Rachel Caine
P C & Kristin Cast
Stephen Chbosky

Beth Goobie
David Klass
E Lockhart
Catherine MacPhail
Richelle Mead
Jaclyn Moriarty

Joyce Carol Oates
Bali Rai
John van de Ruit
Cecily von Ziegesar
Jason Wallace

Science fiction

5-7

Malorie Blackman
David Orme

Paul Stewart
Jonny Zucker

8-11

Linda Buckley-Archer
Philip Caveney
Steve Cole
Jeanne DuPrau

Mark Haddon
Graham Marks
Jenny Nimmo
Andrew Norriss

S F Said
Robert Swindells
Steve Voake

12-14

L J Adlington
Alison Allen-Gray
Steve Augarde
Stephen Baxter
Ian Beck
T E Berry-Hart
Terence Blacker
Jason Bradbury
Andy Briggs
John Brindley
Patrick Cave
Emma Clayton
Stephen Cole
Suzanne Collins
James Dashner
John Dickinson

Sam Enthoven
Brian Falkner
Kat Falls
Roderick Gordon and
     Brian Williams
Matt Groening
Ben Jeapes
Conor Kostick
Tim Lott
Sophie McKenzie
Margaret Mahy
Gemma Malley
Benjamin J Myers
Garth Nix
Kenneth Oppel
James Patterson

Susan Price
Alex Scarrow
Neal Shusterman
Nicky Singer
Jeff Smith
Marc Sumerak
A G Taylor
Kate Thompson
David Thorpe
Steve Voake
Rachel Ward
Robert Westall
Scott Westerfeld
Jeanette Winterson
Chris Wooding

14+

Stephen Baxter
Suzanne Collins
John Dickinson
Garth Ennis
Charlie Higson
Conor Kostick
Margo Lanagan

Saci Lloyd
Tim Lott
Sophie McKenzie
Gemma Malley
Sam Mills
Alan Moore
Patrick Ness

Peadar Ó Guilín
Lauren Oliver
Susan Pfeffer
Nicky Singer
Rachel Ward
Scott Westerfeld

Genres

Sea/boats

8-11
Susan Cooper
Paul Dowswell
Helen Dunmore
Michael Molloy

12-14
Paul Dowswel

Slavery

12-14
Laurie Halse Anderson
Bernard Ashley

Pauline Chancler
Mal Peet

Ann Rinaldi
James Riordan

Social issues

8-11
Malorie Blackman
Georgia Byng
Cathy Cassidy
Chris d'Lacey
Siobhan Dowd
Jack Gantos

Alan Gibbons
Diana Hendry
Elizabeth Laird
Hilary McKay
Michael Morpurgo

Linda Newbery
Kenneth Oppel
Louis Sachar
David Walliams
Jacqueline Wilson

12-14
Randa Abdel-Fattah
David Almond
Laurie Halse Anderson
Bernard Ashley
Lynne Reid Banks
David Belbin
Sophia Bennett
Julie Bertagna
Terence Blacker
Malorie Blackman
Tim Bowler
John Boyne
Ann Brashares
Theresa Breslin
Andy Briggs
Kevin Brooks
Anne Cassidy
Cathy Cassidy
Patrick Cave
Gennifer Choldenko

Lucy Christopher
B R Collins
Gillian Cross
Vanessa Curtis
Sarah Dessen
Narinder Dhami
Peter Dickinson
Berlie Doherty
Julia Donaldson
Siobhan Dowd
Nancy Farmer
Anne Fine
Pauline Fisk
Catherine Forde
Alan Gibbons
Keith Gray
Armin Greder
Mark Haddon
Sonya Hartnett
Julie Hearn

Carl Hiaasen
Nigel Hinton
S E Hinton
Mary Hogan
Mary Hooper
Cathy Hopkins
Pete Johnson
Damian Kelleher
Ally Kennen
Elizabeth Laird
Rhiannon Lassiter
Tim Lott
Karen McCombie
Anthony McGowan
Hilary McKay
Catherine MacPhail
Margaret Mahy
Henning Mankell
Graham Marks
Benjamin J Myers

12-14 (cont)

Beverley Naidoo
Linda Newbery
Kenneth Oppel
James Patterson
Mal Peet
Anna Perera
K M Peyton
Helena Pielichaty
Alison Prince
Sally Prue
Philip Pullman
Bali Rai
Celia Rees

James Riordan
Na'ima B Robert
Malcolm Rose
Meg Rosoff
Rosie Rushton
Chris Ryan
Louis Sachar
Dyan Sheldon
Jerry Spinelli
Suzanne Fisher Staples
Jeremy Strong
Jonathan Stroud
Robert Swindells

Shaun Tan
Mildred D Taylor
Kate Thompson
David Thorpe
Jean Ure
Jenny Valentine
David Walliams
Lee Weatherly
Scott Westerfeld
Jacqueline Wilson
Tim Wynne-Jones
Markus Zusak

14+

Randa Abdel-Fattah
Sherman Alexie
Laurie Halse Anderson
Jay Asher
Sherry Ashworth
Nora Raleigh Baskin
Julia Bell
Malorie Blackman
Tim Bowler
Kevin Brooks
Suzanne Bugler
Julie Burchill
Melvin Burgess
Kate Cann
Anne Cassidy
Stephen Chbosky
B R Collins
Keren David
Melissa de la Cruz
Sharon Dogar
Siobhan Dowd
Stephen Emond
Judith Fathallah

Catherine Forde
Alan Gibbons
Linzi Glass
Sandra Glover
Beth Goobie
Keith Gray
Julia Green
Mark Haddon
Sonya Hartnett
Julie Hearn
Simmone Howell
J A Jarman
Ally Kennen
Joanna Kenrick
David Klass
Tim Lott
Anthony McGowan
Carolyn Mackler
Catherine MacPhail
Paul Magrs
Sarra Manning
Graham Marks
Sam Mills

Nicola Morgan
Jaclyn Moriarty
Patrick Ness
Linda Newbery
Joyce Carol Oates
Mal Peet
Julie Anne Peters
Gillian Philip
Laura Powell
Bali Rai
Meg Rosoff
Nicky Singer
Tabitha Suzuma
Bryan Talbot
Kate Thompson
Jenny Valentine
Cecily von Ziegesar
Jason Wallace
Scott Westerfeld
Matt Whyman
Lili Wilkinson
Benjamin Zephaniah

Genres

Space

5-7

Simon Bartram
Tony Bradman
Anna Maxted

8-11

Guy Bass
Mark Haddon
Joshua Mowl
Shoo Rayner

Sport

5-7

David Bedford
Judy Brown
Keith Brumpton

Janet Burchett and
   Sara Vogler
Rob Childs
Malachy Doyle

Alan Durant
Sophie Smiley
Martin Waddell
Bob Wilson

8-11

David Bedford
Terence Blacker
Chris Bradford
Tony Bradman
Bob Cattell

Rob Childs
Michael Coleman
Narinder Dhami
Alan Gibbons
Candy Gourlay

Barry Hutchison
Tom Palmer
Bali Rai
Jonny Zucker

12-14

Brian Falkner
Alan Gibbons

Candy Gourlay
Mal Peet

Theresa Tomlinson

14+

Nick Hornby

Mal Peet

Markus Zusak

Stage

8-11

Julia Golding
Noel Streatfeild

12-14

Rowan Coleman
Yvonne Collins and
   Sandy Rideout
Julia Golding

Superhero

14+

Garth Ennis

Neil Gaiman

Teen pregnancy

12-14
Berlie Doherty

14+
Malorie Blackman
Suzanne Bugler
Siobhan Dowd
Julia Green
Catherine MacPhail

Thrillers

8-11

Paul Bajoria	Catherine Fisher	Chris Priestley
Andy Baxter	H I Larry	Sebastian Rook
Cathy Cassidy	Dan Lee	Lauren St John
Alex Cliff	Graham Marks	Steve Voake
Gillian Cross	Tom Palmer	Mark Walden

12-14

R J Anderson	Julia Donaldson	Andy McNab and
Bernard Ashley	Patricia Elliott	Robert Rigby
Paul Bajoria	Sam Enthoven	Margaret Mahy
Ian Beck	Catherine Fisher	Graham Marks
Tom Becker	Catherine Forde	Stephenie Meyer
David Belbin	David Gilman	Robert Muchamore
Malorie Blackman	Julia Golding	Anna Perera
Tim Bowler	Helen Grant	Will Peterson
Jason Bradbury	Philip Gross	Philip Pullman
John Brindley	J A Henderson	Celia Rees
A J Butcher	Jack Higgins with	Ann Rinaldi
Anne Cassidy	Justin Richards	Malcolm Rose
Cathy Cassidy	Charlie Higson	Chris Ryan
Patrick Cave	Nigel Hinton	Craig Simpson
Stephen Cole	Anthony Horowitz	R L Stine
Eoin Colfer	Ben Jeapes	Robert Swindells
B R Collins	Ally Kennen	Steve Voake
Joe Craig	Conor Kostick	Mark Walden
Gillian Cross	Y S Lee	Sarah Wray
James Dashner	Geraldine McCaughrean	Tim Wynne-Jones
Jeremy de Quidt	Sophie McKenzie	Rick Yancey

14+

Bernard Ashley	Kate Cann	Monika Feth
Sherry Ashworth	Dean Vincent Carter	Catherine Forde
Malorie Blackman	Anne Cassidy	Helen Grant
Tim Bowler	Keren David	James Jauncey

Genres

Thrillers (cont)

14+ (cont)

Lauren Kate
Ally Kennen
Conor Kostick
Andy McNab
Catherine MacPhail

Gemma Malley
Graham Marks
Sam Mills
Kate Morgenroth

Craig Simpson
Tabitha Suzuma
Rachel Ward
Matt Whyman

Time travel

5-7

Mark Skelton

8-11

Sophie McKenzie
Graham Marks
Mark Skelton

12-14

Linda Buckley-Archer
Henry Chancellor
Susan Cooper
Ben Jeapes
Michael Lawrence
Alex Scarrow

Toys

5-7

Mick Inkpen

Michael Rosen

Traditional

5-7

Anne Fine
Rose Impey
Geraldine McCaughrean

Mal Peet and
    Elspeth Graham

Russell Punter
Barrie Wade

8-11

Kevin Crossley-Holland   Mal Peet and Elspeth Graham

Transport

5-7

Jenny Alexander

Benedict Blathwayt

Jon Scieszka

8-11

Roy Apps	Tommy Donbavand	Pete Johnson

12-14

Tom Becker	Catherine Jinks	L J Smith
Tim Collins	Stephenie Meyer	G P Taylor
Claudia Gray	Darren Shan	Scott Westerfeld

14+

Rachel Caine	Claudia Gray	Christopher Pike
P C & Kristin Cast	Matt Haig	Darren Shan
Cassandra Clare	Alyxandra Harvey	Cynthia Leitich Smith
Tim Collins	Catherine Jinks	L J Smith
Alex Duval	Richelle Mead	Scott Westerfeld

WWI 1914-18 • WWII 1939-45

5-7

Shirley Hughes WWII

8-11

Steve Augarde	Morris Gleitzman WWII	Michael Morpurgo WWI/II
Nina Bawden WWII	Dennis Hamley WWII	Linda Newbery WWII
Thomas Bloor WWII	Anne Holm WWII	Ian Serraillier WWII
Terry Deary WWII	Judith Kerr	Robert Swindells WWII
Paul Dowswell	Sophie McKenzie WWII	Sandi Toksvig WWII
Jackie French WWII	Michelle Magorian WWII	Robert Westall WWII
Yanker Glatshteyn WWII		

12-14

L J Adlington WWII	Morris Gleitzman WWII	Mal Peet WWII
Bernard Ashley	Shannon and Dean Hale	James Riordan WWII
Thomas Bloor WWII	Sonya Hartnett WWII	Meg Rosoff
John Boyne WWII	Michelle Magorian WWII	Craig Simpson WWII
Theresa Breslin WWI	Adeline Yen Mah WWII	Jerry Spinelli WWII
Sharon Dogar WWII	Andy McNab and	Robert Swindells WWII
Paul Dowswell WWII	Robert Rigby	Robert Westall WWII
Jim Eldridge	Michael Morpurgo WWI/II	Scott Westerfeld
Deborah Ellis	Robert Muchamore WWII	Markus Zusak WWII
Yanker Glatshteyn WWII	Linda Newbery WWI/II	

14+

Aidan Chambers WWII	Patrick Ness	Craig Simpson WWII
Sharon Dogar WWII	Linda Newbery WWI/II	Benjamin Zephaniah
Jim Eldridge	Mal Peet WWII	Markus Zusak WWII
Andy McNab	Meg Rosoff	

Genres

Graphic Novels

As mentioned in the previous edition of Who Next...?, graphic novels have become a major part of children's publishing with many successful authors and illustrators of adult graphic novels producing successful children's titles. Publishers also continue to reformat already popular titles and TV characters into graphic novels and these continue to attract boys to reading.

In this edition we have included some titles for older readers. This means that some of the material may depict violent scenes, as well as dealing with difficult subject matter. For more information on the genre, please look up the individual authors in the relevant age group.

Please be aware that the quality and suitability of an individual book may vary because many series have a number of different authors and illustrators.

For more information generally on graphic novels and up to date lists of other titles please visit: www.dr-mel-comics.co.uk/sources run by Mel Gibson, a UK based comics scholar and consultant.

5-7

Ben 10	Ben 10 Comic Books Series
David Orme	Boffin Boy Series
Philip Wooderson	Arf and the Metal Detector

8-11

David Almond	The Savage
Raymond Briggs	Father Christmas Fungus and the Bogeyman
Rob Childs	Moving the Goalposts
Eoin Colfer	Arctic Incident
René Goscinny	Asterix Series
Hergé	Tintin Series
Erin Hunter	Warriors Manga: Seekers Series Warriors: Manga Series
Geronimo Stilton	Geronimo Stilton
J R R Tolkien	The Hobbit

Frank Beddor	*Looking Glass Wars Series*
Meg Cabot	*Avalon High*
Eoin Colfer	*Arctic Incident* *Artemis Fowl*
Neil Gaiman	*Coraline*
Armin Greder	*The City* *The Island*
Matt Groening	*Futurama Series* *The Simpsons Series*
Shannon and Dean Hale	*Calamity Jack* *Rapunzel's Revenge*
Anthony Horowitz	*Killer Camera* *Point Blanc* *Stormbreaker*
Hope Larson	*Gray Horses* *Mercury* *Salamander Dream*
Ted Naifeh	*Courtney Cumrin Series* *Polly and the Pirates Series*
James Patterson	*Maximum Ride Manga Series*
Terry Pratchett	*Guards! Guards!*
Darren Shan	*The Saga of Darren Shan Series*
Jeff Smith	*Bone Series* *Shazam! The Monster Society of Evil*
Marc Sumerak	*Hulk Powerpack Series* *X-Men Powerpack Series*
Natsuki Takaya	*Fruits Basket Series* *Phantom Dream Series* *Tsubasa Series*
Shaun Tan	*The Arrival* *Eric*
J R R Tolkien	*The Hobbit*

Graphic novels

Frank Beddor	*Hatter M Series* *Looking Glass Wars Series*
Holly Black	*Good Neighbors Series*
Garth Ennis	*Dan Dare* *Ghost Rider Series* *The Punisher Series*
Neil Gaiman	*Batman: Whatever Happened to the Caped Crusader?* *Coraline* *Eternals* *Marvel 1602* *The Sandman Series*
Ben Haggarty	*Mezolith*
Shannon and Dean Hale	*Calamity Jack* *Rapunzel's Revenge*
Melissa Marr	*Wicked Lovely Tokyopop Series*
Mike Mignola	*Hellboy Series*
Alan Moore	*Captain Britain* *Tom Strong Series* *V For Vendetta* *Watchman*
Grant Morrison	*All Star Superman* *Arkham Asylum* *Emergency Stop* *Gothic* *World War III*
Terry Pratchett	*Guards! Guards!*
Marjane Satrapi	*Persepolis*
Darren Shan	*The Saga of Darren Shan Series*
Art Spiegelman	*Maus and Maus II*
Bryan Talbot	*Alice in Sunderland* *The Tale of One Bad Rat*

Graphic novels

Short Stories

8-11

Louise Cooper	*Short and Scary*
	Short and Spooky
Kevin Crossley-Holland	*Outsiders*
Paul Jennings	*Uncovered!*
	Unreal!
	Unseen!
Chris Mould	*Fangs 'n' Fire*

12-14

Kevin Crossley-Holland	*Outsiders*
Berlie Doherty	*Running on Ice*
Neil Gaiman	*M is for Magic*
Alan Gibbons	*Dark Spaces and Other Stories*
Anthony Horowitz	*More Bloody Horowitz*
Beverley Naidoo	*Out of Bounds*
J K Rowling	*The Tales of Beedle the Bard*
Shaun Tan	*Tales from Outer Suburbia*

14+

Sarah Dessen	*Infinity*
Neil Gaiman	*M is for Magic*
Margo Lanagan	*Red Spikes*
	White Time

Current Children's Book Prizes

For this edition we have updated those awards listed in previous books and added a new list of awards which are currently in place (probably not exhaustive!). Many local Schools Library Services and public library authorities run ballots locally, involving young people within their areas in voting for their favourite children's books in various categories. Details about all those awards appearing below are easily accessible by entering the name of the award into a search engine.

Bedfordshire Children's Book of the Year

Berkshire Children's Book Award

Best New Illustrators Award

Bisto Book of the Year Awards (CBI - Children's Books Ireland)

Bolton Children's Book Award

Booktrust Early Years Awards

Booktrust Teenage Prize

Calderdale Children's Book Awards

Cambridgeshire Children's Picture Book Award (Read it Again!)

Coventry Inspiration Book Awards

Doncaster Book Award

Dundee City of Discovery Picture Book Award

East Sussex Children's Book Award

English 4-11 Book Awards
(for the best illustrated children's books of the year)

Essex Book Award

Falkirk RED (Read Enjoy Debate) Children's Book Award

Frances Lincoln Diverse Voices Children's Book Award

Gateshead Children's Book Award

Grampian Children's Book Award

Hampshire Book Award

Hampshire Illustrated Book Award

Heart of Hawick Children's Book Award

Kelpies Prize (new Scottish writing for children)

Lancashire Children's Book of the Year

Lincolnshire Young People's Book Award

Marsh Award for Children's Literature in Translation

Norfolk Children's Book Awards

Northern Ireland Book Award

Nottingham Children's Book Award

Phoenix Book Award (London Borough of Lambeth)

Portsmouth Book Awards

Redbridge Children's Book Awards

Renfrewshire Children's Book Award

Roald Dahl Funny Prize

Salford Children's Book Award

Scottish Royal Mail Children's Book Awards

Sefton Super Reads Award

Southern Schools Book Award

Southwark Book Award

Staffordshire Young Teen Fiction Award

Stockport Schools' Book Awards

Stockton Children's Book of the Year

Tower Hamlets Book Award

UKLA (UK Literacy Association) Children's Book Award

West Sussex Children's Book Award

Hans Christian Andersen Awards · Biennial

The highest international recognition given to authors and illustrators, these awards are presented to those whose complete works have made a lasting contribution to children's literature. The nominations are made by the national sections of IBBY, an international jury of children's literature specialists select winners and the awards are presented during the biennial IBBY Congress. For further information contact: International Board on Books for Young People, Nonmenwag 12, Postfach CH-4003-Basel, Switzerland, tel: (+4161) 272 2917, email: ibby@eye.ch.

	Author	Illustrator
2010	David Almond, UK	Jutta Bauer, Germany
2008	Jürg Schubiger, Switzerland	Roberto Innocenti, Italy

Angus Book Award · Annual

An Angus-wide initiative to encourage pupils aged 13/15 to read and enjoy quality teenage fiction. From January to May, third year pupils read the five titles shortlisted by teachers and librarians from books written by UK resident authors and published in paperback in the preceding 12 months. The children discuss the books before they vote in a secret ballot. For further details contact: Moyra Hood, Education Support Officer Literacy, Bruce House Wellgate, Arbroath DD11 3TL tel: 01241 435008, email: hoodm@angus.gov.uk, www.angus.gov.uk/bookaward.

2010 *Numbers* by Rachel Ward (Chicken House)

2009 *Forget Me Not* by Anne Cassidy (Scholastic)

2008 *Leaving Poppy* by Kate Cann (Scholastic)

2007 *Candy* by Kevin Brooks (Chicken House)

Prizes

Launched in 2000, the Blue Peter Book Awards are run by the BBC children's programme Blue Peter. A celebrity judging panel selects the shortlists from paperback titles published in the UK in the previous year. These books are then read by Blue Peter Young Judges chosen as a result of a Blue Peter Book Review Competition. They chose the winners for each of three categories. From these three winning titles, a Book of the Year is selected. For further information: www.booktrust.org.uk/Prizes-and-awards/Blue-Peter-Book-Awards.

Prizes

2011 Favourite Story and the
Blue Peter Book of the Year Award 2011
(NB slight change to categories)
Dead Man's Cove (A Laura Marlin Mystery)
    by Lauren St John (Orion)

The Most Fun Story with Pictures
Lunatics and Luck (The Raven Mysteries)
    by Marcus Sedgwick illus. by Pete Williamson (Orion)

The Best Book with Facts
Do Igloos Have Loos? by Mitchell Symons (Doubleday)

2010 The Book I Couldn't Put Down and the
Blue Peter Book of the Year Award 2010
Frozen in Time by Ali Sparkes (OUP)

The Most Fun Story with Pictures
Dinkin Dings and the Frightening Things
    by Guy Bass illus. by Pete Williamson (Stripes)

The Best Book with Facts
Why Eating Bogeys is Good For You
    by Mitchell Symons (Doubleday)

The 2008/09 awards were merged to coincide with World Book Day
2009 The Book I Couldn't Put Down and the
Blue Peter Book of the Year Award 2009
Shadow Forest by Matt Haig (Corgi)

The Most Fun Story with Pictures
Mr Gum and the Dancing Bear
    by Andy Stanton illus. by David Tazzyman (Egmont)

The Best Book with Facts
Planet in Peril (Horrible Geography)
    by Anita Ganeri (Scholastic))

Blue Peter Children's Book Awards (cont) — Annual

2007 The Book I Couldn't Put down and the
Blue Peter Book of the Year Award 2007
The Outlaw Varjek Paw by S F Said (David Fickling)

The Most Fun Story with Pictures
You're a Bad Man, Mr Gum!
by Andy Stanton illus. by David Tazzyman (Egmont)

The Best Book with Facts
The Worst Children's Jobs in History
by Tony Robinson (Macmillan)

Branford Boase Award — Annual

This award began in 2000 and is in memory of two very important figures in the children's book world, both of whom died of cancer in 1999. Henrietta Branford was a talented, award-winning children's novelist and Wendy Boase was a passionate children's book editor who was the Editorial Director of Walker Books as well as being one of its founders. Sponsored by Dame Jacqueline Wilson OBE and also by Walker Books, this annual prize is awarded to the author and editor of an outstanding first-time novel for children.
For further details contact the administrator, Anne Marley,
tel: 01962 826658, email: anne.marley@tiscali.co.uk,
website: www.branfordboaseaward.org.uk.

2010 *Stolen* by Lucy Christopher (Chicken House)

2009 *The Traitor Game* by B R Collins (Bloomsbury)

2008 *Before I Die* by Jenny Downham (David Fickling)

2007 *A Swift Pure Cry* by Siobhan Dowd (David Fickling)

Carnegie and Greenaway Awards

The Carnegie and Kate Greenaway awards are presented annually by CILIP (Chartered Institute of Library and Information Professionals) and administered by the Youth Libraries Group of CILIP. Nominations are submitted by institute members and winners selected by a panel of 13 children's librarians from the Youth Libraries Group.

Established in 1936, the Carnegie Medal is given for an outstanding book for children. Contenders are appraised for characterisation, plot, style, accuracy, imaginative quality and that indefinable element that lifts the book above the others. The date of the award is based on the date that the books were published, not when the award is announced. Administered by: CILIP, 7 Ridgmount Street, London WC1E 7AE, email: ckg@cilip.org.uk, www.carnegiegreenaway.org.uk/carnegie

2010   *The Graveyard Book* by Neil Gaiman (Bloomsbury)

2009   *Bog Child* by Siobhan Dowd (David Fickling)

2008   *Here Lies Arthur* by Philip Reeve (Scholastic)

2007   *Just in Case* by Meg Rosoff (Penguin)

This award was instituted in 1955 and goes to an artist who has produced the most distinguished work in the illustration of children's books. Nominated books are assessed for design, format and production as well as artistic merit and must have been published in the UK during the previous year. Administered by: CILIP, 7 Ridgmount Street, London WC1E 7AE, email: ckg@cilip.org.uk, www.carnegiegreenaway.org.uk/greenaway

2010   Freya Blackwood   *Harry & Hopper*
                                      text by Margaret Wild (Scholastic)

2009   Catherine Rayner   *Harris Finds His Feet* (Little Tiger Press)

2008   Emily Gravett   *Little Mouse's Big Book of Fears* (Macmillan)

2007   Mini Grey   *The Adventures of the Dish and the Spoon* (Jonathan Cape)

The Children's Laureate is chosen every two years and is somebody who writes or illustrates books that young people love. Their books are the kind that you'll never give away, books you'll remember for the rest of your life. The Children's Laureate is a working prize intended to provide a platform for the winner to stimulate public discussion about the importance of children's literature and reading in a forward looking society.

2011   Julia Donaldson   2007   Michael Rosen

2009   Anthony Browne

Costa Children's Book of the Year Award   Annual

(formerly Whitbread)

The Whitbread awards started in 1971 and the first award for a children's novel was given in 1972. The format changed in 1985 when the Whitbread Book of the Year was launched, and in 1996, children's books were taken out of the main category and given a prize of their own. Costa took over the award in 2006. Entries must be by authors who have been resident in the UK or Eire for three years and whose book has been published between 1 November and 31 October of the year of the prize. The prize is £5,000. The winner is announced in January. 1999 was the first year the winner of the Whitbread Children's Book of the Year Award was also considered for the overall Whitbread Book of the Year Award, with a prize of £25,000. Main contact: Naomi Gane, The Bookseller's Association, tel: 020 7802 0801, email: naomi.gane@bookseller.org.uk

2010   *Out of Shadows* by Jason Wallace (Anderson)

2009   *The Ask and the Answer* by Patrick Ness (David Fickling)

2008   *Just Henry* by Michelle Magorian (Egmont)

2007   *The Bower Bird* by Ann Kelley (Luath Press)

Guardian Children's Fiction Award   Annual

The prize of £1,500 is awarded to an outstanding work of fiction for children (not picture books) written by a British or Commonwealth author and first published in the UK during the calendar year preceding the year in which the award is presented. Following publisher entry only, the winner is chosen by a panel of authors and the review editor for The Guardian's Children's Books section.

2010   *Ghost Hunter* by Michelle Paver (Orion)

2009   *Exposure* by Mal Peet (Walker)

2008   *The Knife of Never Letting Go* by Patrick Ness (David Fickling)

2007   *Finding Violet Park* by Jenny Valentine (Harper Collins)

NASEN/TES Book Award   Annual

This award is sponsored by the National Association for Special Educational Needs and the TES. The award, a prize of £500, is given to the book of any genre that most successfully provides a positive image of children or young people with special needs. The judges look for books that are well written and well presented and which can be appreciated by all children under the age of 16, not just those with special needs.

2009   *Running on the Cracks* by Julia Donaldson (Egmont)

2008   *Best Friends* illus. by Mark Chambers (Tango)

2007   *The London Eye Mystery* by Siobhan Dowd (David Fickling)

Annual — North East Book Award

Initiated in 1999, this prize is awarded to a book written by an author resident in the UK and first published in paperback. A shortlist of five titles is selected by local librarians and teachers in conjunction with Northumberland Schools Library Service and the final winner is chosen by Year 10 pupils from participating schools. For more information contact: Eileen Armstrong, Cramlington High School, Cramlington, Northumberland NE23 6BN, tel: 01670 712 311, fax: 01670 730 598, www.northeastbookaward.wordpress.com.

2009 *The Set-Up* by Sophie McKenzie (Simon & Schuster)

2008 *Ways to Live Forever* by Sally Nicholls (Marion Lloyd Books)

2007 *Skulduggery Pleasant* by Derek Landy (Harper Collins)

Annual — Red House Children's Book Award

The only major book prize in the UK decided by the readers. The award is made annually to the best work of fiction for children after hundreds of books have been read, digested and voted for, by children. The federation of Children's Book Groups co-ordinates the award, acting as an umbrella organisation for autonomous book groups across the UK. Children from within these book groups carry out initial reviewing, and eventually choose a shortlist of ten titles that all children can vote on. As well as deciding who the overall winner will be the votes cast determine three other categories: Book for Younger Children, Book for Younger Readers and Book for Older Readers.
Contact: www.redhousechildrensbookaward.co.uk, 2 Bridge Wood View, Horsforth, Leeds LS18 5PE.

2010 Book for Younger Children

Mondays are Murder by Tanya Landman (Walker)

Book for Younger Readers

Bottoms Up! by Jeanne Willis & Adam Stower (Penguin)

Book for Older Readers & Overall Winner

The Hunger Games by Suzanne Collins (Scholastic)

2009 Book for Younger Children

The Pencil by Allan Ahlberg & Bruce Ingham (Walker)

Book for Younger Readers

Daisy and the Trouble with Zoos by Kes Gray (Random House)

Book for Older Readers & Overall Winner

Blood Ties by Sophie McKenzie (Simon & Schuster)

Prizes

2008 Book for Younger Children
Penguin by Polly Dunbar (Walker)
Book for Younger Readers
Ottoline and the Yellow Cat by Chris Riddell (MacDonald)
Book for Older Readers & Overall Winner
Skulduggery Pleasant by Derek Landy (Harper Collins)

2007 Book for Younger Children
Who's in the Loo? by Jeanne Willis & Adrian Reynolds (Transworld)
Book for Younger Readers & Overal l Winner
You're a Bad Man, Mr Gum!
by Andy Stanton illus. by David Tazzyman (Egmont)
Book for Older Readers
Girl, Missing by Sophie McKenzie (Simon & Schuster)

Sheffield Children's Book Award   Annual

The Sheffield Children's Book Award began in 1989 and is presented annually to the book chosen as the most enjoyable by the children of Sheffield. The majority of the judges look at, read and vote on the shortlisted books within their class at school. There are three category winners and an overall winner. For further details contact: Jennifer Wilson (Book Award Co-ordinator), c/o Schools Library Service Sheffield, tel: 0114 250 6843, email: jennifer.wilson@sheffield.gov.uk.

2010 Picture Book & Overall Winner
Morris the Mankiest Monster
by Giles Andreae & Sarah McIntyre (Corgi)
Shorter Novel
Boom! by Mark Haddon (David Fickling)
Longer Novel
Gone by Michael Grant (Egmont)

2009 Picture Book & Overall Winner
Smelly Peter the Great Pea Eater
by Steve Smallman & Joelle Dreidemy (Little Tiger Press)
Shorter Novel
The Mum Shop by Ceci Jenkinson (Faber)
Longer Novel
Bog Child by Siobhan Dowd (David Fickling)

Prizes

2008 Picture Book

Aliens Love Underpants
by Claire Freedman & Ben Cort (Simon & Schuster)

Shorter Novel & Overall Winner

Beware! Killer Tomatoes by Jeremy Strong (Puffin)

Longer Novel

Before I Die by Jenny Downham (David Fickling)

2007 Picture Book & Overall Winner

Who's in the Loo? by Jeanne Willis & Adrian Reynolds
(Transworld)

Shorter Novel

Help! I'm a Classroom Gambler by Pete Johnson (Yearling)

Longer Novel

A Swift Pure Cry by Siobhan Dowd (David Fickling)

The Tir na n-Og Awards are three prizes of £1,000 awarded annually to acknowledge the work of authors and illustrators in three categories. These are Best Fiction of the Year (original Welsh-language novels, stories and picture-books are considered); Best Welsh-Language Non fiction Book of the Year; and Best English (Anglo-Welsh) Book of the Year (with an authentic Welsh background, fiction and non-fiction). Books must be published during the preceding year. For more details, contact the Administrators: Children's Books Department, Welsh Books Council, Castell Brychan, Aberystwyth SY23 2JB, tel: 01970 624 151 or fax: 01970 625 385, e-mail: wbc.children@wbc.org.uk.

2010 Best Welsh Fiction (Primary Sector)

Cyfres yr Onnen: Trwy'r Tonnau by Manon Steffan Ros (Y Lolfa)

Best Welsh Fiction (Secondary Sector)

Cyfres yr Onnen: Codi Bwganod by Rhiannon Wyn (Y Lolfa)

Best English Fiction

Dear Mr Author by Paul Manship (Pont)

2009 Best Wesh Fiction (Primary Sector)

Brownsio by Emily Huws (Cymdeithas Lyfran)

Best Welsh Fiction (Secondary Sector)

Annwyl Smotyn Bach by Lleuca Roberts (Cyfres y Dderwen)

Best English Fiction

Merlin's Magical Creatures by Graham Howells (Pont)

Prizes

Tir na n-Og Award (cont)   Annual

2008 Best Welsh Fiction (Primary Sector)
Y Llyfr Ryseitiau: Gwaed y Tylwyth
by Nicholas Daniels (Dref Wen)
Best Welsh Fiction (Secondary Sector)
Eira Mân, Eira Mawr by Gareth F Williams (Cyres Whap! Gomer)
Best English Fiction
Finding Minerva by Frances Thomas (Pont)

2007 Best Welsh Fiction (Primary Sector)
Ein Rhyfel Ni by Mair Wynn Jones (Gwas y Bwthyn)
Best Welsh Fiction (Secondary Sector)
Adref Heb Elin by Gareth F Williams (Cyfres Whap! Gomer)
Best English Fiction
Dark Tales From the Woods by Daniel Morden (Pont)

Wirral Paperback of the Year   Annual

Set up in 1995, this award is organised by the Wirral Schools Library Service. It aims to give young people from the area the chance to read exciting new fiction. The Schools Library Service chooses 20 titles, first published in paperback in the preceding year. Copies are lent to up to 20 local secondary schools. Year 8 and 9 pupils from each school choose their own shortlist and a Wirral shortlist is then compiled from these in May. Representatives from each school meet in July to discuss and vote for their favourite book. For further information contact: Wirral Schools Library Service, Wirral Education Centre, Acre Lane, Bromborough, Wirral CH62 7BZ, tel: 0151 346 6502, email: sls@wirral.gov.uk.

2010 *Unwind* by Neal Shusterman (Simon & Schuster)

2009 *Poison Study* by Maria V Snyder (MIRA)

2008 *My Swordhand is Singing* by Marcus Sedgwick (Orion)

2007 *Tamar* by Mal Peet (Walker)

Exploring Further and Keeping up to Date

Oxford Companion to Children's Literature   *1999*
Edited by Humphrey Carpenter and Mari Prichard
ISBN 9780198602286
Oxford University Press

The Cambridge Guide to Children's Books in English   *2001*
Edited by Victor Watson
ISBN 9780521550642
Cambridge University Press

Twentieth Century Children's Writers   *3rd ed 1989*
ISBN 9780912289953
St James Press (USA)

Children's Literature   *2001*
Peter Hunt
ISBN 0 631 21141 1
Blackwell

Great Books to Read Aloud   *2006*
Jacqueline Wilson
ISBN 978-0552554985
Corgi

Riveting Reads 6–8   *2006*
Prue Goodwin
ISBN 9781903446355
School Library Association

Riveting Reads 8–12   *2006*
Jo Sennitt
ISBN 9781903446300
School Library Association

Riveting Reads 12–16   *2006*
Eileen Armstrong
ISBN 9781903446324
School Library Association

Riveting Reads Plus: a View of the World   2006
Oxford Branch of the School Library Association
ISBN 9781903446348
School Library Association

Riveting Reads Plus: Everyone's Reading 11-18   2010
Eileen Armstrong
School Library Association
(Download available from the SLA website)

Riveting Reads Plus: Fantasy Fiction   2008
Frances Sinclair & School Library Association in Scotland
ISBN 9781903446461
School Library Association

Riveting Reads Plus: Boys into Books 5-11   2008
Chris Brown
ISBN 9781903446454
School Library Association

Riveting Reads Plus: Boys into Books   2007
Eileen Armstrong
ISBN 9781903446409
School Library Association

Riveting Reads Plus: Book Ahead 0-7   2008
Julia Eccleshare
ISBN 9781903446430
School Library Association

Boys and Girls Forever: Children's Classics   2003
from Cinderella to Harry Potter
Alison Lurie
ISBN 9780142002520
Penguin

Modern Children's Literature: an Introduction   2004
Kimberley Reynolds
ISBN 9781403916129
Palgrave

The Ultimate Book Guide: Over 700 Great Books for 8–12s   2009
Daniel Hahn, Leonie Flynn & Susan Reuben (Eds)
ISBN 9781408104385 (2nd revised edition)
A & C Black

The Ultimate Teen Book Guide 2010
Daniel Hahn & Leonie Flynn (Eds)
ISBN 9781408104378 (2nd revised edition)
A & C Black

The Ultimate First Book Guide: 2008
Over 500 Great Books for 0- 7s
Leonie Flynn, Daniel Hahn, & Susan Reuben (Eds)
ISBN 9780713673319
A & C Black

1001 Children's Books You Must Read Before You Grow Up 2009
Julia Eccleshare (Ed)
ISBN 9781844036714
Cassell

Books for Keeps: The Children's Book Magazine
Books for Keeps
1 Effingham Road
London SE12 8NZ
Phone: 020 8852 4953
E-mail: enquiries@booksforkeeps.co.uk
Six issues per year available at www.booksforkeeps.co.uk

Carousel: The Guide to Children's Books
Carousel
The Saturn Centre
54–76 Bissell Street
Birmingham B5 7HX
Phone: 0121 622 7458
E-mail: carouselguide@virgin.net
www.carouselguide.co.uk
Three issues per year plus Christmas supplement

The School Librarian
Unit 2
Lotmead Business Village
Lotmead Farm
Wanborough
Swindon SN4 0UY
Phone: 01793 791787
E-mail: info@sla.org.uk
Four issues per year

Exploring further

Websites are a good way of exploring the world of children's literature. These days many authors and illustrators have their own website and it is always worth putting a name into a search engine to see if a site will come up. Many are hosted on publishers' sites or signposted from information or library sites. The sites listed below are helpful, but please note that although they were accurate at the time of going to press, they may change during the life of this edition.

www.achuka.co.uk
News and views about children's books. Information on authors and illustrators.

www.bbc.co.uk
Links to Jackanory, Blue Peter etc. Follow-ups on books appearing on programmes. Games and things to do.

www.booksforkeeps.co.uk
The UK's leading, independent children's book magazine, now online. It was launched in 1980 and ever since has been reviewing hundreds of new children's books each year and publishing articles on every aspect of writing for children.

www.bookheads.org.uk
Site for teenagers developed from Booktrust to promote teenage reading in conjunction with its Teenage Book Prize.

www.channel4learning.com/sites/bookbox/home.htm
Information on popular authors, illustrators and books.

www.childrensbooksequels.co.uk
Useful site for seeing what title is next or what comes where in order of reading.

www.clpe.co.uk
Site of the Centre for Literacy in Primary Education. Aimed at teachers but useful for all interested in children's books and reading.

www.cool-reads.co.uk
Reviews for and by 10–15 year olds.

www.dr-mel-comics.co.uk
UK academic Mel Gibson's site on aspects of graphic novels and comics – useful resource.

www.everyonesreading.org.uk
Website to accompany initiative, see School Library Association above.

www.fcbg.org.uk
Federation of Children's Book Groups site. A network of book groups founded by parents to further the love of books and reading. Has a useful list of links to topics of interest.

www.guardian.co.uk/childrens-books-site
News, reviews (including some by children), author interviews.

www.kidsatrandomhouse.co.uk
News about latest books. Links to authors/illustrators. Interactive book chooser. Fun and games.

www.literacytrust.org.uk
News and views on books and reading. Reports on initiatives. Of interest to anyone involved in children's books. Signposting to areas of interest including an area on websites about children's books and reading.

www.lovereading4kids.co.uk
Access to the biggest children's book store. Recommendations and lists. Reviews.

www.mrsmad.com
For children of all ages plus teachers, parents & librarians. Reviews, lists games and stories.

www.ncll.org.uk
Site of the National Centre for Language and Literacy at Reading University. Great resource for teachers and librarians. Resources, news on events, how to find authors for events.

www.papertigers.org
Site for information on multicultural books from all over the world, in English.

www.readingagency.org.uk
Independent charity set up to inspire people to read more. Works with local authorities and others to run various initiatives most notably, for children, the summer reading challenge.

www.readingforlife.co.uk
Promotes the benefits of reading all stages of life. Came about as a development from the National Year of Reading 2008. Ideas for activities, book recommendations, access to free book-related materials.

www.readingmatters.co.uk
Reviews. Also book chooser – a series of questions are asked about what to read – a selection of titles offered as a result.

Exploring further

www.readingzone.com
Interesting "all round" site for young people, parents, teachers and librarians – access to many resources. Reviews and author interviews.

www.sevenstories.org.uk
Website for Seven Stories, a gallery and archive celebrating some of the best of children's books. Open to the public.

www.scottishbooktrust.com
Details of Scottish book initiatives, awards and resources

www.surlalune.fairytales.com
Wonderful site for information on fairytales – from a precis on the original to all kinds of retellings.

www.ukchildrensbooks.co.uk
Directory of authors, illustrators, publishers, organisations.

www.wordpool.co.uk
Site for parents, teachers, writers and children. Links to: author/ illustrator sites. Information and tips for aspiring writers. No longer being updated but reviews and information remain.

Blogs

Finally, a word about blogs. Blogs have become a very important part of young peoples' lives and are a major form of communication. They are important for spreading the word about books and for sharing books. Don't forget to share! Authors are doing it, as well as young people who enjoy their books, so it's another source.

Index

Author	Age ranges	Page numbers
Abdel-Fattah, Randa	12-14 14+	105, 168
Abela, Deborah	8-11	44
Adams, Richard	8-11	44
Adeney, Anne	5-7	1
Adlington, L J	12-14	105
Ahlberg, Allan	5-7 8-11	1, 44
Aiken, Joan	8-11 12-14	44, 105
Alcott, Louisa May	8-11	44
Alexander, Jenny	5-7	1
Alexander, Lloyd	12-14	105
Alexie, Sherman	14+	168
Allen, Jonathan	5-7	1
Allen-Gray, Alison	12-14	105
Almond, David	5-7 8-11 12-14	2, 45, 106
Anderson, Laurie Halse	12-14 14+	106, 168
Anderson, R J	8-11 12-14	45, 106
Anderson, Scoular	5-7	2
Anderson, Sorrel	5-7	2
Andreae, Giles	5-7 8-11	2, 45
Anholt, Laurence	5-7 8-11	2, 45
Apps, Roy	8-11	45
Arbuthnott, Gill	12-14	106
Archer, Dosh	5-7	3
Ardagh, Philip	5-7 8-11	3, 46
Armitage, Ronda and David	5-7	3
Armstrong, Kelley	14+	168
Arnold, Louise	8-11	46
Asher, Jay	14+	168
Ashley, Bernard	12-14 14+	106, 169
Ashworth, Sherry	14+	169
Asquith, Ros	8-11 12-14	46, 107
Atinuke,	5-7	3
Augarde, Steve	8-11 12-14	46, 107
Bailey, Helen	12-14	107
Bajoria, Paul	8-11 12-14	46, 107
Baker, E D	8-11	47
Balliett, Blue	8-11	47
Banks, Lynne Reid	8-11 12-14	47, 107
Barber, Antonia	5-7	3
Barker, Clive	14+	169
Barker, Dominic	8-11 12-14	47, 108
Barlow, Steve and Steve Skidmore	8-11	47
Barrie, J M	8-11	48
Bartram, Simon	5-7	3
Baskin, Nora Raleigh	14+	169

Bass, Guy	8-11			48
Bates, Michelle	8-11			48
Baum, Frank L	8-11			48
Baumgart, Klaus	5-7			4
Bawden, Nina	8-11			48
Baxter, Andy	8-11			48
Baxter, Stephen	12-14	14+		108, 169
Beardsley, Martyn	5-7	8-11		4, 49
Bearn, Emily	5-7			4
Beck, Ian	8-11	12-14		49, 108
Becker, Tom	12-14			108
Beddor, Frank	12-14	14+		108, 169
Bedford, David	5-7	8-11		4, 49
Belbin, David	12-14	14+		108, 170
Bell, Julia	14+			170
Ben 10,	5-7			4
Bennett, Sophia	12-14			109
Bentley, Sue	5-7			5
Berenstain, Stan and Jan	5-7			5
Berry-Hart, T E	12-14			109
Bertagna, Julie	12-14			109
Birdsall, Jeanne	8-11			49
Birney, Betty G	8-11			49
Black, Holly	8-11	14+		49, 170
Blacker, Terence	5-7	8-11	12-14	5, 50, 109
Blackford, Andy	5-7			5
Blackman, Malorie	5-7	8-11	12-14 14+	6, 50, 109, 170
Blade, Adam	8-11			50
Blake, Jon	5-7			6
Blathwayt, Benedict	5-7			6
Bloor, Thomas	8-11	12-14		50, 110
Blume, Judy	8-11			50
Blyton, Enid	8-11			51
Bond, Michael	8-11			51
Bosch, Pseudonymous	8-11	12-14		51, 110
Boston, Lucy M	8-11			51
Bowler, Tim	12-14	14+		110, 170
Boyce, Frank Cottrell	8-11	12-14		51, 110
Boyne, John	8-11	12-14		51, 110
Bradbury, Jason	12-14			111
Bradford, Chris	8-11	12-14		52, 111
Bradman, Tony	5-7	8-11		6, 52
Brand, Christiana	8-11			52
Brashares, Ann	12-14			111
Bray, Libba	14+			171
Brennan, Herbie	8-11	12-14		52, 111
Brennan, Sarah Rees	12-14			111
Breslin, Theresa	8-11	12-14		52, 112
Brian, Kate	14+			171

Index

Briggs, Andy	12-14	112
Briggs, Raymond	5-7 8-11	7, 53
Brindley, John	12-14	112
Brisley, Joyce Lankester	5-7	7
Broad, Michael	5-7	7
Brooke, Lauren	8-11 12-14	53, 112
Brooks, Kevin	12-14 14+	112, 171
Brooks, Terry	14+	171
Brown, Jeff	5-7	7
Brown, Judy	5-7	7
Brown, Marc	5-7	8
Browne, Anthony	5-7	8
Browne, N M	12-14	113
Brumpton, Keith	5-7	8
Bryant, Ann	5-7 8-11	8, 53
Buckley-Archer, Linda	8-11 12-14	53, 113
Bugler, Suzanne	14+	171
Burchett, Janet and Sara Vogler	5-7	8
Burchill, Julie	14+	171
Burgess, Melvin	14+	172
Burnett, Frances Hodgson	8-11	53
Burningham, John	5-7	9
Burtenshaw, Jenna	12-14	113
Bussell, Darcey	5-7 8-11	9, 53
Butcher, A J	12-14	113
Butterworth, Annette	8-11	54
Butterworth, Nick	5-7	9
Byars, Betsy	8-11	54
Byng, Georgia	8-11	54
Cabot, Meg	8-11 12-14	54, 113
Caine, Rachel	14+	172
Cameron, Ann	5-7	9
Canavan, Trudi	12-14 14+	114, 172
Cann, Kate	14+	172
Carpenter, Humphrey	5-7	9
Carranza, Maite	12-14	114
Carroll, Lewis	8-11	54
Carter, Ally	12-14	114
Carter, Dean Vincent	14+	172
Cassidy, Anne	5-7 12-14 14+	10, 114, 173
Cassidy, Cathy	8-11 12-14	54, 114
Cast P C & Kristin,	14+	173
Castor, Harriet	5-7	10
Cattell, Bob	8-11	55
Cave, Patrick	12-14	115
Cavendish, Grace	8-11 12-14	55, 115
Caveney, Philip	8-11 12-14	55, 115
Chadda, Sarwat	12-14	115
Chambers, Aidan	14+	173
Chancellor, Henry	8-11 12-14	55, 115

Index

Chandler, Pauline	12-14		115
Chapman, Linda	5-7	8-11	10, 55
Cheshire, Simon	8-11		55
Child, Lauren	5-7	8-11	10, 56
Childs, Rob	5-7	8-11	11, 56
Chbosky, Stephen	14+		173
Choldenko, Gennifer	12-14		116
Christopher, Lucy	8-11	12-14	56, 116
Clare, Cassandra	14+		173
Clark, Emma Chichester	5-7		11
Clayton, Emma	12-14		116
Clement-Davies, David	8-11		56
Cliff, Alex	5-7	8-11	11, 56
Cole, Stephen	12-14		116
Cole, Steve	8-11		56
Coleman, Michael	8-11		57
Coleman, Rowan	12-14		116
Colfer, Eoin	8-11	12-14	57, 117
Collins, B R	12-14	14+	117, 173
Collins, Suzanne	12-14	14+	117, 174
Collins, Tim	12-14	14+	117, 174
Collins, Yvonne and Sandy Rideout	12-14		117
Cooper, Helen	5-7		11
Cooper, Louise	8-11		57
Cooper, Paul	5-7		11
Cooper, Susan	8-11	12-14	57, 118
Cope, Andrew	5-7	8-11	12, 57
Corder, Zizou	8-11	12-14	58, 118
Cornish, D M	12-14		118
Cowell, Cressida	8-11		58
Craig, Joe	12-14		118
Crebbin, June	5-7		12
Creech, Sharon	8-11		58
Croggon, Alison	12-14		118
Crompton, Richmal	8-11		58
Cross, Gillian	8-11	12-14	58, 119
Crossick, Matt	8-11		59
Crossley-Holland, Kevin	8-11	12-14	59, 119
Cunliffe, John	5-7		12
Curley, Marianne	12-14		119
Curtis, Vanessa	12-14		119
d'Lacey, Chris	5-7	8-11	12, 59
Dahl, Roald	5-7	8-11	12, 59
Dale, Anna	8-11		59
Dale, Jenny	8-11		60
Dalton, Annie	8-11		60
Daniels, Lucy	5-7	8-11	13, 60
Dann, Colin	8-11		60
Dashner, James	12-14		119
David, Keren	14+		174

Index

Davies, Katie	8-11			60
Daze, Hayley	5-7			13
de Fombelle, Timothee	8-11	12-14		61, 120
de la Cruz, Melissa	14+			174
de Quidt, Jeremy	12-14			120
Deary, Terry	8-11			61
Delaney, Joseph	8-11	12-14		61, 120
Dent, Grace	12-14	14+		120, 174
Dessen, Sarah	12-14	14+		120, 175
Dewan, Ted	5-7			13
Dhami, Narinder	8-11	12-14		61, 121
di Camillo, Kate	8-11			61
Dickinson, John	12-14	14+		121, 175
Dickinson, Peter	12-14			121
Dodd, Lynley	5-7			13
Doder, Joshua	8-11			62
Dogar, Sharon	12-14	14+		121, 175
Doherty, Berlie	8-11	12-14		62, 121
Dolan, Penny	5-7			13
Donaldson, Julia	5-7	12-14		14, 122
Donbavand, Tommy	8-11	12-14		62, 122
Donnelly, Jennifer	12-14			122
Dowd, Siobhan	8-11	12-14	14+	62, 122, 175
Downham, Jenny	12-14	14+		122, 175
Dowswell, Paul	8-11	12-14		62, 122
Doyle, Malachy	5-7			14
Doyle, Roddy	8-11			62
Dunbar, Fiona	8-11			63
Dunmore, Helen	8-11	12-14		63, 123
DuPrau, Jeanne	8-11			63
Durant, Alan	5-7			14
Duval, Alex	14+			176
Dyer, Heather	8-11			63
Eastman, P D	5-7			14
Edwards, Dorothy	5-7			15
Edwards, Eve	12-14			123
Eldridge, Jim	12-14	14+		123, 176
Elliott, Patricia	12-14			123
Ellis, Deborah	12-14			123
Emmett, Jonathan	5-7			15
Emond, Stephen	14+			176
Ennis, Garth	14+			176
Enthoven, Sam	12-14			123
Falconer, Ian	5-7			15
Falkner, Brian	12-14			124
Falls, Kat	12-14			124
Fardell, John	8-11			63
Farmer, Nancy	12-14			124
Fathallah, Judith	12-14	14+		124, 176
Fearnley, Jan	5-7			15

Index

Feasey, Steve	12-14			124
Feth, Monika	14+			176
Fine, Anne	5-7	8-11	12-14	15, 63, 124
Fisher, Catherine	8-11	12-14		64, 125
Fisk, Pauline	12-14			125
Fitzpatrick, Becca	14+			177
Flanagan, John	12-14			125
Fleischman, Paul	5-7			16
Fletcher, Charlie	8-11	12-14		64, 125
Ford, Michael	8-11	12-14		64, 125
Forde, Catherine	12-14	14+		126, 177
Forman, Gayle	12-14	14+		126, 177
Freeman, Hilary	14+			177
Freer, Echo	12-14			126
French, Jackie	8-11			64
French, Vivian	5-7			16
Friedman, Joe	5-7			16
Friel, Maeve	5-7	8-11		16, 64
Funke, Cornelia	8-11	12-14		64, 126
Funnell, Pippa	5-7	8-11		16, 65
Gaarder, Jostein	14+			177
Gaiman, Neil	5-7	8-11	12-14 14+	17, 65, 126, 178
Gantos, Jack	8-11	14+		65, 178
Gardner, Sally	5-7	8-11	12-14	17, 65, 127
Garner, Alan	8-11			65
Gavin, Jamila	12-14			127
Geras, Adèle	8-11	12-14		66, 127
Gibbons, Alan	8-11	12-14	14+	66, 127, 178
Gibson, Maggi	12-14			127
Gilman, David	12-14			128
Glass, Linzi	14+			178
Glatshteyn, Yanker	8-11	12-14		66, 128
Gleitzman, Morris	8-11	12-14		66, 128
Gliori, Debi	8-11			66
Glover, Sandra	14+			178
Godbersen, Anna	14+			178
Golding, Julia	8-11	12-14		67, 128
Goobie, Beth	14+			179
Goodhart, Pippa	5-7			17
Goodman, Alison	12-14			128
Goodwin, Harriet	8-11			67
Gordon, Roderick and Brian Williams	12-14			129
Gordon, John	8-11			67
Goscinny, René	8-11			67
Goudge, Elizabeth	8-11			67
Gourlay, Candy	8-11	12-14		67, 129
Gowar, Mick	5-7			17
Graham, Bob	5-7			17
Graham, Elspeth and Mal Peet	5-7	8-11		31, 88
Grahame, Kenneth	8-11			67

Grant, Helen	12-14 14+		129, 179
Grant, John	5-7		18
Grant, K M	12-14		129
Grant, Michael	12-14		129
Graves, Sue	5-7		18
Gravett, Emily	5-7		18
Gray, Claudia	12-14 14+		129, 179
Gray, Keith	12-14 14+		130, 179
Gray, Kes	5-7 8-11		18, 68
Greder, Armin	12-14		130
Green, John	14+		179
Green, Julia	14+		179
Gregg, Stacy	8-11 12-14		68, 130
Grey, Mini	5-7		19
Griffiths, Andy	8-11		68
Grimstone, David	8-11		68
Grindley, Sally	5-7 8-11		19, 68
Groening, Matt	12-14		130
Gross, Philip	12-14		130
Guène, Faïza	14+		180
Gurney, Stella	5-7		19
Haddon, Mark	8-11 12-14 14+		68, 130, 180
Haggarty, Ben	14+		180
Haig, Matt	8-11 14+		69, 180
Halam, Ann	12-14		131
Hale, Shannon and Dean	12-14 14+		131, 180
Halliwell, Geri	8-11		69
Hamley, Dennis	8-11		69
Hanley, Victoria	12-14		131
Hardinge, Frances	8-11 12-14		69, 131
Hare, Lucinda	8-11		69
Harper, Meg	8-11		69
Harris, Joanne	12-14 14+		131, 180
Harris, M G	12-14		132
Harrison, Michelle	8-11 12-14		69, 132
Hartnett, Sonya	12-14 14+		132, 180
Harvey, Alyxandra	14+		181
Harvey, Damian	5-7		19
Haven, Paul	8-11		70
Hawthorne, Rachel	14+		181
Hearn, Julie	12-14 14+		132, 181
Hearn, Lian	14+		181
Hedderwick, Mairi	5-7		20
Hedges, Carol	8-11 12-14		70, 132
Henderson, J A	12-14		132
Hendry, Diana	8-11		70
Hergé,	8-11		70
Hiaasen, Carl	12-14		133
Higgins, Chris	12-14		133
Higgins, F E	12-14		133

Index

Higgins, Jack with Justin Richards	12-14		133
Hightman, Jason	8-11		70
Higson, Charlie	8-11 12-14 14+		70, 133, 181
Hill, Stuart	12-14		134
Hinton, Nigel	8-11 12-14		71, 134
Hinton, S E	12-14		134
Hoeye, Michael	8-11		71
Hoffman, Mary	5-7 12-14		20, 134
Hogan, Mary	12-14		134
Holm, Anne	8-11		71
Hooper, Mary	8-11 12-14		71, 135
Hopkins, Cathy	12-14		135
Hornby, Nick	14+		181
Horowitz, Anthony	8-11 12-14		71, 135
Horse, Harry	5-7		20
Howell, Simmone	14+		181
Hughes, Shirley	5-7		20
Hughes, Ted	8-11		72
Hunt, Elizabeth Singer	5-7 8-11		20, 72
Hunter, Erin	8-11		72
Hussey, William	12-14 14+		135, 182
Hutchison, Barry	8-11		72
Ibbotson, Eva	8-11 12-14		72, 136
Impey, Rose	5-7 8-11		21, 73
Inkpen, Mick	5-7		21
Jackson, Steve and Ian Livingstone	8-11		73
Jacques, Brian	8-11 12-14		73, 136
Jago, Lucy	12-14		136
Jansen, Hanna	14+		182
Jarman, J A	14+		182
Jarman, Julia	5-7 8-11		21, 73
Jarvis, Robin	8-11 12-14		73, 136
Jauncey, James	14+		182
Jeapes, Ben	12-14		136
Jefferies, Cindy	8-11		74
Jeffers, Oliver	5-7 8-11		21, 74
Jenkinson, Ceci	8-11		74
Jennings, Paul	8-11 12-14		74, 136
Jensen, Marie-Louise	12-14		137
Jinks, Catherine	12-14 14-		137, 182
Jobling, Curtis	14+		182
Johnson, Pete	8-11 12-14		74, 137
Jones, Allan Frewin	8-11		74
Jones, Diana Wynne	8-11 12-14		75, 137
Jungman, Ann	5-7		22
Kate, Lauren	14+		182
Kay, Elizabeth	8-11		75
Keaney, Brian	12-14		137
Kelleher, Damian	12-14		138
Kelley, Ann	12-14		138

Index

Kemp, Gene	8-11			75
Kennen, Ally	8-11	12-14	14+	75, 138, 183
Kenrick, Joanna	14+			183
Kent, Deborah	8-11			75
Kerr, Judith	8-11			75
Kerr, P B	8-11			76
Kessler, Liz	8-11			76
Kilworth, Garry	8-11			76
Kimpton, Diana	5-7	8-11		22, 76
King, Caro	8-11			76
King, Clive	8-11			76
King, Daren	5-7	8-11		22, 77
King-Smith, Dick	5-7	8-11		22, 77
Kinney, Jeff	8-11	12-14		77, 138
Kitamura, Satoshi	5-7			23
Klass, David	14+			183
Knapman, Timothy	5-7			23
Kostick, Conor	12-14	14+		138, 183
Kuipers, Alice	14+			183
LaFleur, Suzanne	8-11	12-14		77, 138
Laird, Elizabeth	8-11	12-14		77, 139
Lanagan, Margo	14+			183
Landman, Tanya	12-14			139
Landy, Derek	8-11	12-14		78, 139
Lane, Andrew	8-11			78
Langrish, Katherine	8-11			78
Larry, H I	5-7	8-11		23, 78
Larson, Hope	12-14			139
Lassiter, Rhiannon	12-14			139
Law, Karina	5-7			23
Lawhead, Stephen R	12-14	14+		140, 183
Lawrence, Caroline	8-11	12-14		78, 140
Lawrence, Michael	5-7	8-11	12-14	23, 79, 140
Layton, Neal	5-7			23
Le Guin, Ursula	12-14			140
le Vann, Kate	14+			184
Lee, Dan	8-11			79
Lee, Ingrid	8-11			79
Lee, Tanith	12-14			140
Lee, Y S	12-14			140
Lennon, Joan	8-11			79
Lewis, C S	8-11			79
Lewis, Paeony	5-7			24
Limb, Sue	12-14			141
Lindgren, Astrid	5-7			24
Lindsay, Elizabeth	5-7	8-11		24, 79
Lively, Penelope	8-11			80
Livingstone, Ian and Steve Jackson	8-11			73
Llewellyn, Sam	8-11	12-14		80, 141
Lloyd, Saci	12-14	14+		141, 184

Index

Lloyd, Sam	5-7			24
Lockhart, E	14-			184
Lott, Tim	12-14	14+		141, 184
Lowry, Lois	8-11			80
McCaughrean, Geraldine	5-7	8-11	12-14	24, 80, 141
McCombie, Karen	8-11	12-14		80, 142
MacDonald, Alan	5-7	8-11		25, 81
McDonald, Megan	5-7	8-11		25, 81
McGowan, Anthony	8-11	12-14	14+	81, 142, 184
McKain, Kelly	5-7	8-11		25, 81
McKay, Hilary	5-7	8-11	12-14	25, 81, 142
McKee, David	5-7			25
Mackenzie, Ross	8-11			82
McKenzie, Sophie	8-11	12-14	14+	82, 142, 184
Mackler, Carolyn	14+			185
McNab, Andy and Robert Rigby	12-14			143
McNab, Andy	14+			185
McNaughton, Colin	5-7			26
McNish, Cliff	12-14			143
MacPhail, Catherine	12-14	14+		143, 185
Magorian, Michelle	8-11	12-14		82, 143
Magrs, Paul	14+			185
Maguire, Eden	12-14			144
Mah, Adeline Yen	12-14			144
Mahy, Margaret	12-14			144
Malley, Gemma	12-14	14+		144, 185
Mandrake, Tiffany	5-7			26
Mankell, Henning	12-14			144
Manning, Sarra	14+			186
Marks, Graham	8-11	12-14	14+	82, 144, 186
Marr, Melissa	14+			186
Marriott, Zoe	12-14			145
Marshall, Hazel	8-11			82
Marshall, James	5-7			26
Marshall, Jill	8-11			82
Masini, Beatrice	5-7	8-11		26, 82
Maxted, Anna	5-7	8-11		26, 83
May, Natasha	5-7			27
Mayhew, James	5-7			27
Mayo, Margaret	5-7			27
Mead, Richelle	14+			186
Meadows, Daisy	5-7	8-11		27, 83
Melling, David	5-7	8-11		27, 83
Mendes, Valerie	14+			186
Meyer, Carolyn	12-14			145
Meyer, Kai	12-14			145
Meyer, Stephenie	12-14	14+		145, 187
Michael, Livi	8-11			83
Mignola, Mike	14+			187
Miller, David	8-11	12-14		83, 145

Index

Mills, Sam	14+			187
Milne, A A	8-11			83
Mitchelhill, Barbara	5-7	8-11		27, 84
Mitton, Tony	5-7			28
Molloy, Michael	8-11	12-14		84, 145
Mongredien, Sue	5-7			28
Montgomery, L M	8-11			84
Mooney, Bel	5-7			28
Moore, Alan	14+			187
Moore, Maggie	5-7			28
Morgan, Nicola	12-14	14+		146, 187
Morgenroth, Kate	14+			188
Moriarty, Jaclyn	14+			188
Morpurgo, Michael	5-7	8-11	12-14	29, 84, 146
Morrison, Grant	14+			188
Mould, Chris	8-11			84
Mowll, Joshua	8-11	12-14		85, 146
Muchamore, Robert	12-14			146
Murphy, Jill	5-7	8-11		29, 85
Murray, Martine	5-7			29
Myers, Benjamin J	12-14			146
Nadin, Joanna	14+			188
Naidoo, Beverley	12-14			147
Naifeh, Ted	12-14			147
Nash, Margaret	5-7			29
Nelson, Jandy	14+			188
Nesbit, E	8-11			85
Ness, Patrick	14+			188
Newbery, Linda	5-7 8-11 12-14 14+			30, 85, 147, 189
Newbound, Andrew	8-11			85
Nicholls, Sally	12-14			147
Nicholson, William	8-11	12-14		86, 147
Nimmo, Jenny	5-7	8-11		30, 86
Nix, Garth	12-14			148
Noel, Alyson	14+			189
Norriss, Andrew	8-11			86
North, Laura	5-7			30
Norton, Mary	8-11			86
Noyes, Deborah	14+			189
O'Brien, Robert C	8-11			86
ÓGuilin, Peadar	14+			189
Oates, Joyce Carol	14+			189
Offen, Hilda	5-7			30
Ogilvy, Ian	8-11			87
Oldfield, Jenny	5-7	8-11		30, 87
Oliver, Lauren	14+			189
Oppel, Kenneth	8-11	12-14		87, 148
Oram, Hiawyn	5-7			31
Orme, David	5-7			31
Orr, Wendy	8-11			87

Osman, Sam	8-11	12-14		87, 148
Owen, James A	12-14			148
Owen, Joanne	12-14			148
Owen, Laura	5-7	8-11		31, 88
Palmer, Tom	8-11			88
Paolini, Christopher	12-14			148
Patterson, James	12-14			149
Paver, Michelle	8-11	12-14		88, 149
Pearce, Philippa	8-11			88
Peet, Mal and Elspeth Graham	5-7	8-11		31, 88
Peet, Mal	12-14	14+		149, 190
Pennac, Daniel	8-11			89
Pennypacker, Sara	8-11			89
Perera, Anna	12-14			149
Peters, Julie Anne	14+			190
Peterson, Will	12-14			149
Peyton, K M	12-14			150
Pfeffer, Susan	14+			190
Philip, Gillian	14+			190
Pielichaty, Helena	8-11	12-14		89, 150
Pike, Aprilynne	12-14			150
Pike, Christopher	14+			190
Pilkey, Dav	5-7	8-11		31, 89
Pirotta, Saviour	5-7			32
Plaisted, Caroline	8-11			89
Platt, Richard	8-11			89
Postgate, Daniel	5-7			32
Potter, Beatrix	5-7			32
Powell, Jillian	5-7			32
Powell, Laura	14+			190
Powling, Chris	5-7	8-11		32, 90
Pratchett, Terry	8-11	12-14	14+	90, 150, 191
Price, Susan	12-14			150
Priestley, Chris	8-11	12-14		90, 151
Prince, Alison	12-14			151
Prineas, Sarah	8-11			90
Promitzer, Rebecca	12-14			151
Prowse, Jane	12-14			151
Prøysen, Alf	5-7	8-11		33, 90
Prue, Sally	12-14			151
Pullman, Philip	8-11	12-14		90, 152
Punter, Russell	5-7			33
Puttock, Simon	5-7			33
Rai, Bali	8-11	12-14	14+	91, 152, 191
Ransome, Arthur	8-11			91
Rayban, Chloë	12-14			152
Rayner, Shoo	5-7	8-11		33, 91
Read, Anthony	8-11			91
Rees, Celia	12-14			152
Rees, Gwyneth	5-7	8-11		33, 91

Reeve, Philip	8-11	12-14	92, 153
Renner, Ellen	8-11		92
Rennison, Louise	12-14	14+	153, 191
Rettig, Liz	12-14	14+	153, 191
Richards, Justin	8-11		92
Richards, Justin with Jack Higgins	12-14		133
Richardson, E E	12-14		153
Riddell, Chris	5-7		34
Rideout, Sandy and Yvonne Collins	12-14		117
Ridley, Philip	8-11		92
Rigby, Robert and Andy McNab	12-14		143
Rinaldi, Ann	12-14		153
Riordan, James	12-14		154
Riordan, Rick	8-11	12-14	92, 154
Rix, Jamie	8-11		93
Robert, Na'ima B	12-14		154
Roberts, Katherine	8-11	12-14	93, 154
Robinson, Hilary	5-7		34
Robson, Mark	12-14		154
Rodda, Emily	8-11		93
Rodgers, Frank	5-7		34
Rook, Sebastian	8-11		93
Rose, Malcolm	12-14		155
Rosen, Michael	5-7		34
Rosoff, Meg	12-14	14+	155, 191
Ross, Tony	5-7		34
Rowling, J K	8-11	12-14	93, 155
Rusbridger, Alan	5-7		35
Rushton, Rosie	12-14		155
Ryan, Chris	12-14		156
Ryan, Margaret	5-7	8-11	35, 94
Sachar, Louis	5-7 8-11	12-14	35, 94, 156
Sage, Angie	8-11		94
Said, S F	8-11		94
Salter, Helen	14+		192
Satrapi, Marjane	14+		192
Saunders, Kate	8-11		94
Scarrow, Alex	12-14		156
Scieszka, Jon	5-7		35
Scott, Michael	12-14		156
Sedgwick, Marcus	8-11	12-14	95, 156
Serraillier, Ian	8-11		95
Seuss, Dr	5-7		35
Sewell, Anna	8-11		95
Shadow, Nick	8-11		95
Shan, Darren	12-14	14+	157, 192
Sharratt, Nick	5-7		36
Shaw, Hannah	5-7		36
Sheldon, Dyan	5-7 8-11	12-14	36, 95, 157
Shipton, Paul	8-11		95

Index

265

Shulman, Dee	5-7		36
Shusterman, Neal	12-14		157
Simmons, Jane	5-7		36
Simon, Francesca	5-7 8-11		37, 96
Simpson, Craig	12-14 14+		157, 192
Singer, Nicky	12-14 14+		157, 192
Singleton, Sarah	12-14		158
Skelton, Mark	5-7 8-11		37, 96
Skelton, Matthew	8-11 12-14		96, 158
Skidmore, Steve and Steve Barlow	8-11		47
Small, Charlie	8-11		96
Smiley, Sophie	5-7		37
Smith, Cynthia Leitich	14+		192
Smith, Dodie	8-11		96
Smith, Jeff	12-14		158
Smith, L J	12-14 14+		158, 193
Smith, Wendy	5-7		37
Snicket, Lemony	8-11		96
Somper, Justin	8-11 12-14		97, 158
Sparkes, Ali	8-11 12-14		97, 158
Spiegelman, Art	14+		193
Spinelli, Jerry	12-14		159
Spyri, Johanna	8-11		97
St John, Lauren	8-11		97
Stanton, Andy	5-7 8-11		37, 97
Staples, Suzanne Fisher	12-14		159
Steer, Dugald	8-11		98
Stewart, Paul	5-7 8-11 12-14		37, 98, 159
Stewart, Trenton Lee	8-11 12-14		98, 159
Stiefvater, Maggie	14+		193
Stilton, Geronimo	5-7 8-11		38, 98
Stimson, Joan	5-7		38
Stine, R L	8-11 12-14		98, 159
Stone, David Lee	8-11 12-14		98, 159
Stone, Jeff	8-11		99
Stone, Rex	5-7 8-11		38, 99
Streatfeild, Noel	8-11		99
Strong, Jeremy	5-7 8-11 12-14		38, 99, 160
Stroud, Jonathan	12-14		160
Sumerak, Marc	12-14		160
Sutcliff, Rosemary	8-11		99
Suzuma, Tabitha	14+		193
Swindells, Robert	8-11 12-14		99, 160
Sykes, Julie	5-7		38
Takaya, Natsuki	12-14		160
Talbot, Bryan	14+		193
Talbot, Shaun	5-7 8-11 12-14		39, 100, 161
Taylor, A G	12-14		161
Taylor, G P	12-14		161
Taylor, Mildred D	12-14		161

Thomas, Valerie	5-7			37
Thompson, Colin	5-7			39
Thompson, Kate	8-11 12-14 14+			100, 161, 194
Thorpe, David	12-14			162
Tiernan, Cate	12-14			162
Toft, Di	8-11			100
Toksvig, Sandi	8-11			100
Tolkien, J R R	8-11 12-14 14+			100, 162, 194
Tomlinson, Jill	5-7			39
Tomlinson, Theresa	12-14			162
Townsend, Sue	12-14 14+			162, 194
Travers, P L	8-11			100
Turnbull, Ann	12-14 14+			162, 194
Umansky, Kaye	5-7 8-11			39, 101
Updale, Eleanor	12-14			163
Ure, Jean	8-11 12-14			101, 163
Uttley, Alison	5-7			40
Valentine, Jenny	5-7 12-14 14+			40, 163, 194
van de Ruit, John	14+			194
Voake, Steve	8-11 12-14			101, 163
Vogler, Sara and Janet Burchett	5-7			8
von Ziegesar, Cecily	14+			195
Vornholt, John	8-11			101
Waddell, Martin	5-7			40
Wade, Barrie	5-7			40
Walden, Mark	8-11 12-14			101, 163
Wallace, Jason	14+			195
Wallace, Karen	5-7 8-11 12-14			40, 102, 164
Walliams, David	8-11 12-14			102, 164
Walsh, Pat	8-11			102
Ward, Rachel	12-14 14+			164, 195
Waters, Summer	5-7			41
Weatherill, Cat	8-11			102
Weatherly, Lee	12-14			164
Webb, Beth	12-14			164
Webb, Catherine	12-14			164
Webb, Holly	5-7 8-11			41, 102
Webb, Sarah	12-14			165
West, Colin	5-7			41
Westall, Robert	8-11 12-14			102, 165
Westerfeld, Scott	12-14 14+			165, 195
White, E B	8-11			103
White, T H	8-11			103
Whitley, David	12-14			165
Whybrow, Ian	5-7			41
Whyman, Matt	14+			95
Wilder, Laura Ingalls	8-11			
Wilkinson, Lili	14+			
Willems, Mo	5-7			
Williams, Brian and Roderick Gordon	12-14			

Williams, Ursula Moray	8-11		103
Willis, Jeanne	5-7		42
Wilson, Anna	5-7	8-11	42, 103
Wilson, Bob	5-7		42
Wilson, David Henry	5-7		43
Wilson, Jacqueline	5-7 8-11 12-14		43, 104, 165
Winkler, Henry	8-11		104
Winterson, Jeanette	12-14		166
Woodall, Clive	12-14		166
Wooderson, Philip	5-7		43
Wooding, Chris	12-14		166
Woods, Titania	8-11		104
Woodward, Kay	12-14		166
Wormell, Chris	5-7		43
Wray, Sarah	12-14		166
Wright, Rachel	12-14		166
Wynne-Jones, Tim	12-14		167
Yancey, Rick	12-14		167
Yolen, Jane	5-7		43
Zephaniah, Benjamin	14+		196
Zevin, Gabrielle	14+		196
Zucker, Jonny	5-7 8-11		43, 104
Zusak, Markus	12-14 14+		167, 196

Index